Sexual Discretion

Sexual Discretion

Black Masculinity and the Politics of Passing

JEFFREY Q. MCCUNE, JR.

The University of Chicago Press
Chicago and London

Jeffrey Q. McCune, Jr., is an associate professor of Women, Gender, and Sexuality Studies and an associate professor of Performing Studies in the Department of Performing Arts at Washington University.

The University of Chicago Press, Chicago 60637
The University of Chicago Press, Ltd., London
© 2014 by The University of Chicago
All rights reserved. Published 2014.
Printed in the United States of America

23 22 21 20 19 18 17 16 15 14   1 2 3 4 5

ISBN-13: 978-0-226-09636-0 (cloth)
ISBN-13: 978-0-226-09653-7 (paper)
ISBN-13: 978-0-226-09667-4 (e-book)

DOI: 10.7208/chicago/9780226096674.001.0001

Library of Congress Cataloging-in-Publication Data

McCune, Jeffrey Q., Jr., author.
    Sexual discretion: black masculinity and the politics of passing /
  Jeffrey Q. McCune, Jr.
        pages; cm
    Includes bibliographical references and index.
    ISBN 978-0-226-09636-0 (cloth : alk. paper) — ISBN 978-0-226-09653-7
(pbk. : alk. paper)—ISBN 978-0-226-09667-4 (e-book) 1. African American
gay men. 2. Closeted gays. 3. Gay men—Relations with heterosexual women.
4. Masculinity.   I. Title.
    HQ76.27.A37M33 2014
    306.76'6208996073—dc23   2013021535

♾ This paper meets the requirements of ANSI/NISO Z39.48-1992
(Permanence of Paper).

For my parents,
my siblings, Monique and Melissa Brown and Aaron McCune,
and my loving grandparents.
May you always know that I am,
because you are.

CONTENTS

In 2005 I wrote, directed, produced, and accidentally starred in *Dancin' the Down Low*, a play based on narratives from interviews collected doing ethnographic research with men who have sex with men and who sometimes have wives/girlfriends. Act II of this play opens with the character Antwon upstage center with his back turned to the audience, while an anonymous man kneels before him performing fellatio. Antwon turns his head, looking over his shoulder, and directly addresses the audience, saying, "What y'all starin' at? Y'all never seen a man get his dick sucked?" As if this were call and response in the black church, my grandmother, who had sneaked into the theater without my knowledge, screamed in her most emphatic damsel-in-distress tone, "*Nooooooooo!!!!*" The whole audience laughed, and I sat backstage thinking, "Uh-oh, what have I done?!" Or more pointedly, "What will I do or say when my mom and I take my grandmother back to her South Side Chicago residence?" How would I explain this moment of sexual taboo in the midst of what I am sure my grandmother understood would be a strictly academic performance? In essence, my own sexual identity and politics would be subject to exposure and scrutiny by the McCune family at large, as well as being an embarrassment to them. This was what I had spent my life trying to avoid.

Sexual Discretion: Black Masculinity and the Politics of Passing is about the lives and representations of men who have sex with other men and who view their sexual practices and proclivities as private. In essence, this is a project about black masculinity and its demands on black men, in multiple spaces—physical and discursive. I attempt to explain how the stigma around sexual practices, the mandates of a stable identity formation, and the abjection of non-normative masculinity produce a "feeling" that prompts many black men to live "in secret." I critically explore where much of this maintenance of masculinity happens—in the practice of a historical African American politics of *sexual discretion*. Admittedly, my own recognition of and reverence for such politics nearly kept me from writing this book.

My impulse not to write about "taboo" stuff was, like most things, informed by multiple sources. It stemmed from years of sitting in pews while ministers recited passages of the Bible as a tool to quiet sexuality. It emerged from the cultural memo that made all discussions of sex between men an indicator of my "suspect" sexuality and masculinity. This impulse, to keep sex and sexuality in place, was reinforced at my aunt and uncle's dinner table, which forbade conversations about "fleshly" topics that would "complicate" the flow of conversation. It was also informed by the constant odd hush-hush attitude about the cousin, sister, father, or brother who was "that way." Finally, I dare to say, this feeling was fueled by my many black gay friends who chose partners who would try their best to conceal their "sexual perversions" to save face within the community and society at large. This commitment to keeping sex and sexual discourse down low—discreet or private—became a second-nature function, in lieu of a cultural mandate for self-surveillance.

This feeling also emerged from the absence of conversations about sexuality within the institutions that shaped me into the man I am today—schools, churches, workplaces, and community buildings where sex and sexuality were supposed to be checked at the door and were subject to high surveillance. In addition, the everyday walk down Chicago city streets reminded me that "fags" and "fruits" and "punk asses" were to be quiet—even if the only signifier of my sexuality was the malperformance of masculinity in fashion. Together, these institutions and everyday occurrences have called forth a discrete performance of self that attempts to quiet sexuality and avoid sexual taboos. An everyday feeling transforms into an everyday politics—a way of being in the world that privileges privacy and discretion.

On August 3, 2003, this discreet position would ironically be called out of the closet, as a sexually foreign object called the "down low" (DL)—black men who supposedly had sex with other men while also engaging in sexual relationships with their wives/girlfriends. "Double Lives on the Down Low," a peculiar faux-ethnographic exposé of black men, appeared in the *New York Times Magazine*, beginning with this epigraph:

> To their wives and colleagues, they're straight.
> To the men they are having sex with, they're forging an exuberant new identity.

To the gay world, they're kidding themselves.
To health officials, they're spreading AIDS in the black community.
(Denizet-Lewis 2003, 28)

While I was aware of the media buzz around DL men, the presence of this story in the *New York Times Magazine* signaled a new level of visibility for the topic. This article, loaded with its sensational statistics and hyperbolic stories, was clearly shaped to make certain appeals. Benoit Denizet-Lewis's tongue-in-cheek concern for black women's health and welfare, all the while focusing instead on the tricks and trash of black men's duplicity, was most troubling. Having been in conversation with HIV/AIDS epidemic researchers and practitioners like David Malebranche and Ron Simmons and reading the work of Cathy Cohen and Cindy Patton, I knew that this discourse had all the ingredients of not only creating moral/cultural panic, but irresponsibly marking black DL men as sexual suspects who are the new vectors of contagion. Furthermore, the manipulation of black female representation had all the telltale signs of another moment of painting these women as victims without sexual agency—all in the service of furthering once again a construction of black men as criminals of sexual deception. Like the son of a preacher woman, my prophetic vision took hold of my academic trajectory—conjuring a desire not to prove wrong or challenge the discursive constructs of these men, but to gain a richer understanding of the complexity of their lives in the midst of public scrutiny. And in doing so, I was called out of my own position of discretion.

This book represents one entrance into the field of discourse, through an examination of media discourse and life narratives, while situating sexual discretion within a history of masculinity constructs. As much I was burdened by the implications of this work for my personal life, this media event was the straw that broke the camel's back—an unveiling of the greater stakes for those who reside in environments where certain brands of masculinity were made premium and necessary for survival. Most black men in urban America do not sit with the privilege of a PhD in hand, writing and researching within institutions where LGBT research has begun to have a certain cache. With this knowledge, I cautiously entered their lifeworld (underworld) by way of personal narrative. Importantly, I have always recognized the uniqueness of black men and masculinities in America, carefully drawing out the (dis)similarities between us—our different investments in keeping the closet closed, cracked, or open. I am attentive to my position as a professor of sexuality studies, in a world where the salience of sexuality in everyday life may be liminal and limited.

Sexual Discretion explores black men's negotiation of queer sexuality[1] and masculinity, as they recuperate and recapitulate passing performances. Here, individuals must construct gender within scenes of high social constraint. They improvise every day to manage multiple identities, which stand in tension with not only their own masculine imagining of self, but also the larger public imagination. The role of proper gender performance in the sexual politics of discretion (how, and with whom, one chooses to engage in homoerotic desires) is central to this project. With this awareness, *Sexual Discretion* moves between the spaces where black men discreetly come together and the thick lines of historic literature, public discourse, and gossip. Together, these performative texts enliven and illuminate the complexity of black men's negotiations between masculine ideals and non-normative sexuality. This book represents my journey through physical space, my attention to gendered performances, and my engagement with literary and media texts that offer constructive grounds to develop a greater understanding of the promises and pitfalls of sexual discretion.

Peoples and Terrance Wooten—my graduate students and "extra eyes and ears"—my engagement with your minds and your present/future dissertation projects provided much insight and inspiration. The conversations, feedback, and collegial exchanges at University of Maryland were most valuable and unforgettable. Finally, to my friends and colleagues Faedra Carpenter and Christina Hanhardt, the worlds we create together—wherever we are—provide enough energy to get one hundred books done!

I have been blessed to be a part of scholarly networks and affiliations that enhance and enrich my intellectual and academic experience. The Black Sexual Economies Collective, the Scholars' Network on Black Men and Boys, and the Black Performance Theory Group have all been critical incubators for ideas and creativity. I wish to personally recognize Adrienne Davis, Alford Young Jr., and Omi Jones, who make generous mentorship appear so smooth and effortless. N. Fadeke Castor and Marlon Bailey, together we have walked this thing out—laughing and crying all the way to this moment! A host of other scholars have been a part of this book in direct, or more subtle, ways—representing a network of a different sort: Jack Halberstam, Roderick Ferguson, Jose Munoz, Tavia Nyong'o, Mark Anthony Neal, Tommy DeFrantz, Maurice Wallace, Marlon Ross, John L. Jackson Jr., Imani Perry, Wallace Best, Jonathan Holloway, Bryant Keith Alexander, Venita Kelley, Gust Yep, Brenda J. Allen, Phyllis Jap, Ronald Lee, Ronald Jackson, Robin R. Means Coleman, D. Soyini Madison, Mary Weismantel, Celeste Watkins-Hayes, C. Riley Snorton, Ramon Rivera-Servera, Jasmine Cobb, Harvey Young, Erica Edwards, Deb Vargas, Keith Harris, Mignon Moore, Kai Green, David B. Green, Darius Bost, Frank Leon Roberts, Kwama Holmes, Nicole Fleetwood, Carlos DeCena, Deriek Scott, Brandi Catanese, Robin Bernstein, Charlton Copeland, Victor Anderson, Josef Sorett, Alondra Nelson, Stephanie Batiste, Mireille Miller-Young, Felice Blake, Xavier Livermon, Matt Richardson, LaMonda Horton Stallings, Scott Herring, Shane Vogel, Michael Jeffries, Byron Hurt, Jason King, Martin Manalansan, Vershawn Young, Rudolph Byrd (I miss you), Gwendolyn Pough, Kevin Mumford, Hershini Young, David Ikard, Shanti Parikh, Rebecca Wanzo, and countless others. In their own way, each of these folk (and anyone I may have omitted) have been an inspiration and an intellectual contributor to this work.

As this book finished, I began a new chapter with many colleagues, whom I feel I have known for years. To the faculty of Women, Gender, and Sexuality Studies and the Department of Performing Arts at Washington University in St. Louis, I say thank you for supporting my work even before I was "official." The support, both intellectually and personally, has been unmatched and exceptional.

Without a doubt, this books owes much to its readers and its production team. To my anonymous readers, thank you for providing direction that would push this project for greater interdisciplinarity and to reach its fullest potential. To Doug Mitchell, you are a drummer who never misses a beat! From day one, I knew my book was in good hands. Tim McGovern and Erin DeWitt, words cannot express how your eyes and hands have been miracle-makers for this book. Indeed, the whole staff at University of Chicago Press handled this project with much care.

Finally, I must thank the anchors of my being. Thank God for keeping me. My parents, Sandra and Ronald Brown (and Jeffrey McCune Sr.), thank you for undying support. To my brother, Aaron McCune (who wrote two books before me), and my sisters, Monique and Melissa Brown (who will probably write more articles than I ever have), I honor you with this writing. For this book's finish has your existence to thank. My partner, Terence Pleasant, I know this book was discreetly "the other man." Thank you for sharing me; but mostly thanks for making the writing easier through encouragement and prayer. To all of my family and friends, words cannot express how grateful I am for your active roles in all of my many lives.

Chapter 2 was previously published in part in *Black Sexualities: Probing Powers, Passions, Practices, and Policies*, edited by Juan Battle and Sandra L. Barnes (New Brunswick, NJ: Rutgers University Press, 2009). Chapter 3 was previously published in part as "'Out' in the Club: The Down Low, Hip-Hop, and the Architexture of Black Masculinity," *Text and Performance Quarterly* 28, no. 3 (2008): 298–314.

ONE

Introduction:
Discrete/Discreet Acts, Goin' Down Low

The contemporary lesbian and gay movement since Stonewall has made living one's life as an openly gay or lesbian person a criterion of "liberation."

—Mark Blasius, "An Ethos of Lesbian and Gay Experience"

Driving the mechanism of these performed identities is a need to blend in, not to be noticed. The power of the "unseen" community lies in its ability to cohere outside the system of observation which seeks to patrol it.

—Peggy Phelan, *Unmarked: The Politics of Performance*

. . . a lot of black folks don't come out . . . doesn't mean they are closeted, but that they wish not to utilize terms that have too many distant associations, intentions, and connotations.

—Tim'm West[1]

In 2005 controversial and creative R & B superstar R. Kelly introduced to the world *Trapped in the Closet*, an innovative twelve-part music video epic—dramatized through the unraveling of social and sexual secrets, while also suggesting their centrality within everyday black life. In a sense, Kelly opened the closet narrative, filling it with cultural specificity and multiple possibilities. The series begins with Sylvester—taken from Kelly's middle name and played by Kelly—literally in a closet. From this vantage point, Sylvester narrates how what was supposed to be a one-night sexual event turned into a morning after. In Chapter 1, Sylvester explains how he woke up, lying in the bed of a woman (Cathy) after he fell asleep and "lost track of time." In a rush to get to his "wife at home," he attempts to leave but discovers that Cathy's husband, Rufus, "is coming up the stairs." To avoid

1.1 Sylvester (R. Kelly), in *Trapped in the Closet* (2005).

conflict or a confrontation, Sylvester first ridiculously considers exiting by way of a window, but then decides to hide inside of a closet.

As Cathy welcomes her husband home with an Oscar-worthy performance, they begin erotic play, as Sylvester waits in the closet. Each chapter in the series follows the same plot formula, unfolding the angst and anxiety of a particular clandestine relationship, while the uncovering of secret acts becomes the rising tension that leads to a cliff-hanging close. One of the most fascinating features of this series is the construction of each filmic music video: dramatic plots (absent a chorus), stylized employment of half-sung/half-spoken lyrics, and the God-like omniscient narrator that Kelly employs and embodies. Indeed, this ability to conjoin these often disconnected components is a masterful artistic accomplishment, as well as a site of pop-cultural fascination and controversy. The cliff-hanging tension—in this particular chapter, the potential of Sylvester being discovered in the closet—drives the narrative in each episode. As Cathy and Rufus are entangled in heated passion, Sylvester's phone rings. Here the plot thickens, as Rufus searches all over the house for the mysterious guest. Finally, in exhaustion and anger, he comes to the closet door—opening it slowly—as Sylvester stands inside with a raised Beretta in his hand. The sense of "what will happen next?" is the dramatic device that created high anticipation for Kelly's strategic release of each chapter within mass media and among his fans. Radio stations, television networks, and even billboards promoted the arrival of each of Kelly's episodes of high drama. Indeed, the opportunity to peek into the "closet"—to enter into what was a discreet space—offered people insights into an unknown world, even if it was only a construction of Kelly's imagination. However, what is most memorable about this moment of Kelly's artistry is the public controversy that he evoked with the closing of chapter 2 in the *Trapped in the Closet* series.[2]

Chapter 2 starts up at the moment when Sylvester is found in the closet holding a gun. He steps out of the closet, with gun raised, and engages in a conversation with Rufus that reveals that Sylvester was unaware of Rufus's relationship with Cathy, who wore a wig to disguise her identity and asked him to come home with her. It is also revealed that Rufus is a pastor.

The tension of the flailing gun is tempered as Rufus decides that "since we're all coming out of the closet today," he would too. Rufus then makes a phone call and says, "Baby . . . I just need for you to get back right here now." As we, the audience, anticipate the entrance of his mystery lover, Sylvester and Cathy also wait tensely for the arrival. There is a creak up the stairs and then a knock, and Sylvester narrates, "A knock on the door . . . and

1.2 Sylvester (with gun), Rufus, and his wife, Cathy, in *Trapped in the Closet* (2005).

1.3 Sylvester and Chuck, in *Trapped in the Closet* (2005).

the gun's in my hand . . . he opens the door . . . I can't believe it's a man!"
And out of the liminal space of the hallway comes Chuck.

This positionality, the clandestine relationship of these two men, not only becomes accentuated by Kelly as director, but is also a signature moment in public memory. Seemingly, the masses of people who witnessed the debut of this chapter of the series were in shock; I counted approximately twenty radio conversations on the day of its release that posed the question, "Sister, what would you do if your man was sleeping with another man?"[3]

This question has been central to black public discourse since 2004, with black men who sleep with other men while maintaining relationships with women receiving a considerable amount of critical mass-media attention. These men who often disidentify with traditional descriptors of sexuality (gay, bisexual, etc.) have been referred to and refer to themselves as "men on the down low" (DL). Often DL men practice discreet sexual acts while privileging spaces that are more heteronormative and that often protect or conceal their male-male sexual desires/practices. Indeed, the momentum of the DL topic within media caught my interest, as the discourse conjoined issues of black masculinity and sexuality. While mass-media attention has focused almost exclusively on those men who travel between sexes, the term "DL" is often employed by men who only have sex with men and employ a sexual politics of discretion. The disinterest by mass media in the men who solely have discreet relations with other men makes it clear what is at the core of popular fascination with this phenomenon: a crisis over sexual certainty.

The press has often framed "DL brothas" as being the primary carriers of HIV/AIDS, while implying that the solution is for DL men to "come out" to the black "community," as the anxiety around sexual uncertainty grows.[4] Consequently, it is the ability of some men to "pass for straight" that has become the central focus of mass media. While on the one hand, it is clear that there are valid concerns over transmission of disease (especially considering the lack of explanation for rising cases of HIV/AIDS among black women), the rhetoric around this subject still signals more angst over ownership of black men's (hetero)sexuality and an expected correlation between gender presentation and sexual desires. The anxiety created through this perpetuation of "black male crisis" has cast DL men's "private" practices as fodder for public consumption and obsession. *Sexual Discretion: Black Masculinity and the Politics of Passing* is an attempt to situate the DL and black men's private sexual practices within a larger historical and cultural framework, while also attending to the labor of black masculinity as an organizing structure for how these communities are constituted, as well as represented in media. While much of the public interest is fixed on deception and the potential of disease, my book pushes beyond this focus and reveals how the DL phenomena illuminates a complex working politics among black men (and women) called *sexual discretion*. As Juan Battle and Sandra Barnes suggest in their important anthology *Black Sexualities*:

> The nature and scope of the Black experience means considering what sexualities mean and how they manifest across the life course as well as how structural forces associated with poverty, political, and legal systems influence sexual decision making. (2009, 6)

Therefore, to answer their call, I look closely at articulations of sexual passing (performing discretion to move into respectable categories of sexual identity), while following men of various class backgrounds into virtual and physical spaces of erotic desire, and examining media and popular handlings of black male sexuality. I contend that the DL illuminates the centrality and complexity of black sexual politics—particularly unmasking the creative possibilities and dangers that emerge at the site of sexual and gender regulation. In order to understand how the DL both regulates and produces possibilities for black men, it is important to explore the etymological roots of the down low, which illuminate its relationship to the larger construct of sexual discretion.

The Down Low: A Case of Sexual Discretion

The term "down low" (DL) has come to be understood as describing a group of problematic black men who sleep with other men while having relationships with wives/girlfriends. But within the black community, the DL has always been more than an identity. The DL, in its long history within the black expressive tradition, has most commonly been understood as "something kept very quiet and secretive; also something done on the sly" (Smitherman 1994, 109). The DL acts as an epistemology—a knowing and doing outside of the common eye, or more aptly the scenes of surveillance. This way of doing and knowing was made evident through the "hush-hush," "quiet as kept," literally down-low positioning of things in both our communities and within our minds. This DL epistemological presence was articulated in the "hush" and "quiet" in slave songs and Negro spirituals, as well as the everyday adages that emphasized logics such as "be still and know." As black people have always been subject to social and juridical rule, they have attempted to move outside of the realm of discipline and punish. As they employed a discreet life (DL), which hid their innermost thoughts, they exemplified an early recognition of visibility's trap. Visibility seems to endanger the subject's individual agency—as bodies and cultures on display become available for control and usurpation. In this logic, spectacles—visible subjects and their personal repertoire—become controlled by those who have the power to determine their meaning and make public those things that marginal subjects hide for safekeeping. Therefore, these performative utterances and cultural vernacular expressions are not simply catchphrases, but indicative of the ways in which many black people deploy language to negotiate the safety of their identities. The importance given to such terms and discreet doings in scenes of high social constraint (slavery, lynching, Jim Crow) speaks to a recognition of how integral the "out of sight" moments were for those whose freedoms have historically been tied to secrets and careful renderings of information.

Of particular interest is how blacks use various maxims to signify not only the location of the information to be protected, but also to assert an evaluative judgment on the "nature" of the protecting. As early as the 1920s, there were maxims that accentuated the spatial register of those things that people dare not speak aloud. Kevin Mumford has excavated the term "low life" as a way to describe the black underground culture (cabarets, vice districts, balls) that enabled a commingling of queers, blacks and whites, as well as transgendered subjects. The use of the term "low life" here is not only a way to describe *where* in the community these activities took place, but also *how* the larger community may have interpreted participation in such venues outside the scene of black respectability. Nonetheless, practitioners of "deviance" had to move from up high (visibility) to places down low (clandestine), in order to express their desires, pleasures, and understandings of community.

This latter point can be seen most explicitly in a groundbreaking essay by Darlene Clark Hine, which I argue inadvertently speaks to the presence of sexual discretion within black life. Hine's essay "Rape and the Inner Lives of Black Women in the Middle West: Preliminary Thoughts on the Culture of Dissemblance" anticipates sexual discretion, as she narrates "a cult of secrecy, a culture of dissemblance, to protect the sanctity of inner aspects of their lives" (1998, 915). Since this essay, there has been no serious treatment of dissemblance, especially in terms of how it works within masculine contexts. Indeed, the DL is often understood as an "enigmatic" registering of silence, which conceals the inner and/or outer tensions between race, gender, and sexuality in black men's lives. While Hine rightfully situates the politics of dissemblance (discretion) as a coping mechanism within a history of rape and violence toward women, my aim here is to recognize the mechanics of this presence within black men's lives. Though most men with whom I spoke in this book were not victims of sexual violence, they were often governed by a world that committed violence against them when they acted outside of the gender norms for black men. Physical and verbal violence that policed their gender performance and sexual desire were often the norm of their day—teaching them what deemed them as proper black men in the context of urban regimes of masculinity. As one man said to me matter-of-factly, "You knew what was questionable and what should never be discussed." This current position of dissemblance and discretion speaks back to the histories of "coping" that have been a part of black male and female worlds. The DL, like the culture of dissemblance, offers a way for men to navigate the complex web of gender, race, class, and sexuality. The DL can also be traced to its most literal manifestation, the Underground Railroad, where thousands of slaves went "down low" to protect themselves from the demonizing gaze and hold of white supremacy. This example, like the life histories of the men with whom I spoke, illustrates how subjection can dangerously animate DL subjectivity. Late scholar Charles Clifton cited the presence of "homoerotic images, potential homoerotic relations, and alternative interpretations of same-sex relations" (2000, 355) during slavery as examples of early DL sexual realities. When coupling this with how black slaves would secretly teach their families how to read in clandestine areas with secret codes, it becomes clear that DL activity is not new nor contained to only certain dimensions of black cultural practices. While it may seem odd to employ the DL to these earlier happenings, in times where such language was unavailable, the social/sexual/cultural performances by many black subjects have historically occupied a space or location that can possibly be understood as the "underworld" (Herring 2007, 201). When one looks closely at the social worlds of the Harlem Renaissance and through time up to the present hip-hop culture, we witness how artists, politicians, and intellectuals employ discrete performances of social and sexual identities that often defy notions of respectability. To follow the DL backward or forward is to begin to follow the "ghosts"[5] that Avery Gordon notes may be instructive to understanding the "dense site where history and subjectivity make social life" (2008, 8). DL men and women exemplify a "complex personhood"—where they negotiate between the acceptable and unacceptable, the respectable and disrespectable, the queer and the non-queer. This navigation, a DL way of being in the world, is an articulation of a politics of discretion—which is not exclusive to sexual acts or outsiders, but rather available to all who seek agency under the constraints of surveillance.

The DL has always acted as an imaginative and physical space where blacks create, produce, and pronounce their own meanings outside of surveillance. Indeed, the men of this study utilize the DL as a way to describe their location outside of sexual surveillance and as a way to mark their masculinity as legibly truculent, guarded, and non-queer. These men travel and engage in desire in spaces that are outside of dominant culture, and they create lifeworlds that allow them to often celebrate the ideals of black masculinity while acting on queer desire. This is the function of the DL that speaks most to what I have called *sexual discretion*, as this term not only explains the use of secret and privacy (discreet), but also speaks to men's individual partner selection (discrete). My attention to the double function of discretion enables this project to not only deal with the phenomenological, but also the ethnographic and material machinations of ideal masculinity in the lives of black men. This, of course, is significantly different from other studies of black masculinity,[6] as this project is attentive to *how* men privilege ideal masculinities in order to move outside of queer affiliation and suspicion. For many of the men discussed here, the DL is not simply a sexual nomenclature, but a way to mark a desirable performance of gender. In this book, there is intentional slippage between "discreet" (showing good judgment in conduct) and "discrete" (individually distinct), as particular commitments to normative gender muddies the ability to mark a clear distinction between these terms. For those who are under repeated surveillance, they often dance between the discreet and discrete, sometimes embodying both in one moment—signaling the collapse of these terms, especially for those who are very clear that they are sexually distinct, but also sexually protective.

This latter move, to protect and move outside of deviant associations, is ever apparent in the discourse surrounding the DL in contemporary media. The DL, as noted earlier, has always had a dark valence, ascriptions that demonize those things that challenge notions of black "respectability" and "uplift." On these occasions, the DL is used to name those things that are deemed dissident and outside of black normative traditions. More pointedly, as the DL is coupled with sexual acts, it becomes taboo—or troubling even[7]—as the moniker gets attached to queer sexual subjects. The subject of sex and sexuality is often thought to be relegated to private quarters, underground clubs, and literature. For the sixty men with whom I spoke in this study, in both interviews and surveys, the DL was a way to articulate how they could make sense of their sexual experiences with men, without having to mark themselves as queer. Thus, for the majority of these men, the desire was not simply an aversion to visibility, but a rejection of the sexual liberation rooted in an articulated sexual identity. For the larger public, the DL quickly became a new, threatening queer presence that could not be disaggregated from disease, deviance, and a defiling of black manhood. In this book, my aim is not simply to explore the construction or maintenance of a DL identity, but to map how men "use their positional perspectives as a place from where values are interpreted and constructed" (Alcoff 1995, 434). Therefore, the DL as a positionality will be my common refrain—emphasizing *how* and *where* black men see themselves and their sexuality, in lieu of both media and historical framings of their subjectivity. In this way, the DL as a positionality for black men who have sex with men produces an alternative epistemology, wherein they can articulate sexual discretion on their own terms.

Rather than committing the sin of understanding the DL as epiphenomenal—a new emergent culture—I insist upon mapping the connection between the new articulation by men who have sex with men and historic presences, or silences, within the black community. *Sexual Discretion* is as much about the silence in the black community about sexuality as it is about the sexual silences that have always existed but remained unspoken. This project unveils a historical mode of performance that has been reincarnated, or remixed, under a new name: the down low. This nomenclature is not only a contemporary metaphor for discreet sexual acts, but also a signifier of a people's being in the world—a location that conceals private desires for the sake of pleasure, protection, and politics.

Most importantly, *Sexual Discretion* argues that in our focus on the DL as an illusory category, we have missed an opportunity to unpack the complexity of black masculinity and black silences around sex and sexuality. The role of sexual discretion as a coping mechanism within black queer life is underwritten in contemporary scholarship. In an attempt to correct this oversight, this project turns its attention toward public discourse and DL men in public and private spaces, as well as drawing lines between the DL and historic passing (discreet/discrete) subjects. How is the DL shaped through various modes of representation, and what role does the intersection of race, gender, class, and sexuality play? Who are the participants in DL culture, and how is this culture or community maintained and sustained? What genealogies of performance are in conversation with this contemporary manifestation of discreet sexual identity? How might we read historical performances using this contemporary presence and vice versa? How did sexual discretion as public fodder produce a sexual suspect or criminal?

Trapped in the Closet: Carceral Logics and the Architexture of Black Masculinity

R. Kelly's *Trapped in the Closet* video series clearly capitalizes on the popularity and heightened public awareness of the DL as phenomena and as sexually suspicious. In a sense, sexual discretion has become a product for public consumption. Kelly's awareness of the DL subject as in vogue is made most clear in his use of the male-male affair as the cliff-hanger for chapter 2 of his series, and this plays into the mass hysteria that sustains the public's interest. When the CDC distributed their 2001 HIV/AIDS statistics, stating that black heterosexual women accounted for 64 percent of new infections,[8] almost instantaneously fingers pointed to the down low: the deviant sexuality that would slowly become the new "closeted" face of AIDS. In 2005 the four-year stretch of heightened alarm had fueled much discourse—making the DL a central topic of interest for those most concerned with black sexual health. Thus, Kelly's production of the *Trapped in the Closet* series was both timely and economically savvy.

However, what is most compelling for me, as a scholar who engages in work that interrogates critical race theory and queer studies, is how Kelly forges a conversation between a historical racial trope and the construction of what can be called the black "epistemology of queer sexuality." Though the public focuses on the male-male sexual affair, the most sophisticated element of Kelly's creation is the exposure of the many "closets" within black experience more generally. What Kelly accomplishes in this artistic experiment is the crafting of a video series that uniquely adapts the "closet" as a stand-in for the black vernacular phrase "down low." Inadvertently, Kelly's framing supports my understanding of the DL as a continuum of histori-cal passing performances, which embraces a positionality that privileges a discrete way of being in the world. In the video series, it is clear that this is a functional theme, as characters wish not to draw attention to themselves or their doings. Rather, they move in and out of various positions—contingent upon who is looking—preferring to avoid surveillance and to contain their private desires.

What is odd about Kelly's hip-hopera is his employment of the closet as a generic metaphor for various types of discreet human behaviors rather than embracing the colloquial "down low," which has more racial specificity. This move is instructive as to the ways in which dominant terms penetrate marginal life and often become the "official" terms of use, rather than those that are more indigenous. In this case, though the DL may actually better encapsulate the experience of black male sexuality, the "closet" is employed for the sake of clarity or coherency. The common assumption, within and outside of mass media, is that umbrella terms produce simplicity and re-duce ambiguity about meaning. However, Kelly's move here seems to elide the importance of the cultural vernacular of black people, ignoring the clos-et's function as a term outside the black lexicon. Instead, he appropriates the closet and conjures all of its cultural baggage as a historically white and monolithic term—which Patricia Hill Collins reminds us in *Black Sex-ual Politics* predicates itself on being a prison-state and a place from which people want and need to escape (2004, 91–93). The DL, as one manifesta-tion of sexual discretion, cannot be so easily mapped on to a carceral struc-ture. The DL men with whom I spoke with do not have a yearning or desire for an "escape," but often find ways to navigate within an unmarked space that provides sexual autonomy and agency. In addition, to situate DL prac-tices within the prison continuum is to extend what Rashad Shabazz has discussed as the "carceral logic"—the act of limiting black male behavior and representations to prison productions (2009, 285). Like Shabazz, I imag-ine the larger community where black masculinities are produced—urban locations where prison and housing projects are commonplace—as having an adverse reaction to markers that may recapitulate high degrees of regula-tion and containment. In other words, the closet—unlike the DL—does not offer a space for freedom.

DL men, like other subjects who employ sexual discretion, use a "practice of freedom," whereby "the subject deliberately acts upon the self in an effort to alter the dimensions already imposed upon it, to reconstitute the energies already shaped by existing relations of power" (Scott 1999, 213–14). Like David Scott, I understand the unique articulations of the DL positionality as gesturing back at regimes of power. Tucked away in DL spaces, these men work within, around, and against dominant forms of black masculinity, heteronormativity, and urban surveilling mechanisms that attempt to organize their lives. The DL offers a space where they may imagine differently and organize sites where black masculine ideals and queer desire can coexist. While creative, this coexistence—in its contradiction—often casts these men into a discursive pit of double negation. On the one hand, they become the stereotypical black figures that represent the dangers of black manhood, while, on the other, they defy heteronormative expectations—appearing to be subjects of deception, rather than discretion. While some men do operate within the frame of dishonesty, the willingness to reduce all DL men to such figurations should be met with great pause. Rather, what is most clear in this study is that DL men who practice sexual discretion are much less preoccupied with deceptions than they are with crafting a presentation of self that signifies a heterogender, without requiring heterosexuality. Thus, the appeal and necessity of the DL as positionality is the access it provides to a "freedom" that is unavailable within the dominant cultural framing of black manhood and traditional understandings of the "closet."

In general, the closet has become a universal metaphor for secret-holding containers that have little to no agency. For Eve Kosofsky Sedgwick, the closet is "the defining structure for gay oppression in this century" (1990, 71)—it is the space that houses homophobia, the binarism of homo/hetero, and hatred. In his film *The Celluloid Closet* (1987), Vito Russo understands the closet as a container of hidden stereotypes and visual repression. Patricia Boling argues in *Privacy and the Politics of Intimate Life* that the closet is a space where "all are urged to come out in order to do their part in breaking down stereotypes by giving gay America a human face" (1996, 135). And today the closet is often still employed as the metaphor that houses all the "discourse" and debris of society—a space that eventually implodes or explodes. These closets, though descriptive and generative in their use in queer theory and queer life, implicitly attach a carceral logic to discrete sexual acts—both as a configuration that traps sexual subjects and sexual discourses. For all these "closets," the anticipated act of resistance is "coming out": the act of opening the container and revealing one's secrets to the world. As the opening epigraph by Mark Blasius suggests, "coming out the closet" is now the criterion for "gay liberation." Because the closet has become a universal apparatus that describes an oppressive space where individuals dwell, the given solution for finding freedom is located within the process of "coming out." This move from the closet outward, however, commonly describes the sexual development and experience of only some men and women whose understanding of sexual identities is often not informed by an a priori marginal position within society. In his powerful essay "Beyond the Closet as a Raceless Paradigm," Marlon Ross puts it this way:

> . . . the fascination with the closet as a primary epistemological device defining sexual modernity—results in a sort of racial claustrophobia, the tendency to bind both intragender desire and modernity within a small but deep closet containing elite European men maneuvering to find a way out. Beyond the claustrophobic closet, these men's discourses—and the closet that functions in them—are shaped by cultures whose deeply embedded and thus invisible racial identifications play a large unanalyzed role in the conceptualization of desire and sexuality, knowledge and normativity. (2005, 171)

While I accept Ross's premise that the closet's popular construction as a pre-Stonewall (pre-modern) apparatus is dangerous, I question whether the closet has utility at all when discussing raced men and women. For how does one who disidentifies with white homonormative descriptors find his or her "liberation" or freedom? This question is central to Ross's analysis of the whitened "closet," as he interprets the closet as a continued separator of the white "progressives" from the colored "digressives." However, his discussion of the closet as a "raceless paradigm" does not fully address how those who are always already under surveillance, as Peggy Phelan's epigraph alludes to, find efficacy in the act of being "unmarked" rather than marking oneself through public confession. Therefore, it is as important to delineate the moments where the closet does not end in an outing or an "identity," as it is to recognize those who live on the "down low." As various cultural groups employ discretion as politic, we must recognize how material differences move or eliminate the closet as an epistemological construct, as individuals move from a place of pain to one of possibilities. Thus, I refuse the notion of the closet as an explanation to encapsulate where many men of color reside, because of its naturalized link to carceral logics, which black men face in the everyday. No black man in America can escape the meanings of what Michelle Alexander has called the "new Jim Crow," or the prison-industrial complex where "more black men are incarcerated today than at any other moment in our nation's history" (180). The awareness of prison and the overall carceral state in black men's everyday lives is undeniable. The closet as a default frame—seeing its carceral structure—is, for me, unimaginable.

My contested relationship with the closet also emerges as a response to the reality that produced this book: many black men and women have utilized the down low as a structure of choice, to best name and represent the creative, generative, and transgressive space for discreet acts. For these men and women, agency is the ability to articulate sexual freedom through an indigenous frame, rather than to operate with some compulsory out-of-the-closet formula. To employ the concept of the closet in this project is to capture black men. Such incarcerating paradigms foreclose our recognition of sexual autonomy and moments where agency abounds and complex personhood is managed, even within discrete communities. Moreover, in worlds structured by constant negotiation, the presumptive limitations of a closet structure are challenged and turned on their heads—illuminating the need for alternative understandings of sexual discretion. Tim'm West, in the epigraph that begins this introduction, captures the essence of my argument as he explains how queers of color more generally "wish not to utilize terms that have too many distant associations, intentions, and connotations." While West's emphasis in the film *Pick Up the Mic* is about LGBT identities, this is equally applicable to "the closet" as a term. The closet assumes too much and describes so little of what happens in the lives of queers of color; for DL men, it misnames and misframes discretion as a foreign register, which endangers the development and freedom of the given subject.

As we witness R. Kelly's narration of the closet in blackface within his epic video series, the rubric of the traditional closet is apparent as its construction is riddled with ideas of pain and embarrassment. As the title suggests, the individuals in his series are "trapped" in the closet. While typically the word "trapped" connotes a feeling of no escape, I argue that Kelly accidentally narrates a state of being not applicable to the conventional closet metaphor. As the cycle of secrecy within his epic continues to manifest itself, from the beginning of his video series to the end, the idea of the trap becomes a natural state of unfolding possibilities. In other words, Kelly's closet—unlike Sedgwick's or others'—has agency and envisions other experiences outside of "shame."[9] The closet metaphor is typically employed to suggest that there is little or no agency. In Kelly's rendering, Sylvester (Kelly) still has agency in his version of the closet, as the first and second chapters show him narrating (almost directing) the whole video. Though he has limited mobility, he clearly has control over the action and outcome, as his words speak the scene into being. He even stages his exit from the closet. Here, the pain of the closet for Sylvester is that the door is opened—that he is exposed to the gaze of the "other" man in the room. This is an important distinction between notions of the closet and the DL, as the latter does not typically end in a "coming out," but sees the "privacy of intimate life" as a liberating experience.[10] The danger is often not in feeling conflicted or trapped in a closet per se, but the anticipated stigmatization that arises as marks of abject sexuality, or sexual behavior, are revealed.

This awareness is made most evident when Rufus's male partner Chuck arrives on the scene. Immediately, for the audience and for Sylvester (as he points the gun at them), they become the target as the most-wanted and suspicious suspects. They are asked more questions and are met with most surprise and scrutiny than Sylvester was when he was discovered in the closet. In this way, Kelly's framing of the closet in the video series may be similar to the traditional closet in form, but the content is different. Inside Kelly's appropriation of the closet, there is room for agency and pleasure. He utilizes the "closet" but actually unveils the workings of the DL in black communities or society in general. Though he does not mention the DL specifically, its presence and meaning are invoked, as the DL is a part of the current media discourse, as well as a key notion in Kelly's own repertoire. In 1995 Kelly released a song entitled "Down Low (Nobody Has to Know)," which details the life of a man who is propositioned by a woman who is already involved in a committed relationship for an affair "on the down low" or "in secret." *Trapped in the Closet* is like a remix of "Down Low"—in its change in structure, characters, and the use of the closet instead of the DL. Like a good remix, the medium of the song is changed—though not the message—to tell a similar story, with additional riffs and re-visions. Indeed, Kelly is "doin' the down low," while remixing the closet.[11]

The significance of Kelly's choices is emblematic of how individuals can (mis)appropriate terms for the sake of clarity. The real importance of Kelly's creative arrangement for this project is his ability to construct a narrative that revisits sexual discretion for black people, vis-à-vis the DL. Unconsciously, it calls back to black traditions of using the DL to avoid the mark of stigma and move outside the gaze of surveillance. Kelly's video series draws parallels between the down low as a traditional trope within black life, while illustrating the ways in which the DL also serves as a sexual metaphor. Though much of public attention has been given to the queer version of the DL, Kelly's video series recognizes that this "remix of the closet" has utility across sexual lines. Practices of discretion are not specific to those who engage in marginalized sexual acts. Neither are such acts of discretion specific to the sexual realm—the DL, specifically, has been employed in various sociocultural situations where careful judgment and concealment seem the most affordable options. While Kelly's artistic efforts serve as examples of how one can, and should, understand the sexualized DL as a product of history, the public interest in the queer side of his series gestures toward varying anxieties present because of the ideals set for black men and their acts of sexual passing.

Kelly's closet is architecturally genius in its ability to capture how black men are policed at once by institutions and the construct of black masculinity. *Trapped in the Closet*—vis-à-vis a good ethnographic eye—illuminates spatial and affective dimensions of the black masculine queer subjects' dilemma and the DL as a space of negotiation. Kelly's hip-hopera represents black men on the DL on a liminal plane, where the demands of gender ideals and sexual non-normative practices create tension. In chapter 1 of the series, Sylvester goes into the closet as a necessity, as protection from all that would evolve in the bedroom adjacent to the closet. Indeed, as he is coaxed out of the closet by the husband of his mistress, like clockwork everyone in the room begins to "come out" with confessions. While the video reverts to some typical DL narratives (Sylvester and his mistress confess that they are both "stepping out" on their marriages), it also introduces the queer DL figure. While the other discreet sexual acts were delivered with ease and almost nonchalance, Sylvester narrates the queer story line with a legato stretch, offering an overrepresentation (or emphasis) on the husband's male-male love affair. I believe that here, while Kelly's attempt to capture the hype surrounding black male-male discreet sex is most salient, he accidentally unveils what I call the *architexture* of black masculinity. This nomenclature is used throughout this book to illuminate how space (the physical frame) and the texture of the space (the ideological frames of gender) can create a vernacular of understanding of what constitutes appropriate gender presentation and sexual behavior. The thickness of black masculinity as an organizing structure is central to an understanding of sexual discretion in Kelly's video series, as well as the larger public understanding of the DL.

In the process of the minister husband's queer confession, Sylvester uses the quick punitive glance to indicate a greater disapproval of the DL in queer face than his own masquerade. This scopic discipline increases as the wife—who was just caught in an affair with Sylvester—tells her husband how his male-male affair is "a little extreme" since the presumed "she is a he." Together, Sylvester's gaze and the wife's words become symbolic representations of how heteronormativity and the rubrics of masculinity collaborate in the making of discrete queer subjects and an understanding of abject queer subjectivity. Here, Kelly enlivens how surveilling mechanisms such as the black church, marriage, and other institutions—while operating as an aside—are salient and significant in the everyday lives of black men.

Understanding this surveillance through triangulation means understanding how the architexture of black masculinity can be a stronghold on black male subjectivity. The demand for what is deemed properly masculine is narrated by individuals and institutions—providing the backdrop for varying needs of discretion. As I struggled to develop a research methodology for this work, I had to account for the ways my body was deemed less masculine and carried a history, which could only be challenged by a critical and conscious performance of (an)other. In other words, the arbiters of my masculine sincerity or authenticity—in the context of this work—were the men with whom I would speak. Knowing this, my approach to this project was safest when trudging through media clippings and old articles, than the moments where my body was on the line—performing as carefully as the men who questioned not only my intent, but also my gendered subjectivity. My critical-methodological dance—as I often refer to it—exposed the DL as a mode of living or a method of interaction with space and cultural politics, which involves a complex set of considerations and, at times, an exacting distillation of kinetic energy.

The DL Methodology: Discretion in Practice

As an openly gay man, it was sometimes very difficult to sit in rooms where my openness was muted—my queer comportment was tempered—in order to have DL men open up to me about their lives, relationships, and tenets of masculinity. As you can imagine, to perform this study I could not put out a call for all DL men to e-mail or call me nor could I announce myself as a "university professor wanting to know all about your life, your sex practices, and sexuality." Rather, I had to be quite careful. I had to be discreet. I had to be attentive to how I asked questions, got information, and managed verbal and physical vocabularies. Due to the nature of the subject— the transient quality of the topic—I also had to be open to going to nontraditional places. For this reason, I could not be bound to just interviews or participant observation—as the DL was as much a media event as it was a literary presence. Thus, this study, though primarily ethnographic, had to call upon discourse analysis and literary criticism. Like a scholar trained in performance studies, I followed the performance phenomena—in this case, the DL as subject—to better understand the processes and politics of sexual discretion. This book is therefore the result of what John Jackson has called a "peripatetic" ethnographic method (2005, 10), where the ethnographer follows the shifting boundaries of the field. While this project utilizes this methodological approach, space is not just contained to the sociocultural but also includes the intertextual. In order to unveil the richness of this terrain, *Sexual Discretion* makes a concerted effort to maintain a productive tension between traditional participant observation with textual/discursive/ literary analyses.

Sexual Discretion, being the first of its kind to document DL doings and to map the terrain of the larger discourse surrounding them, could not just perform observation and recording without being attentive to its larger cultural significations. On the one hand, I had to embody the sexual and social discretion I studied, while, on the other, I was attentive to how the sexually discrete/discreet was being written about and understood broadly. For me, to explore DL culture and then to write about it was to always be engaged with everyday life and representation. In order to do much of the work for this project, I had to literally go "down low." My entry into the field began at the level of discourse—as the DL arose as the centerpiece of twenty-first-century conversations around the rise of HIV/AIDS among black women. I sat with newspaper articles, media clippings, and even participated in a few public media outlets[12]—witnessing the evolution of the bogeyman, the scapegoat, the deviant subject, and the tensions of sexual discretion. As I gained more understanding of the "Why now?," I became interested in the "How now?"—as in *how* does this descriptor and its discourse operate in the twenty-first century? Or *how* do DL men navigate what I know about traditional structures of black manhood and their queer desire?

To address these questions required me to be both careful in conversation with DL men and in my own presentation of self; ethnography is almost always a discrete/discreet practice. Central to my methodological approach is my own move to a DL positionality, as I had to learn how to navigate within spaces and collect information in a way that did not endanger the "privacy" of those with whom I spoke. As discrete populations are hard to reach, I identified openly gay men who had sex with men who considered themselves to be on the DL to not only secure interviewees, but to learn codes, terms, and practices that were specific to DL men and the construction and maintenance of their positionality. Over a four-year period (2003–7), I secured approximately sixty interviews with DL men in Chicago, with men ranging from eighteen to forty-six years of age. In addition, I was able to establish a way of being in the world that was essentially representative of me, while lending itself to gender norms and expectations of those I would encounter. Through gay-identified men's mini-tutorials, I learned patterns of behavior that would mute some of my non-normative gender attributes and highlight those traits that would make me attractive (or of interest) to men "on the DL."[13] And of course, as I performed more and more interviews, I mastered a masculine delivery that appealed to most of the men with whom I spoke—as they felt more comfortable in sharing personal desires, secrets, vulnerabilities, and conflicted aspects of their lives. Without a doubt, it was imperative that I adopt a "DL way of being in the world" to gain credibility and access into DL spaces and DL men's lives.

My gender performance was as important as the gender presentation of the men in this study. Therefore, throughout the book I am often reflective of my own positionality within various spaces—alerting the reader of how my role as ethnographer is complex and equally creative. This project understands the DL as both a liminal and creative positionality, which accounts for the necessity of sexual discretion. One of the first ethnographic observations I made was that the men with whom I spoke never said, "I am a DL man"; but, rather, they said, "I am on the DL." This is a crucial distinction, as one maxim traffics in the field of naming an identity, while the other speaks to the liminal location of the subject. This difference is remarkable and instructive to understanding how DL men articulate their being caught between two worlds—idealized black masculinity and queer desire. DL men, indeed, are passing subjects.

As I wandered in the field, themes of "passing" saturated my field notes and conjured a return to historic texts, which unbeknownst to me would become a feature of this project. I repeatedly recorded in my field notes questions like, "Where do these men pass each other?" and "Why does it seem like men are trying to pass for something?" or "Can I pass for straight?" I was boggled by the implications of these questions as essentializing projects, but more provoked by the active presence they seemed to have in men's lives. While I was traditionally unconcerned with what Brooke Kroeger has referred to as moments "when people can't be who they are,"[14] I found that passing politics was a more complicated mechanism for DL men, as chapter 5 illustrates by showing how aspirations to perform respectable blackness and acceptable masculinity were given privilege. While mass media is transfixed by this process as one of deception (the passing for) through the frame of the "dreadful bisexual" figure, most of the men with whom I spoke *passed into* a heterosexual identity in public space, while having primary male-male sex. While there were some who navigated between men and women, the large majority employed the DL as a descriptor of sociosexual location but did not participate in sexual relationships beyond male-male formations. The quality of the pass, for these men, was largely contingent upon social and cultural adjudications of gender performance. In other words, the pass into straightness—often thought to be consummated by actual sex—was often maintained through proper performances of gendered expectations.

Indeed, space was highly significant in maintaining and fostering a politics of discretion—as much could be gathered from not only where DL men laid their head at night, but *how* they navigated various social and cultural locations. The sharing of these "space stories" and experiences as significant propelled me to travel into the chat rooms, "real time" phone chat lines, and to the Gate dance club—where I began to understand not only the exterior performances of black masculinity, but also the interior work that is so complicated yet palpable. To map such flow and flux, I employ a multi-sited ethnographic approach,[15] which allows me to move between lived experience, historical texts, and media constructions of black male "scripts."[16] Dwight Conquergood, George Marcus, and William Hawkeswood are the most recent critical influences on my understanding of critical ethnography. Critical ethnography's account of "subjugated knowledges"—those everyday ways of knowing, often illegible to those not in the know, that are often placed at the bottom of the sociopolitical ladder—excites me both intellectually and personally.[17] This commitment to uncovering the multi-layered dimensions of cultural communities undergirds my desire to utilize this disciplinary tradition in my own research. Ethnography, as I envision it, is "committed to unveiling the political stakes that anchor cultural practices-research and scholarly practices no less than the everyday" (Conquergood 1991, 179). This emphasis on the "everyday" and its "stakes" elucidates the importance of my research examining the DL, both as a discursively constructed identity and as an individually embraced concept. So many DL men have shared with me a commitment to black masculinity, which holds as its primary concern finding a way to negotiate everyday performances of masculinity and the stakes of engaging in non-normative sexual practices in non-normative sociosexual environments.

As I built closer relationships with DL men—traveling into social spaces and watching them engage in virtual life, I became an embodiment of Conquergood's notion of "co-performative witnessing." Conquergood conceives of ethnography as "an embodied practice; it is an intensely sensuous way of knowing. The embodied researcher is the instrument" (1991, 180). This conception of ethnography as performance, a doing and a dialogue, situates the ethnographer in a position not above but alongside the people with which we work. Co-performative witnessing demands that I never forget my role as an "uninvited guest," while working toward relationships that establish open lines of communicative exchange.[18] This becomes most important as I discuss with men the intimate details of their sexuality and the inner/outer workings of their masculinity. As a black male in the academy talking to black males outside of the academy, I situate myself at a position that enables dialogue, not distance. This was only accomplished through "deep listening" and never forgetting that "opening and interpreting lives is very different from opening and closing books" (Conquergood 1985, 2). When I encountered DL men in chat rooms, clubs, and phone chat lines, my role as "scholar" coexisted alongside that of "brotha," "homie," and even friend. As I moved in and out of spaces/zones of interaction where I might normally not be invited, I acted strategically—learning codes, performances, and attitudes that would not only provide welcomed entry, but also encourage disclosure and trust. The performative dimensions of this project mark this as more of a "performance ethnography," which signifies my sensitivity to not only history and its constructions, but also the necessary transformations or alterations that the ethnographer's body must make in order to do rigorous and substantive research.

DL men are often hyperaware of their bodies, space, and the markers of masculinity. As they disidentify with the noted politics of visibility, these men occupy sites where anonymity is guaranteed or can at least be achieved. As a "co-performative witness," I had to also acknowledge the shift in landscape and remember that in these many sites the "identity of the ethnographer requires renegotiation" (Marcus 1998, 97). In this study, I witnessed three major sites of inquiry: Internet sites for men who wish to meet other men (commonly known as "m2m" chat rooms), the "Bi-Blade" phone chat line, and a club called the Gate on Chicago's Northwest Side. With a critical consciousness, I transformed, transplanted, and made myself translatable in order to gain access to DL (br)others and to learn more about the inner workings of DL culture and its various meanings. Like a good witness, my sight is not limited to the parameters of formal space, but moves between and beyond literary and historical texts—making way for the unveiling of multiple performances of sexual discretion.

On some levels, this book moves from the outside in, beginning with discursive renderings of the DL in chapter 2, "Yo Daddy's Dysfunctional: Risk, Blame, and Necessary Fictions in Down-Low Discourse," where I explore how the DL is constructed within mass media. This chapter looks closely at mass media because the DL as a subject of interest arises as a media event or frenzy. In this chapter, I extend the discussion beyond the effect of discourse on the understanding of the DL, to also examine how this "scripting" of the black masculine body has (re)constructed black female sexuality, as well as the black community in general. Central to my unpacking of the evolution of DL media discourse are articulations of "risks"—in terms of HIV/AIDS—and "blame," as corroborators in further black male demonization. As this chapter travels within different visual frameworks—from HIV/AIDS prevention posters and materials to the *Oprah Winfrey Show*—I illustrate how various modes of representation enact violence upon black bodies, using agents of the state and understood actors of benevolence. Chapter 3, " 'Out' in the Club: The Down Low, Hip-Hop, and the Architexture of Black Masculinity," moves inside the community and explores how DL men negotiate their identity in spaces of desire. What does it mean for DL men to go "out" to a black, predominantly gay club? To understand this contradictory performance, I enact a "deep listening" and discover how the shape and style of masculinity in the club unexpectedly enables, or unleashes, queer desire and queer (dis)comfort. In chapter 4, I examine how DL men navigate voice-centered and virtual spaces, to produce a certain "masculine sincerity," which at once secures and endangers a DL positionality. This chapter, "Goin' Down Low: Virtual Space and the Performance of the Masculine Sincerity," explores the "doings" of DL men on phone chat lines, as well as on Internet sites for male-male sexual desire. Here, DL men illustrate how they circumvent certain demonizing narratives, while also dangerously enforcing others. Specifically, this chapter explores how DL men represent themselves in voice-centered and virtual space, in the absence of the body. While being self-reflexive about my own use of these mechanisms for communication, I am able to practice, navigate, and examine the coded DL that men use to perform queer desire in virtual space and beyond. Indeed, the navigation of identity boundaries and expectations is central to DL men's social lives and follows the pulse of new media studies, which identifies connection and collaboration between various mechanisms of technological representation. Chapter 5, "The Pages Are Ridden with Discretion: Pedagogy of the Pass and Present," situates the DL within a history of passing narratives. In this chapter, I draw parallels and dissimilarities between racial and sexual passing. Through a rereading of James Weldon Johnson's *Autobiography of an Ex-Colored Man* up against E. Lynn Harris's *Any Way the Wind Blows*, the chapter introduces the contemporary sexual-passing novel—marking the significant differences between the historical and contemporary passing narratives. Shifting the critical paradigm from a *passing for* of identity, this chapter poses the question "What does it mean to imagine this act of transgression as *passing into*?" Before the mainstream attention to the DL, novelist E. Lynn Harris had written several books about the glamorous life of what we now know as DL men. His novels, like race-passing novels, take us on a journey into the life of a sexual, rather than a racial, subject who expiores and navigates his dual identity. E. Lynn Harris novels, however, rarely articulate this process with as much rigor and complexity as writers of race-passing novels. In this chapter, therefore, I examine E. Lynn Harris's novel *Any Way the Wind Blows*, which coincides with the popularization of the DL in popular media. I analyze media responses to his novels, personal reflections, and materials from my "talk sessions" with readers. Ultimately, I argue that his books function as a kind of pedagogy or "epistemology of the DL" that "teaches" black women how to discern whether a man is "passing" and to "beware" of his performance "down low." The chapter concludes with a close examination of *Essence* magazine's DL exposé, which further elucidates the "E. Lynn Harris effect" and how discourses of passing have permeated the larger consuming public.

The concluding chapter, "From Sexual Discretion to Sexual Suspicion," illuminates how the DL serves as a strong case study of how black men's practices of sexual discretion are transmogrified into the suspect sexual subject—as black male sexuality is made illegible to the larger public via mass media. This chapter illustrates not only how DL men's bodies are policed through discourse, but also how heterosexual black men's gender performance is ridden with scrutiny—conjuring impulses to self-police and move away from non-normative gender expressions. Through an engagement of multiple sites of cultural performance, while moving outside of what is considered "traditional" spaces of inquiry, *Sexual Discretion* allows us to see how the DL as cultural spectacle frames sexual discretion as both anomaly and a grotesque racial anatomy. *Sexual Discretion*'s focus on discreet, non-normative sexuality challenges the conventional practice of examining queer practice through attention to the queerly visible. In turn, it naturally pushes what may be accepted as "common sense" for how sexuality is articulated, particularly in the context of black male surveillance. While the DL is used as a contemporary case study, this project does more than investigate this particular group of men—but, rather, it challenges how we may understand the *doing* of sexual discretion, under the constraints of public surveillance and gender policing.

TWO

Yo' Daddy's Dysfunctional:
Risk, Blame, and Necessary Fictions in
Down-Low Discourse

... the statistics—figures—regarding HIV infection are fraught with complications, not merely because they are changing so rapidly, but because they have an uncanny way of slipping into figuration. This means two things: on the one hand, these numbers seem to lift off the page and signify to us something other than literal, living, dying men and women. On the other hand, they are often read too literally—as representing the "reality" of a situation that is in fact much more complex, and implicates many more people.

—Barbara Browning, *Infectious Rhythms: Metaphors of Contagion and the Spread of African Culture*

We have to get used to these anxieties, this mathematics of probability intruding into our intimate concerns, this bogus objectivity, this coding of risks in our present culture. If anyone ever thought that the complex coding of taboos was more restrictive, the work of the modern safety officer should give them pause.

—Mary Douglas, *Risk and Blame: Essays in Cultural Theory*

Where is the origin of this robust interest in and anxiety over black male discreet (bi)sexual acts? For me, it began with a candid conversation at Starbucks, where a woman told me that "there is so little information out here on *these* [DL] men, that *anything* seems helpful." Her search for, and acceptance of, "anything" alerted me to what would be the complex consumption of discursive material around the "down low" (DL). As the DL arose out of media texts as a sexual nomenclature, it became the new buzz-word for racially deviant sexuality—the blame for the rising spread of HIV/AIDS—a product of "spectacular consumption."[1] In the course of a year, the DL moved from being the ironic, contradictory, and paradoxical hip-hop "homo-thug" of simple intrigue to the linchpin in the 2001 report that black women comprised 64 percent of all new HIV/AIDS cases among U.S. women.[2] Somehow, the previously unknown "homo-thug" was pegged as the culprit of transmission, and "Brothas on the Down Low" became the metonym for the new plague within many black houses. In other words, as the discourse transitioned from a more oxymoronic term (homo-thug) to one from within the black vernacular (down low, or DL), there was more attention given to how these men allegedly infected and endangered black women, as well as threatened the imagined stability of black heteronormativity. This threat to black women—and particularly the black heterosexual, often middle-class family—issued an alarm that would spark articles in almost every major news press in this country (*USA Today, Los Angeles Times, Washington Post, St. Louis Dispatch*), black magazines (*Essence, Ebony, Jet*), as well as mainstream television (*ER, Law & Order, Girlfriends*), including the incomparable *Oprah Winfrey Show*. As discursive interests spread throughout the country, the myth that the DL threatened to infect all facets of black life spread concomitantly. The possibility for media to propel a myth of DL ubiquity and contagion speaks to the power of discourse in the construction of not only social fear, but also social drama. In some senses, sexual discretion performed by these men—the unavailability of their narratives to the public—conjured a discursive frenzy to piece a cultural puzzle together, without proper context and consideration. And like a drama without clear characters, the plot thickens in conjunction with a historical, social, and political imaginary.

The beginning of a discursive explosion almost always determines the future of a "thing."[3] The media has taught us most of what we know about the DL and black men's sexual desire and discretion. In this chapter, I attend to constructions and contradictions present within media that frame DL men and attempt to make sense of black men's sexuality and sexual discretion. Mostly I am interested in the conversation that media discourses forge between the public imaginary and black men's lives. Norman Fairclough illuminates the scope and importance of critical discourse analysis:

> Critical discourse analysis of a communicative event is the analysis of the relationships between three dimensions or facets of that event, which I can call text, discourse practice, and sociocultural practice. (1995, 57)

I am interested in these dimensions and attend to how the consequence, or punishment, for contemporary sexual-passing performances[4] is constructed in terms of disease. This construction of the "new black phenomenon" as the blame for the disheartening and startling HIV/AIDS rates is not only a response to the reasonable fear that black women are at high risk, but also the historic tradition of panic over the health of the black family.[5] Most importantly, this defense of family rhetoric appropriates the narrative of dysfunctionality, historically ascribed to black women, and inscribes this fiction upon black male bodies. This so-called discursive strategy frames black men as irresponsible figures within a heterosexual sphere; thus, in some ways rewarding black women while punishing black men.[6] Whereas the Moynihan report attributed much of the detriment of the black family to black women playing "untraditional" roles, in a moment of perceived high black female mobility, it is easy to flip this narrative—using the DL as an example of how black men destroy black families. Unfortunately, the DL arrived at a time when black men were already stricken with the image of "deadbeat dad," "absent father," and "irresponsible partner." These images, while mythological and not metonymic, collaborate with the DL and prescribe a strong formula for the doom of black community health and welfare. My start here, at the place of discursive demonization, is informed by my being in the ethnographic thick of things—watching the discourse unfold, urging a greater engagement of how the men understand themselves and work in contrast to these questionable and dangerous characterizations.

I first realized this reconfiguration of the black family destruction narrative in the DL context when I encountered a privately produced DL-targeted "outreach" poster. The "prevention" poster has an image of a smiling young black girl with her chin resting on her knuckles (as if thinking) and reads:

> You Hurt My Mommy!
> It's more than just about you
> Always Practice Safer Sex

Beyond the problematic use of a young prepubescent girl in the service of sexual welfare, the poster speaks loudly to and points directly at men who infect black women via heterosexual sex. The young girl asks on behalf of the mother, as an innocent yet personal representative of the mother's "hurt"—a result of the black man's, or her daddy's, dysfunctional behavior. Here, the narrative of the father acting out recalls not only a historical understanding of black men's natural inclination toward deviance, but suggests an intent to do harm to black women. The young girl's body is used as a tactic to invoke empathy and sympathy, and a punitive gaze from those who identify with her concern for her "mommy," while also sympathizing with her obscure awareness of what Daddy did to Mommy.

However, one of the most problematic components of this construction is how it assumes that DL men are selfishly ("It's more than just about you") acting out their sexual desire, without concern or care for the women with whom they may, or may not, be involved. In addition, it presumes that DL men have kids and participate in heterosexual sex. Largely, this is representative of the DL discourse. This representation has become the template of the DL type: a black man who has sex with men, who lies to his wife/girlfriend, putting them at risk for sexually transmitted diseases. This poster is emblematic of how DL discourse and various other "official" discourses are highly informed by the mythologies and historical constructions surrounding black men's sexual behaviors and historical constructions, rather than the DL men's sociosexual realities. As the subtitle of this chapter suggests, "risk, blame, and necessary fictions" are at the center of DL discourse. For this reason, this chapter is organized to illuminate how "risks" and "threat" are constructed as media engage in reading DL men's culture; the role of blame (and shame) as a (dis)empowering technique for those who enter DL discourse in search of power, or "mission work";[7] ultimately, this discourse—predicated upon the misconstruction of risk and threat—relies upon the necessary fiction of black women as non-agents and passive victims, who are solely the recipients of black men's disease and pathology. Together, these demonizing inscriptions upon the black male body mark him and the larger black community as dysfunctional—substantiating the urgency of a moral and health crisis.

Indeed, DL discourse explains more about the working ideologies among consumers of DL discourse than the complex network of male subjects who engage in same-sex desire "down low." In this way, the thirst for any possible knowledge about this "new (sexual) phenomenon" is akin to the common excitement over anything representatively black. As the DL subject has arisen out of a media context, as well as been sustained within this domain, the so-called DL phenomenon can more aptly be understood as what John Fiske calls a "media event," in which "we can no longer rely on a stable relationship between a 'real event' and its mediated representation" (1996, 2). The DL has been constructed as a new phenomenon—a construction I challenge in all parts of this project—while also being framed as the "major vector of HIV/AIDS contagion within the black community" (Browning 1998, 12). Important here is that neither claim has ever been empirically or socially substantiated. Indeed, the DL story is not simply a representation but "has its own reality" (Fiske 1996, 2). This narrative is a summation of historic understandings of sexualized black bodies, contemporary mythologies around disease and contagion, as well as a by-product of certain perpetuations of hysteria by those who understand themselves as the "safety officers" of the black community and, more often, black women's bodies. While there are some differences between black and dominant media coverage of the DL in terms of perspective, much of the representation acts like ready-made press material, constructing a slightly modified version of black men acting out. At the core of DL representation is the need to make sense of the seemingly hyper-presence of disease; DL men provide a convenient sense of clarity and a body upon which we can inscribe blame. In one of the epigraphs that begins this chapter, anthropologist Mary Douglas clearly predicts the moment of down-low frenzy that now preoccupies much of media's discussions of HIV/AIDS within the black community. Sexuality outside of heterosexuality is, still indeed, a taboo subject in American society. Sexual taboos undeniably facilitate and encourage comfort in more normative sexualities, pushing all outside performances to the margins in order to retain some kind of moral center. When non-heterosexual relationships are placed at the margins, they are removed from having the cultural intelligibility that is often associated with normative sexuality. As a result, many rely on the decoding of sexual taboos by those whom they believe to have greater knowledge, or authority, in terms of discussing sexuality and its complexities. In the case of DL men—or any performance of non-normative sexuality—media, health officials, and self-appointed "experts" are too often the generators of inaccurate and incomplete explanations of queer sexual presences for the general public. Most pointedly, media, along with its texts, is often accepted as *the* authority on issues of sexuality, removing the power from the voice of the actual sexual subject, neglecting more nuanced discussions of the sociocultural aspects of our constructions of sexual identities. Instead, DL discourse provides a necessary fiction that attempts to reconcile the enigmatic nature of the sexual uncertainty within our society. Public and official discourse, in this case, work in tandem to explicate not only what constitutes the DL, but also how it functions in relationship to what is often thought to be the sexually certain—heterosexuality. Often we use the ideological tools given by history and contemporary constructions of blackness to do what Ronald Jackson II (2006) has referred to as "scripting the black body." Here, the DL is scripted not only with the cultural baggage of the demonized and dangerous male of yesterday, but also with the threat to the future of black community well-being.

This chapter looks closely at the rhetorical implications of media discourse around the DL—how the black male body is scripted—the dual effect of media representation on hetero/homo constructions of community. I am interested in the seemingly insistent effacing of the complexity of sexuality, for the sake of uncovering the potential mystery of the rapid growth of HIV/AIDS in black America. Media, and even state agencies, enact three types of violence in their public renderings of the "official" DL narrative: (1) As the DL is labeled a new *black* phenomenon, which is dangerous and a spin-off of the homo-*thug*, it unfairly constructs black queer, and non-queer, men as being sexually irresponsible, peculiar, criminal, and generally dysfunctional; (2) when the rising HIV/AIDS rates among black women are placed as central to public inquiry, black women are positioned as convenient conduits for demonizing black men—enabling continued gender tensions between black men and women—while framing women as being simple "victims" of black male sexuality; and (3) when emphasis is placed on both the lack of "outness" among DL men and the "heightened homophobia" within black communities, an image of black people as unreasonably backward and socially underdeveloped emerges—without giving recognition to racism's effects in static constructions of blackness. Because of this lack of recognition, this chapter engages more than just discourse, enabling a "critical pedagogy," which, as Douglas Kellner explains in *Media Culture*,

> develops concepts and analyses that will enable readers to critically dissect the artifacts of contemporary media and consumer culture, help them to unfold the meanings and effects on their culture, and thus give individuals power over their cultural environment. (1995, 10)

As I have engaged questions around DL men and their performances of sexuality, one of the most problematic tendencies among consumers and producers of discourse has been the lack of scrutiny given to source material, as well as the case studies used within quasi-documentary narratives. This chapter rereads the discourse in a historical context, understanding how, as Patricia Hill Collins puts it, "the past is ever present. . . . [T]he new racism relies heavily on the manipulation of the ideas within mass media" (2004, 54). Rather than seeing the construction of the DL as an extension of black male criminalization, much more attention has been given to the intent, ethics, and behaviors of the DL subject. As one woman told me, "I wish these men would just come from down low, put it out in front and on the table!" Her imperative echoes the sentiments of many women and men who embrace circulating narratives of DL men as irresponsibly parading as straight, while infecting "our sisters" with HIV/AIDS—often left to assume that the motive behind these men's secrecy is simple deception, without accounting for the sociopolitical circumstances of men of color, more generally.

Such conclusions are too simple, leading to reductive renderings of black male sexuality, as well as of the complexities of HIV/AIDS transmission. Because DL men typically remain "down low" or choose discretion in terms of their (homo)sexual behavior, there is little opportunity to hear actual explanations for discreet sexual practices by DL men themselves. For this reason, the voice of the subject is often absent, leaving the general public to absorb information that reflects more about those who do the reporting, as well as their own anxieties around issues of sexual uncertainty, more than actually representing the population of men on the DL. Specifically, the construction of "disease might be read as a literalizing or making manifest of the social atrocities against those afflicted . . . here, gays, the urban poor, women of color . . ." (Browning 1998, 23).

In this sense, the dominant reading of the down low is an interpretation of absence. DL discourse attempts to give textuality to an inaccessible/invisible presence that is void of cultural recognition. This, in turn, produces more negative attitudes toward black men, facilitating intra-margin tensions, whereby "brothas" are always scrutinized and policed. As black women search for the "signs" of DL men—often finding nothing—they collect misleading data on DL men. I argue that this desire for *any* information, as well as the robust dissemination of "knowledge," has led many to embrace and perpetually recycle incomplete narratives, which purport to provide greater clarity and valuable answers to those concerned with the "deadly" and "dangerous" deceivers. Through close readings of popular media texts and their constructions of the DL subject, I uncover the somewhat coded meanings that are inscribed within DL discourse. First, through an examination of the shift in DL men's construction from "homo-thug" to "down low," I map and trace the residue of the "thug" representation, which, I argue, is never detachable from its most recent manifestations in popular mediums. Second, I look closely at the emergence of a physical representation of the down low, through J. L. King, who provides a visual image and affirms highly scrupulous explanations for the presence and "prevalence" of DL men. Since the beginning of the down-low media frenzy, King has been a central figure in its momentum. As a self-proclaimed "DL brotha," he "outed" the culture, and himself, to the public. Here, I am really interested in how black popular discourse makes use of and relies on what I call a "messenger mythology" as a mode of understanding King and his "knowledge" of community health issues. Third, I reevaluate the popular ethos of "Save our women," which has become the central explanation for discussion around the "dreadful bisexual." Finally, I offer some examples of HIV/AIDS outreach in communities of color, as well as pose a challenge for cultural constructions of "queers of color" in terms of disease. Most important, I argue that these contemporary portrayals of DL men recall historic laments of black men as poor fathers, always acting out, and leading to the dysfunction of black society. Similar to various representations of black women—where they are framed as the central problem within black families[8]—a new working-class "monster"[9] has now invaded black familial territory, endangering all that has been gained post–civil rights: DL men.

From the "Homo-Thug" to "Down Low": Constructing Black Sexual Deviance

The negro is eclipsed. He is made into a member. He is the penis.

—Frantz Fanon, *Black Skin, White Masks*

To be an American Negro male is to be a kind of walking phallic symbol; which means that one pays, in one's own personality, for the sexual insecurity of others.

—James Baldwin, "The Black Boy Looks at the White Boy"

As black men who have sex with other men while sometimes maintaining relations with black women have received much public attention, their moniker "down low" (DL) is often discursively flipped to "low-down" (LD). Rather than providing information that is descriptive in nature, many journalists focus on the dark stories that highlight men's sexual deception. Generally, DL discourse offers contemporary representations whereby black men are reduced to what David Malebranche has called "a black weapon of mass destruction."[10] As discourse preoccupies itself with "the secret sex" that black men have with other men, it only draws attention to how the black man functions sexually, ignoring the sociocultural factors of DL life. Thus, the black man is reduced to how his penis performs in his everyday life, rather than how either sociocultural forces act upon him (such as homophobia), or how he negotiates sociocultural expectations or constraints. Yet when journalists or so-called activists do attend to such issues, they construct a picture of the black community as being peculiarly homophobic or "backward." For example, an April 22, 2002, *St. Louis Post-Dispatch* article explains that "homophobia—the irrational fear or hatred of homosexuals—has deep roots throughout the world. But in America, the fear of ostracism may be greatest in the black community, where masculinity is especially prized" (Hollinshed 2002, A1). Such renderings juxtapose the "black community" against the larger American society, viewing it as a unique space that enacts homophobia at higher proportions. In the context of a post-Stonewall America, then, the black community becomes backward and "underdeveloped." The discourse assumes a certain advancement in addressing homophobia and acceptance of homosexuality in other communities, while black communities appear bound to some age-old commitment to masculinity that is less present in other communities. While there is some merit to the centrality of masculinity in creating the necessity of the down low, this is not culturally specific to black people. Nonetheless, this telling of the narrative in the *St. Louis Post-Dispatch*, and in many other newspapers and magazines across the country, unfairly racializes the down low as always already black, not to mention "homosexual." In this way, the Fanon epigraph above is fitting—as these men and their way of being in the world is eclipsed, while focus is placed on what they do with their penises and the dangers caused by them. Rather than viewing these men and their everyday encounters, we are presented with a fragment—penile activity—which acts as the representative "member" of black male dysfunction and destructiveness.

Before the *St. Louis Post-Dispatch* or the now-popular Benoit Denizet-Lewis's *New York Times* exposé of the DL, there were other media representations of black men who had sex with other black men, who allegedly claimed a heterosexual identity. The initial conversation taking the "down low" as subject began exactly where it most likely will end—the black male as (homo-)thug.[11] In July 2001 Malcolm Venable published an article in *Vibe* magazine that featured the "homo-thug," a descriptor for men on the DL in a hip-hop context. This presumably paradoxical nomenclature, "homo-thug," is as provocative as it is problematic, particularly in a black sociopolitical economy that tells us that "there is no homo in hip-hop."[12] In this value system, hip-hop culture is at the center of the thug's life, while gay culture is often assumed to be its antithesis. Though the *Vibe* article's central focus is the "unmarked" heterosexuality of DL men that becomes possible through a stylized masculinity, its usage of "homo-thug" overpowers and reconfigures the potential possibilities for any critical exploration. The incorporation of such a loaded term, while potentially transgressive in its connection of seemingly disparate representations, highlights the discord between societal constructions of homosexuality and hip-hop. Consequently, as both homosexuality and thugism are often static within public imaginings, the transgressive possibilities for the presence of a "homo-thug" dialogue is limited. The homosexual is largely (mis)understood as white and effeminate, while the thug is often (mis)interpreted as black and virulently masculine. Nonetheless, one may propose that if we understand hip-hop and homosexuality as polysemic entities, then we can see that the economy of hip-hop makes room for a space where the homosexual and hip-hop are in conversation. As both respectively disrupt the normative structures of sexual and musical histories, they call forth a politics of resistance and disidentification. In this way, hip-hop and homosexuality may be seen as two peas in the same pod. Thus, their meeting at the nexus of DL discourse seems more appropriate than oddly placed.

Vibe's introduction to the DL has largely framed the popular aesthetic that would become the prominent representational figure for DL men. Pitted above its large caption "A Question of Identity," the *Vibe* article begins with a photograph: black men and a woman dressed in hip-hop fashions, dancing asymmetrically, while postured in a way that suggests an identification with everything that is considered properly masculine within a hip-hop sphere. These men dance at the Warehouse, a once historical black gay club space in the South Bronx of New York City. Venable emphasizes that we are "more likely to see them in rap videos, in music videos, or hanging out on the nearest corner of the hood" (2001, 100–101). While Venable's painting of these men as those in "rap videos" and living in the "hood" conjures all that is problematic and essentialist in many contemporary constructions of black hip-hop figures, it attempts to articulate how certain bodies are unexpected in identifiably queer spaces. The figure of the "unclockable" thug-like figure, in his malleability and inaccessibility to the larger public, has become the enabling device for more punitive discussions of DL men—rather than the middle-class affluent brothers who also participate in discreet performances of same-sex desire.[13] In *Vibe*'s framing of the DL, the black male is often dressed in baggy clothes (read: hip-hop gear), which clearly associates him with a certain class of sexual deviancy. The "DL brother" in this article is never suited, or even dressed in khakis, but posed against the backdrop of hip-hop—a historical marker for the black poor or working class. Though this has been contested by several scholars, hip-hop apparel is still classed this way—though it is often appropriated by those who are not of the working class. This classed character, the illusion of the "irresponsible" and "non-committal" thug, enlivens the possibility for the pathologizing of black men. Here, in the context of "thugdom," the alleged deceit and harm of DL men toward black men and black women becomes more palpable. The career of the thug as a violent and deadly hip-hop icon inexplicably explains the photographic images of the black male bodies clubbing in the shadows of their supposed heterosexual lives, engaging in criminal drug activity, "hating themselves," and participating in what is often understood as black sexual deviant acts.

In many ways, the coupling of hip-hop and queerness has accelerated the circulation of this "deviant" figure within media, as this "new" combination suggests that the presence of DL men within hip-hop space is, in itself, a new manifestation. As this performance of discreet sexuality has been predominantly located within the world of hyper-masculine hip-hop culture, it appears anomalous and is easily set apart from previous historical black cultural productions. Yet, as we reflect honestly upon history, we know this is a highly inaccurate and incomplete claim. Though the DL is new in terms of its mnemonic use, it has been a part of a black queer genealogy, as well as a historical tradition of controlling images, whereby black men are reduced to the dysfunction—the acting out of their sexual instrument—rather than their negotiation of desire, queer or otherwise, often deemed "deviant" within a white racist, often classist, American imaginary.

In much of the DL discourse, black men are reduced to their penises—the use of it, the misuse of it, and the danger of it. I argue that the prevalence of the DL within the hip-hop frame of the homo-thug constructs black men as class characters acting out through engagements in "risky" and irresponsible sex—giving greater traction to narratives of dysfunctionality and danger. Venable affirms such beliefs when he situates the "thug" within a specific lineage:

> A few of today's successful and popular rappers—DMX and LL Cool J, for example—have that buffed, just-got-out-of-prison appeal. What some of the other leaders of the hip-hop pack may lack in gym body—Jay-Z, Mobb Deep, Master P, and Shyne come to mind—they make up for in general thuggishness. And if the scenes in social environments are any indication, young, gay, black men have mimicked their example. (2001, 104)

Venable suggests that there is something not only about the anatomical structure and nonverbal presence of these men that speaks "thuggishness" but also excludes "young, gay, black men" from the creation of this aesthetic posturing. Vibe's construction of thug works to affirm historical mythologies, while placing the DL within a construction that is always already loaded with criminality and danger; or, at least, construed as such in the retelling in Vibe magazine.

What is missing in DL discourse, however, are the ways in which the so-called "thug" persona is often activated to simply stylize, or aestheticize, a brand of masculinity. Put simply, there is often an incongruous relationship between what one wears and what one "actually is." It seems most appropriate to initiate a critique of the thug as essentially black, as well as always constructed as necessarily violent, irresponsible, uncouth, and working class. If we begin to understand the variant uses of the thug aesthetic, we become better readers of what actually occurs within this domain of discourse: black men are made deviant, only as much as our historical and mythological fantasies work to limit the possibilities of their performances of masculinity. Often the thug aesthetic is a strategic device used to command a certain amount of respect or power through an association with what may be understood as properly masculine. For example, when the main figure in the *Vibe* article, Malik, expresses his commitment to "doing things to prove [he's] a nigga" (Venable 2001, 102), he articulates the performative and powerful component of such aesthetics in the context of homophobic and masculinist surveillance. Malik is engaged in somewhat of a strategic assimilation, whereby he uses a strategically essentialist representation for his own purposes. Malik's understanding of the DL embraces a central theme within hip-hop culture and queer politics, as he "articulates a sense of entitlement and takes pleasure in aggressive insubordination" (Rose 1994b, 60). Yet instead of reading between the lines, so to speak, the discourse continues to produce simpler, more linear notions of the "thug"—whereas this representation of the black masculine satisfies the need for a cohesive, though problematic, understanding of all that is wrong in the scene "down low."[14] Rather than understand DL men in terms of how they understand themselves, this article is committed to circulating a new term in order to provide coherency for the reader. The general reading of the "thug" in this article does not examine what lies beneath the aesthetic of both the space of the club or the clothes worn by DL men. Instead, it refuses to engage in a discussion about an exotic other who does "gay" in thug apparel. The invocation of Baldwin's epigraph above, used as well at the outset of the *Vibe* article, speaks loudly. While I believe Venable's use of Baldwin in *Vibe* speaks directly to the pains and pitfalls of black men satisfying dominant notions of the properly masculine, I believe Venable missed the most important component of this quote. Baldwin appears to engage in double-speak, as he insinuates how men "pay" in order to attain power and appease the gaze of others. Indeed, the image of DL men as homo-thugs, then, is less a confirmation of their subscription to the hip-hop masculinist, homophobic regime than, more accurately, a symbolic script used by these black queer men to access power in a world that compensates them for the propensity to "violently act out" (hooks 2003, 57).

I recognize, however, that the previous reading does not make interesting headlines. While readers are more attracted to provocations of fear, writers have much to gain from the construction of crisis (Altheide 2002, 11). Indeed, DL discourse conjures fear through the construction of the black male thug, while also creating a sense of crisis by locating the origin of rising HIV/AIDS rates within one group of men who sleep with men. When I began this project a few months after the *Vibe* article, the DL was literally "down low." Within months, it not only piqued my interest but emerged as a site of media attention throughout the nation. However, over the next few years, DL discourse would serve to produce more questions than provide working solutions. Between 2001 and 2003, several articles appeared in print media that continued in the trend of shaping the fear of HIV/AIDS "risks" and pointing blame down low—through various forms of tracing the unrecognizable but present sexual "thug" endangering the black community, distorting HIV/AIDS facts and statistics, and reducing the DL to a simplistic subcategory of underdeveloped gay black men. Though it is impossible here to recount the many essays that were written on the topic between 2001–3, it seems instructive to highlight some writings that are quite representative of this trend in the larger discourse to provoke fear, at the risk of demonizing not only DL men but black men in general.[15]

On July 23, 2001, *Jet* magazine published an article entitled "Why AIDS Is Rising among Black Women," which attributed the increase in HIV/AIDS rates to DL men. The article focused on a central female figure who contracted HIV in 1991 during a pre-DL moment. In an *Essence* magazine article problematically titled "Men Who Sleep with Men: AIDS Risk to African American Women," published in October 2001, Tamela Edwards attempts to make sense of the rise of HIV/AIDS by unraveling the possibilities and practicality of DL men being the sole carriers of HIV into the black community. Though she makes a strong effort to complicate the traditional narrative by scrutinizing popular discourses of "blame," her title alone points the finger not only at DL men but all men who have sex with other men. This disconnect between her goal and her rhetoric is symbolic of something highly significant yet commonly elided when examining the discourse: rhetoric often doesn't match intended meaning. While DL men are often constructed as "dreadful bisexuals," they are also simply reduced to dangerous "men who have sex with other men." In this logic, the sex between men is constructed as the "risk factor" and the blame for disease. Here, DL discourse has great implications for its implicit threat to any potential gains in terms of black gay and straight relationships. Though Edwards admits in her article that the problem is unprotected heterosexual sex in terms of the high rates among heterosexual women, she is unclear as to whether the issue is "men having sex with other men" or "men having unprotected sex with other men and their wives." I argue that the opacity in her construction illustrates her own ambivalence. For while the central concern propagated by media is black women's health and safety, the undergirding theme is that men who have sex with other men are inherently dangerous and deviant.

Interestingly, the main narrative in Edwards's *Essence* article, which acts as a case study for how DL men "spread" HIV, is a woman who was married to a DL man, had children, and was never infected. Her use of this example speaks to the type of panic produced through media representations of the "innocent" family who is always in queer danger. While Edwards clearly suggests in this narrative the danger of homoerotic possibilities to heterosexual men and their families, it does not substantiate any evidence of HIV infection as a result of their acts. Likewise, a *Los Angeles Times* article, published on December 7, 2001, pathologizes black men in prison as having an almost natural connection to the down low but does not provide any solid examples that this is at the center of HIV transmission among black women. As Keith Boykin informs us in his book *Beyond the Down Low: Sex, Lies, and Denial in Black America*, "After a year of media hype in 2001, the media could not produce a single example of a man on the down low who had recently given HIV to his female partner" (2005, 105). He later goes on to explain that the actual HIV/AIDS statistics were potentially too "boring" and "complicated" for the general public, whereas the DL provided an easy target.[16] Boykin then adds that between 1991 and 2001, according to the Centers for Disease Control and Prevention's 2001 report, there had only been a 3 percent increase in the number of black women who contracted HIV/AIDS from heterosexual sex—a minor increase considering that only 1.6 percent of those women admitted bisexual sex as a possible means (107). This reading corroborates with the research and findings of Greg Millett and Dr. David Malebranche, who have spent much time examining both DL discourse and public health implications. Millet and Malebranche argue that "few studies of MSM (men who have sex with men) recruit sufficient samples of men of color or collect information on bisexual activity to properly evaluate the level of risk that bisexual men pose to women in minority communities" (Millet et al. 2005, 52S). With no real substantive evidence, just a circulation of articles and blurry images of DL men, the face of the AIDS victim became the black woman, while the criminal agent became not only the enigmatic discreet black man but all men who have sex with other men.

Though the aforementioned media attention was important in the construction of the DL phenomenon, particularly within black communities, its momentum became most prominent in an August 3, 2003, *New York Times Magazine* article. The front cover of the magazine was almost predictable, its caption reading: "Living (and Dying) on the Down Low: Double Lives, AIDS, and the Black Homosexual Underground."[17] This article, which looks closely at the lives of black men who have sex with other men, not only positions their discussion within the context of AIDS, but it also calls back to the "homo-thug." On the front cover, underneath the caption emblazoned in white bold lettering, we witness an extremely problematic urban setting. Two black men face each other, standing between two older vehicles, in front of a crackled wall—staring at each other, dressed in so-called hip-hop gear. Both men place their hands in their pockets, a suggestion of being closed off, yet their stares operate to signal desire or interest. Placed below the larger font of "DOWN LOW," these two bodies—though not clearly recognizable—are representations of DL men. While the static dress code poses questions, the lack of clear recognition is clearly an apt, yet strategic, choice. The down low, up to this point, has no face—except the images that are conjured within the American imaginary when black men are posed as "thugs" or criminals and are painted as silhouettes in the background of the queer club space.

Inside this issue of the *New York Times Magazine* is French gay journalist Benoit Denizet-Lewis's article, which attempts to better explain the image on the front cover. This article, "Double Lives on the Down Low," begins with somewhat of a definition, with the tone of an elegy:

> To their wives and colleagues, they're straight.
> To the men they are having sex with, they're forging an exuberant new identity.
> To the gay world, they're kidding themselves.
> To health officials, they're spreading AIDS in the black community.
> (2003, 28)

First, it is important to note that the *New York Times Magazine*'s patrons are largely middle-upper class and white, and accordingly the article begins with a discussion of "wives and colleagues." Unlike the earlier *Vibe* article, it quickly addresses the audience that it serves most frequently. Consequently, I argue that the discussion begins with attention on the infiltration of the

DL within middle-class communities. This moment is worth noting, as this article prompted what I call the "mainstreaming of the DL"—making its entrance into larger public discourse. As I will discuss later, this article not only became the sort of biblical text for popular understandings of the down low, but also began a cycle of attention by way of other newspaper and magazine articles, television shows, and public discussions. Nonetheless, the residue of the "homo-thug" past always seems to inadvertently find its way within DL discourse. As this introductory poem/elegy/news report gives a sense of urgency to the DL topic, it operates as a signal of crisis, as well as a device to captivate interest. In this passage, DL men are constructed as men masquerading as "straight"—participating in a grotesque drag—which brings forth the presence of disease within the "black community." It is this latter concern that makes the DL a strange bedfellow within the *New York Times Magazine*. In the context of this magazine, a cover story discussing black men who have sex with other men is a historical phenomenon within itself. What makes the *New York Times Magazine*, after all these years of silence on the topic of black queer men, publish an article about the DL? What work does this supposed problematic DL subject perform that sparks more interest than gay black men? In this upper-middle-class media context, I believe that it alleviates this reading public from having to be accountable for the disproportionate rates of HIV/AIDS within the black community. Specifically, this article distracts us from the realities of the disparaging lack of health care treatment and prevention methods geared toward minorities in general. Instead, it refocuses our attention as it situates black men in a position of blame—as the new "vectors of contagion" for HIV/AIDS. Whether conscious or unconscious, such representations within popular media provide a moment where white men can define themselves against black men—as having more courage, strength, and progression (in terms of sexual freedom/safety). Such affirmations negate the strength of these black men in order to affirm the place of not only white middle-class heterosexual men, but also the lives of those who are white and queer. As is common in discourses that take HIV/AIDS as its nucleus, this article participates in the tradition of locating new "risk groups, a community of pariahs" (Sontag 1989, 25). In the popular and highly regarded *New York Times Magazine*, this article could further reconstruct the face of HIV/AIDS as being everything but white and/or gay, reinforcing the circulation of blame placed upon the black and sexually deviant.

Denizet-Lewis's article did everything *but* veer away from the sexiness of the "thug," as he paints a scandalous picture of the two lives of DL men—one that involves dishonesty with women and the other that involves unsafe, unapologetic practices with men. By his title, one may assume, as with many articles written about the DL, that the conversation would include the "double" lives that DL men lead, as they travel in and out of homo- and heteronormative spaces. Such a text would undoubtedly explore how DL men negotiate travel, cleverly and strategically, between two distinct but often overlapping cultural spaces—heterosexual and "queer" communities—particularly examining the language employed within specific spaces and perhaps the impact of the DL presence on the social climate of certain institutions. However, such negotiations are rarely discussed or pursued in this article or in media discourses surrounding the DL more generally. Instead, we see another representation of the black male sexual subject as both deviant, deceptive, and downright irresponsible. Unlike most articles, with a central location of interest, Denizet-Lewis travels across the country. This approach, of course, allows him to implicitly map the presence of DL men nationally, rather than locally. While this might offer a comparative viewpoint, which could illustrate the heterogeneity within DL populations, the article further homogenizes this group. As he travels from place to place, he makes no assessment of how geography changes the expressions of race, masculinity, or sexuality. Rather, he provides a sort of filmic pan across the nation, "framing blackness (and queerness)" as always already deviant and, thus, in need of white surveillance and explication. After all, as a young white female scholar-friend told me, until the Denizet-Lewis article, "there had never been a sustained study of DL men across this country." While this may be the longest article written about the topic, it neither sustains a consistent reading of any one particular scene, nor does it provide critical insights as to what is happening in terms of disease in the black community and DL men's negotiations of sexual identity. This article, like much of popular discourse, participates in the exoticization of black sexuality in order to perpetuate fantasy and deem the black male body as a site of sexual intrigue and disgust, simultaneously.

This trend to exoticize is most obvious as we follow Denizet-Lewis, at the start of his article, into a Cleveland bathhouse called Flex. This space is one riddled with negative historical baggage, as it is often thought of as one of the first institutions implicated as a birth site of the American AIDS epidemic. Beginning the conversation here, right after the public service announcement opening, solidifies speculations that DL men are frequent travelers in what was once, and arguably still is, considered a haven of HIV/AIDS transmission. Throughout this article, the author exoticizes the life of these men, while implicating them as almost conscious criminals who purposely engage in immoral acts. Though he asserts that DL men are not gay men, he also posits: "While intravenous drug use is a large part of the problem, experts say that the leading cause of H.I.V. in black men is homosexual sex" (2003, 30). This preposterous statement was, I believe, an unconscious rendering of the logic that is guiding Denizet-Lewis's article. The problem here is not the DL (indeed, in some ways it is considered "sexy and interesting"), but rather the "revolutionary" act of black men loving black men (Beam 1986, 240). It is this perpetuation of same-sex desire as dangerous and contaminating that fuels homophobia; in this case, taking a historical white homophobic mythology and putting it in blackface.

The *New York Times Magazine* article also dismisses the different articulations of sexuality by these men. For example, as Denizet-Lewis travels to Atlanta and New York, he meets several men who describe themselves as being on the "DL." Though some men state that they still engage in sexual relations with women, while others do not, he reduces them all to being "gay." He dismisses their description of identity, in order to position them within a more legible frame for his reader. Whereas if he was to accept their claims of "DL" or initiate the term "bisexual" in order to more fully explain sexual behavior, Denizet-Lewis would be mandated to provide a more complicated reading. In focusing on the male-male relations, Denizet-Lewis is able to simplify this article while averting any confusion or uncertainty on the part of his reading audience. By utilizing the term "gay," he calls forth a historically homophobic expectation for "gay" deviance—the difference is that here his discussion brings forth both sexual and racial cultural prejudice. His, like earlier texts, provides a necessary fiction—one that explains, though haphazardly and incompletely, the crisis situation in black communities: HIV/AIDS. Moreover, his narrative brings together stereotypical depictions of racialized and sexualized subjects to manifest what he calls "concern" but is interpreted as "crisis." This act of constructing "crisis" is apparent as he moves through the narrative, highlighting sexually charged spaces and "risky" sexual acts between men, while masquerading as a simple tourist of DL culture.

Indeed, Denizet-Lewis's article utilizes the voice of its interviewees—particularly their articulations of masculinity—to illustrate the rhetorical significance and attractiveness of the DL as a cultural group. Through a focus on the interviewees' commitment to black masculinity, a structure I also critique, Denizet-Lewis can establish a central problem in black male life, as well as within the black community. While there is some truth to this claim, he does not complicate this simple equation with other co-constitutive elements of black life—such as dominant ideals of masculinity and the white racist gaze. With flippant remarks such as black men live "secret lives, products of a black culture that deems masculinity and father-hood as a black man's primary responsibility" (32), he demonstrates a very limited perspective on not only the black community, but also black mas-culinity. His readings of black masculinity—constructed as linear—provide an easy point of critique. Here, Denizet-Lewis participates in a style of jour-nalism that employs the KISS method—Keep It Simple, Stupid—showing a problematic, reductionist version of black male life that is easily digestible and relies on stereotypes. Like the *Vibe* magazine article, he shapes the dis-course of the DL within thug-like images. In his mind, the thug aesthetic is not only the dominant motif of black male subjectivity, but also the way in which black masculinity gets performed. Indeed, there is a presence of thugisms within the everyday performances of some black men, but it is not the only example of an idolized black masculine figure. Denizet-Lewis, in relying on the image of the thug, forfeits the opportunity to get at the true complexity of black masculinity—a construction where values, rather than images, are often at its core. In Ronald Jackson's *Scripting the Black Masculine Body*, he defines "thug" as follows:

> A thug by nature does not abide by the rules, and that is the work of pride, not disdain. Thugs seek to reposition the black male body as being in control of himself and his women. . . . [I]t is contrary to the definition of the mack to be weak. One of the hallmark characteristics of a thug is his desensitization, his emotional paralysis. (2006, 112)

While Jackson attempts to problematize this linear narrative through a longer explanation in the text, he more fully characterizes the imaginary at work in Denizet-Lewis's construction. Jackson's passage above may sound like a description of thug discourse; however, it becomes clear that he is committed to the idea that this is an actual embodied manifestation that produces "black masculine scripts." I argue that his distillation is a script of-ten not read, or performed, by all who do what they understand to be black and masculine. The *New York Times Magazine*'s article highlights in bold or-ange letters, in the middle of its DL exposé, a section where a self-identified gay man seems to side with these linear portrayals of the black masculine as thug-centered. The interviewee, whose name is William, explains, "Part of the attraction to thugs is that they're careless and carefree. Putting on a condom doesn't fit in with that" (Denizet-Lewis 2003, 32). Denizet-Lewis offers no critique or explanation for such an essentialist remark, nor does he even add an alternative reading to this construction, but rather affirms that condom negotiation would "shatter the [DL man's] denial." Not only does

Denizet-Lewis make acts of denial an ontological presence among DL men; he also validates a thug persona as being natural and uniquely black. Indeed, Jackson's discussion that the "thug is a modern brute, which is revered for his Stagoleean disposition and feared for his out-of-control, haphazard, and volatile behavior" (113), speaks more to Denizet-Lewis's discursive rendering rather than affirming a belief in the ontological outrageousness, immorality, or irresponsibility of black men. William's explication of his attraction to the thug, as well as Jackson's framing of him, are simply individual responses to isolated situations and circumstances. Rather than allowing such framings to theorize DL men, as Denizet-Lewis does, it may be more productive to examine these statements within the historical contexts of black male demonization and demoralization—particularly the ways in which racial doubt is infiltrated within the black community by means of media, society, and cultural understandings. The words of these men, in terms of defining the thug, are not finite voices, but versions of racist/homophobic understandings beings internalized by those who sit at the margins themselves.

Interestingly, the hinge of the demonization and demoralization of black men in Jackson's visualization of the thug and Denizet-Lewis's article is the black woman. Denizet-Lewis's piece, like most writings on the topic, starts from the premise that "two-thirds of the women who found out they had AIDS were black" (30). However, similar to most other articles, the black woman is the subject who never returns in the article, but who acts as an illusory mammy figure—used to help carry out racist imaginings of black men. In Denizet-Lewis's article, we see a broad sweep over the actual voice of black women and how they understand themselves within the discourse. Yet an overwhelming focus is on DL men's activities within black "queer" settings with one female "scholarly" representative of the black female voice—who never is asked to discuss her black femaleness. Such broad sketching of DL life only serves to exoticize the "queer" potential of black men on the DL, rather than to address issues announced as significant from the article's outset:

> DL culture has grown, in recent years, out of the shadows and developed its own contemporary institutions, for those who know where to look . . . . Over the same period, Down Low Culture has come to the attention of alarmed public officials, some of whom regard men on the DL as an infectious bridge spreading HIV to unsuspecting wives and girlfriends. In 2001, almost two-thirds of the women in the United States who found out that they had AIDS were black. (Denizet-Lewis 2003, 30)

The core issue, often noted as the impetus for the majority of media texts about men on the DL, is the impact of HIV/AIDS among black women. Whether there is a direct relationship between DL men and black heterosexual women's contraction of HIV is irrelevant. The issue of concern here is *how* and *why*, and to what end, are black women's bodies being called forth as "wives and girlfriends." In Philip Brian Harper's *Are We Not Men?: Masculine Anxiety and the Problem of African-American Identity*, he argues that in the case of Magic Johnson his heterosexuality was called forth as a "shoring up of masculinity" (1996, 33). How does the black woman factor into the DL equation? Here, she is the exponential factor who hides in the shadows of the "hot" details of DL men's sexual explorations—who only appears when necessary to further criminalize black men. Though she is often a symbol that raises the value of black male demonization, she is always already present. Throughout Denizet-Lewis's framing, she appears to challenge DL manhood, and/or masculinity, as the DL man is often framed in the process of acting irresponsibly. She is the diseased body haunting the consciousness of the *New York Times Magazine* article, as well as that of DL men. She is the wife who birthed the child sitting in the backseat; she is the woman to whom phone calls are made to explain why he is not home; and she is the specter that always appears when DL men affirm their heterosexuality or disavow homosexuality. In the case of Magic Johnson, the black woman was conjured to affirm his masculine status; within this discourse, the black woman is simultaneously marked invisible and visibly marked. The distinction here is significant. Magic Johnson in one sense controlled his image, as he constructed his public narrative and his wife was made highly visible. At this point this is not the privilege of DL men, as there are no men and women who represent themselves and make themselves visible. This would be contrary to the whole notion of a DL positionality. Consequently, the "sexy" tales of DL men are reported to the public by pop ethnographers, while the women are merely used as bodies to make a point, rather than persons of significance in the HIV/AIDS discourse.

The constant displacement of black female subjectivity marks her as insignificant and indispensable to the construction of DL sexuality, while simultaneously positioning her as a victim of DL sex. This black female as "victim" is a highly problematic and limiting frame. First, it poses the black female as an open cavity, with no sexual agency. It also pinpoints black male homosexual acts as the problem, locating homosexuality as the key vector in the spread of HIV/AIDS. In this equation, DL sexual acts are always already unsafe and irresponsible, while black women are seemingly always available for transmission. In the context of working racist American mythologies around black sexuality, Leo Bersani's insight in "Is the Rectum a Grave?" is instructive:

> This is a fantasy of [black] female sexuality as intrinsically diseased; and promiscuity, in this fantasy, far from merely increasing the risk of infection, is the sign of infection. Women and gay men spread their legs with an unquenchable appetite for destruction. (1987, 24)

Thus, in the racist American imaginary, the myth perpetuated by the *New York Times Magazine* article may, in fact, be in conversation with ideas about black female and gay sexual deviance as natural annihilators of their own humanity. The black queer man infecting the whole community is clearly a part of Denizet-Lewis's understanding of the DL—being played out from his opening sentence to the very last. Nonetheless, in his article, the presence of HIV/AIDS among black women is only acknowledged as a brief aside, marking this sociocultural reality as unimportant, or at least uninteresting. Through his manipulation of the black female body for his discursive purpose, Denizet-Lewis participates in the misogynist tradition of privileging both the male body and voice, while hiding or silencing the "other" until she is "useful" to him: bell hooks refers to this agenda as the "dick-thing," or phallocentrism, where men align themselves with each other under the identification of power, which is not contingent upon but related to the possession of the penis (2003, 87–113). hooks clearly directs our attention to the ways in which such devaluing, through media representation, is deeply entrenched in an indirect version of male bonding, which sacrifices female subjectivity for male power. In the omission of black women in these discourses, the homoerotic tension between the writer and his male subjects is most evident through the pulse and detail of his pop-ethnographic descriptions.

Within the *New York Times Magazine* article, the only follow-up on the relationship between HIV/AIDS, black women, and the DL comes through the voice of a gay man infected with HIV/AIDS. The late Chris Bell, then a local HIV/AIDS activist in Chicago, critically analyzes the framing of DL men, yet unconsciously supports Denizet-Lewis's erasure of black women within his article:

> They [DL men] became the "modern" version of [a] highly sexualized, dangerous, irresponsible black man who doesn't care about anyone and just wants to get off. . . . Black men had been dying of AIDS for years, it wasn't until "innocent" black women became infected that the black community bothered to notice. (2004, 32)

This final claim does hold some truth. In the context of this article, however, Bell provides ammunition for Denizet-Lewis's silencing of women's voices. Denizet-Lewis's focus on DL men, when combined with Bell's voice, is both justified and necessary. The marking of "innocent" with quotation marks questions black female "unknowingness" and sexuality. It satisfies a racist imaginary that has continued to hypersexualize the black female body. The question of "innocence," or chastity, is one that has historically been posed to black female bodies (Smith 1982; hooks 1981) and clearly resonates within the contemporary discourses around HIV/AIDS. In the context of this article, such a suggestion, briefly but significantly, feeds the master narrative of a sexually irresponsible and uncontrollable black "gay" community. Such scrutiny over who has the right to speak, however, distracts from the role of racism in systematically silencing both black gay and female voices, within and outside the black "community."

The cynical tone of Bell's statement, while it denotes frustration with certain black community politics, can be read in this context as an invocation of the tension between society and the imagined "sapphire." This figure, as Pamela Smith informs us, is often seen as the "threatening, intimidating, angry" black woman (2000, 124). The black female body is seen as excessive; she is too combative to be taken seriously. By discounting the black female voice and/or attitude, Denizet-Lewis removes the black woman from the sexual equation of the down low, in order to keep the narrative sleek and sexy. This aversion strategy allows the reader to engage in Denizet-Lewis's fetishistic fantasy, rather than the complex and multi-layered public concerns about the DL. Concomitantly, Bell's statement in the context of this article's frame reenacts what Evelyn Hammonds has located as the early problems with HIV/AIDS media discourses:

> The sense of powerlessness that African American women who are HIV-positive experience [is] used to emphasize their irresponsibility. Such comments leave unexamined the personal and economic difficulties that these women face in their attempts to get access to good health care and counseling. . . . We are not told about the different opportunistic infections in women that could possibly mask early diagnosis. We are not told how many of these women have lost their homes and custody of children when their HIV status is made known. (1995, 437)

Hammonds not only demonstrates the importance of the black female voice in any discussion of HIV/AIDS, but also critiques the manipulation of women's experience to filter questions of responsibility. Hammonds's insights are quite instructive. In examining women's role in the discourse of the DL, they are often only evoked to criminalize black men as the physical evidence that these men are "vectors of contagion." Though this does not always prove to be the case, discourse about thuggishness or brute violence convinces us of the possibility. In addition, the suggestion that black women are receivers of HIV/AIDS and that DL men are givers grossly genders who is affected by this disease for the reading public. This positing of the victim/villain dichotomy facilitates a discursive rendering that may quickly mention the impact of HIV/AIDS on black women, while neglecting to address those DL men who are HIV-positive. My point here is not to make a move for representational equality, but to illustrate how discourse can be constructed to focus our attention on one body over another. In essence, the *New York Times Magazine* article exploits black women's HIV/AIDS rates in order to make a stronger case for the importance and relevance of the down low. Further, it perpetuates a value system of bodies where the queer black body (here, the DL man) is given less discursive weight than that of black women. I argue that this article established a format, or protocol, for all discussions of the DL to, first, present statistics and concerns for black women and HIV/AIDS in order to generate relevance and concern within the public: to only encourage a formulaic dismissal of black female relevance, where they are utilized as simple attention-getters for the rhetoric of DL deviance.[18]

If black female voices are going to be underrepresented or absent from the printed page, why invoke their presence at all? Why employ this sound bite on HIV/AIDS that quickly exits stage left? I contend that Denizet-Lewis and others invoke the black woman as specter in order to contextualize and consequently fuel the antagonistic and anxious attitudes toward black men, specifically those who participate in "queer sexuality." This is another moment where black women, in this spectral position, are positioned as an illusory "mammy" figure who *carries* the racist imaginary throughout the piece, persuading us to see all of DL interactions and sexual discoveries in relationship to the rise of HIV/AIDS in the black community.

The power of organization is important in understanding Denizet-Lewis's article and other media engagements with the DL. It is Denizet-Lewis who has the power to construct the narrative of the DL, telling the story he wants to share—no matter how dangerous or incomplete it is. If this article were an anomaly, my analysis would have no grounding and Denizet-Lewis's work would be just another magazine article that poorly addresses the relationship of HIV/AIDS and the DL in the absence of the other parties that are involved. However, the explosion of articles following Denizet-Lewis's that commit such violence illustrates the unconscious workings of a racist, misogynist, and uncritical imaginary, more concerned about the "sexy" than the substantive.

Denizet-Lewis's article positions and crafts both the black woman and the black man as "controlling images," each of which "naturalizes, normalizes, and legitimates racism, sexism, and homophobia against these 'outsiders'" (Collins 2000, 70–71)—be it the women who don't matter or the men who only matter as sexualized beings with no guiding ethics or ethical responsibility. In the midst of the circulating discourse, this text has received the most public attention, as it is often used as primary source material in news media coverage on television, other newspaper-magazine representations, and even within academic texts. The *New York Times Magazine* piece set forth a cycle of newspaper articles that continued in the demonization of black men—painting a picture of DL men as villains or culprits. Even academic experts rely on its accuracy to explain, analyze, and critique this so-called new sexual phenomenon (Collins 2004; Neal 2005; Guy-Sheftall and Cole 2003). In addition, it was one of the first articles to mention J. L. King as a "former DL man" who speaks out, and it initiated the conversations that would lead to the publication of King's *New York Times* best-selling publication of *On the Down Low: A Journey into the Lives of "Straight" Black Men Who Sleep with Men*.[19] Indeed, this article has had much impact on the future career of the DL within public discourse.

While it is understandable that the *New York Times Magazine* article may have been the most lengthy and detailed discussion of the DL to date, its romanticizing and exploitative tone deserves a critique that has been heretofore absent from the general discourse. Denizet-Lewis's article teaches us less about DL men and HIV/AIDS, and more about how black culture and sexuality remain exotic topics of interests. Consequently, we are left with a narrow view of DL men as peculiar, sexually deviant subjects who continue a historical representation of black men—queer or not—as sexual savages to be hated, not loved. The only potentially promising characteristic of this DL discourse is the absence of an actual body for reference. The DL man was conspicuously without a face, yet represented as a collage of social imaginings of deviance.[20] While he was constructed as a working-class brute, he was still an ambiguous figure who potentially threatened black women's lives. The absence of real bodies meant that the public could only speculate about who is DL, and it was this very absence of a face—this unseen "presence"— that fueled the sense of hysteria and fear of those who have investments in the politics of the visible. Thus, while this is significantly important in deterring a conscious profiling of DL men, it enlivens a Foucauldian sense of mass surveillance—the need to always know, or get to know, for those who are most concerned about this "sexual bogeyman."

The Bogeyman Comes Out?:
J. L. King as the Messenger of DL Mythology

In February 2004 I sat onstage at the new haven for Chicago's black social discourse, the Spoken Word Cafe. I waited to be a part of a community conversation, a "relationship chat" turned town hall meeting, which would discuss the dynamics of the "down-low phenomenon." As I walked around the space, I listened as an audience of about 80 percent black women expressed concerns such as "this DL thing is getting out of control!"; "How do we know some of these men are not on the down low?"; and "Girl, I swear, you almost have to go the other way [as in, date white men], in order to find a good one." As I walked past a group of women, I heard one woman say, "See him, he looks like he could be on the down low." As a young, openly gay man, I could not help but be implicated as a "DL brotha." This moment spoke to the urgency and currency of this thirst for knowing, as one woman said, "who is and who ain't on the DL." In addition to these women, there were several reporters dispersed throughout the audience, as well as news cameras. Indeed, this was a high-profile event. About thirty minutes after the publicized starting time, "Chat Daddy" Art Sims, the emcee and host for this Sunday event, enters. As he walked out onstage, dressed in an all-black suit, he spoke in a somewhat sultry but talk-show host voice:

> Good evening and welcome to this Sunday's relationship chat. . . . [He then, in the voice of a car salesman, made a pitch for the next chat session, then switched to a serious preacher-like tone.] HIV/AIDS is a real issue in the black community. It is not a gay male disease; it is a behavior disease. It does not matter if you are male, black, white, whatever, and you are not protecting yourself, *you are putting yourself at risk*. My guest tonight we met about three years ago. . . . He was taking his message out to people in Cleveland. I am honored to have him here, first, as my friend. Second, I am pleased to have him as an educator; and third of all, to have him as a black man with a positive *message*. Whether you feel the vibe, understand what he's saying, at least he's *speaking up* to let *you* know what's goin' on! I ask everybody to rise from your seats and welcome Mr. J. L. King. (field notes, February 2004)

With a great sense of anticipation and angst, about three hundred men and women stood up with enthusiasm to greet the "messenger." There was something unique about the audience's gaze toward the stage. As I peered around, I witnessed people assessing King's body, examining his clothes, commenting on his "look"—gathering together a sense of what this man, the self-proclaimed member of and expert on the down low, represented. Indeed, they were trying to figure out how the poster boy of the DL incarnate figured in the discursive fragments they had received elsewhere. In addition, they were, as I teach in my speech classes, adjudicating the credibility (or authenticity) of the speaker. Nonetheless, they were here—comprising the largest audience this chat session had ever witnessed—to receive J. L. King's message.

While the "chat" began as a dialogue between Chat Daddy and King, it became more of a rehearsal for King's then forthcoming book, *On the Down Low: A Journey into the Lives of "Straight" Black Men Who Sleep with Men.* In this conversation, Chat Daddy began with a key question:

CHAT DADDY: Who is J. L. King and why *now?*

J. L. KING: First of all—this mission, this ministry, this journey that I've been on, was not something that I asked for. You have to be careful what you pray for. . . . I was living in Atlanta . . . I had a great job, wonderful family . . . I was a pretty successful brotha. I was still kinda confused about my life situation and purpose. I was living this life of destruction: I had women all over the country, I had brothas sweatin' me all over the country—I had it going on for real [many audience members begin to look at each other like "yeah, right!"]. I was living this life and didn't have any guilt about it . . . then something said, "Tell your story, tell your story." Now I didn't know anything about the stats, HIV—I had never been tested, didn't really want to be tested. I really didn't care. And then it happened . . . the spirit said, "Do your thang." . . . But then I was at a conference and a brotha in LA said he had "a secret that women need to know about." And it was like a train. Keep in mind, I didn't start this DL phenomenon—J. L. King did not start it. . . . I was just the first brotha to step forward and say: "Look at me, let me tell you about my life." (field notes, February 2004)

Besides the conceit that exudes from King's words and gestures, the "mission, ministry, journey" narrative aligns him within what I call the "historical messenger mythology." This narrative construction, I argue, is the leading paradigm through which black leaders have historically articulated their spiritual, intellectual, and political agendas. It is this figuring of being "called by God" that operates as a legitimating device for those who wish to situate their knowledge as "official" and most appropriate for whatever cause. Here, King positions himself within this tradition by selecting a revelatory narrative, which works to encourage his audience to both listen and believe.

Thus, it is intuitive for King to choose to ignore Chat Daddy's initial question of "Who is J. L. King?" and instead move to the second part of the question, which establishes his credibility. He recited the common narrative of the "calling" or "epiphany"—a classic revelatory move that is common in traditional religious narratives, whereby a leader (typically a minister) details how he or she was "called" to preach. In this cultural context, among an almost all-black audience, such religious narratives have great currency. Because the black church has been pivotal in producing leaders within the community, the narrative—that a religious epiphany is at the core of one's mission—is more than a passing statement. It is an authenticating narrative that marks one's words as prophetic rather than political, salvation-centered, or self-expressive. In other words, J. L. King's work is not his own, but that of God's. In this scenario, God becomes the sender of the message while King is the ordained messenger. Thus, the confession that he recites in this conversation—as "living a life of destruction"—acts to move him outside of the criminal, guilt-ridden "sinner" into the realm of salvation. Now, after his confession, the audience is more able to accept him as an "ordained" minister—a giver of the gospel. As expected, the audience consumes his rhetoric as if he were the Messiah himself.[21]

As the conversation progressed, King described how to read for "signs" of DL men, as well as provided his own theorizations about why DL culture is "everywhere," particularly in Chicago.[22] King unconsciously, through the telling of his own "dirty laundry" and through specific references to men who "do what they wanna do," misrepresents his own experience as representative of the whole population, while also constructing another illustration of a thug persona at work among black men. The idea that these men "do what they wanna do" suggests that there is a "carefree and careless" nature within DL men. While King may interpret his desires in this way, the rendering of this explication for a mass population is unfair and irresponsible. Yet King is able to manipulate the audience to set him apart from "other" DL men, as he frames his critics as attempting to "silence the messenger."[23] Like a historic move within the evangelism discourses of the Christian church, King is delegated as a messenger of truth by constructing a me/them dichotomy between himself, DL men, and his critics. According to this theology, sinners do not want to be conscious of their wrongdoing; it is through evasion of sin that the unrighteous can continue in their "wicked ways." King, as a public figure, utilizes religious metaphors and configurations to further authenticate himself as *the* DL spokesperson, while also separating himself from the black sexual deviant.

When Chat Daddy inquired as to his motivation for writing his book on the topic, King responded:

> I was not going to write a book . . . They [agents/publishers] read about me in the *New York Times* . . . and then I got all these calls from all these agents . . . saying, "You going write a book about your life?" I said, "Naw." Then they said, "If you write a book, you could make a whooooooole lot of money!" And so, I said "cool!"[24]

This statement contradicts the spiritual motivation that King cited as the initial impetus for his "HIV/AIDS prevention journey." As King's career as the DL messenger continues, it becomes evident that his "mission" is less about being a messenger and more about being a mess-maker. Though I believe that King's intention is not to make a mess, his rather brash discursive choices prompt messy outcomes. In a sense, King's choice of offering himself as a spokesperson complicates the discourse. Because of the enigmatic nature of the DL in discourse, it becomes difficult for King to be understood as a single irresponsible individual; rather, his narrative becomes a metonymic voice and characterization for the whole community of men. King's physical presence and the publication of his autobiographical narrative fulfill the appetite of those most hungry for an embodied representation of the DL. While the DL man was once a disembodied subject, now he is inscribed with meaning, as King positions himself as the DL poster boy. In her book *Volatile Bodies*, Elizabeth Grosz explains that "inscriptions on the subject's body coagulate corporeal signifiers into signs, producing all the effects of meaning, representation, depth, within or subtending our social order" (1994, 141). In the case of the DL, King is the representative body on which all public discourse that preceded his physical presence is inscribed, compared, and authenticated.

The ways in which J. L. King, who is often mistakenly called "D.L." King, has become the representative voice of DL men was never more apparent than in his appearance on the *Oprah Winfrey Show* in 2004. Oprah Winfrey and her producers were intrigued by the DL after a special segment on ABC television that featured King and a host of other community voices, academic affiliates, and public health officials.[25] In addition to these individual voices, the segment featured excerpts from the conversation between Chat

Daddy and King, while also showing HIV/AIDS statistics. The ABC segment, filled with a range of perspectives, was a strong example of news reporting that was more descriptive than prescriptive. This special segment not only exemplifies the tensions surrounding the DL, but also challenges the dangerous discourse perpetuated by print media and public conversation. This was a great accomplishment for a seven-minute segment. To my dismay, the *Oprah Winfrey Show*—in its forty-five minutes—would not have the same impact.

Oprah begins her show with an awkward but obvious statement: "I'm an African American woman." This statement positions her in relationship to an issue that has been largely constructed as a "woman's problem" within the popular press: DL men. She then proceeds to cite what is now an oft-quoted public health statistic, marking "AIDS as the leading form of death for black people ages twenty-five to forty-four." Perhaps most important for my purposes here are her remarks and responses to these "startling statistics":

> Not only are more black people getting AIDS in record numbers, more women—listen to me now, *more women*—more college students, and people over fifty are at greater risk than ever before. Here's a shocker. It's one of the big reasons why so many women are getting AIDS—their husbands and their boyfriends are having secret sex with other men. (*Oprah Winfrey Show*, "A Secret Sex World")

Immediately, the audience gasps, and the camera focuses on a black woman taken aback, as well as a white woman in utter shock. These visceral responses speak loudly to the types of hysteria and fear present and produced through a somewhat sensational handling of the DL, especially the emphasis on disease and extramarital/relational sex between men. For Oprah, however, this cautionary tale of men "in a lifestyle called living on the down low" operates to call women once again to their televisions, to consume the latest media event per the *Oprah Winfrey Show*. It is Oprah's mission to educate through the titillation of those things we treasure and value every day, our public and mental health. It is fair to say that Oprah targets a female audience, and it is the common "mission, ministry, journey" for black women that necessitates J. L. King's appearance on the *Oprah Winfrey Show*. Indeed, after this experience, his calling would lead to a "whoooooooole lot of money!"

Together, Winfrey and King "crack the lid on this sexual underground," a goal she signals in her preshow voice-over. This show was going to unveil something that was, as Oprah announced, "shocking and unbelievable."

Quite different, I may add, than how in prior shows Oprah refers to the underground railroad—a down-low way of doing "freedom" during slavery. This episode of the *Oprah Winfrey Show* definitely employs the DL template set by dominant media: it invokes the gross HIV/AIDS statistics, then proceeds to frame the DL as a central problem in HIV/AIDS transmission, blaming the "risky" sex that married or committed men have with other men. To her credit, Oprah does attempt to veer away from the male-centered focus of HIV/AIDS discourse in the time of the DL, as she allows for HIV-positive women to speak on the show. Surprisingly, these women stand not as simply victims of black male sex, but as agents in their own sexual behavior and health maintenance. More importantly, these women are framed as living with HIV, rather than dying of AIDS. I believe this distinction is only implicit in the actual show, but its presence is made clearer through the actual bodily presence of these women, rather than the rhetorical renderings in media. As Oprah actually places the women, as well as college students and health officials, in conversation with King's rhetoric, she arrives at a more democratic representation of the DL. However, within the overwhelming presence of King's autobiographical voice, the book hype, and Oprah's sensational remarks, we lose the radical potential of this occasion.

It is the format of this *Oprah Winfrey Show* that limits the opportunity for the valuable and dialogic experience within this DL episode. As is the case with many of her shows where she features celebrities or soon-to-be-celebrity figures and their written work, the *Oprah Winfrey Show* is less equipped to entertain serious dialogue. These "meet the writer and his/her work" shows often act as more of an advertisement for the text and its author, rather than an informative, dialogic situation. This was, indeed, the case for this DL episode, in which the focus is placed on King as a way through which we can better understand "living on the down low." For example, approximately thirty-five minutes of the forty-five-minute show (once you extract commercials) is devoted to Oprah's attempt to understand King and his explication of DL culture. His narrative, here again, becomes *the* essential (or essentialized) voice for DL men. As King promotes his forthcoming book, this conversation benefits him most economically and socially. Meanwhile, DL men are literally left in the shadows of this conversation.

Before the *Oprah Winfrey Show* becomes a J. L. King show, Oprah features prerecorded footage of three DL men who remain hidden in a poorly lit room to avoid identification. In almost identical confessional tones and narrative structure, these men individually discuss their guilt and pain as they navigate between male and female sexual partners. The way in which

2.1 Oprah Winfrey and self-proclaimed DL expert, J. L. King (April 2004).

the interviews are spliced suggests a cohesiveness that appears, at best, suspect, at worst, dishonest and odd. For example, as one man says, "What we do is very promiscuous," the footage moves to another male figure who chimes in almost the same tone, "Sometimes I practice safe sex; sometimes I don't." In this splicing, we are left to believe the age-old adage that "birds of a feather flock together." In other words, as we hear these almost-identical narratives looped so smoothly, we can conclude that all DL men are promiscuous and sexually irresponsible. This coherency, which often reads as sameness, hides the strategic editorial choices that shape each narrative as responses to identical questions with almost identical answers. Thus, while Oprah features several DL men, we essentially witness one coherent narrative. Not surprisingly, the *Oprah Winfrey Show* seems to mirror dominant discourses on this topic.

Nonetheless, the *Oprah Winfrey Show*'s choice to shadow the faces of the interviewed DL men makes it difficult to believe the claims that King—as he repeats on the show—is still a real-life "DL brotha." According to the narratives presented by the men in the video footage, as well as those within the popular press, visibility is not the mode of representation for those who dwell "down low." However, on the flipside, it also made King into somewhat of a heroic figure, as he commenced to "bring it up high, out front," as commanded by one woman who attended the chat session mentioned earlier. This visibility on a global network, while it can be construed as courageous, disrupts all that we know about DL men through the media. For many gay men, the representation of King as DL in itself seems fabricated, as he was "popular within the Chicago black gay community for hosting parties exclusively for same-sex couples."[26] This may explain his constant disidentification with this community, who are already critical of his work. In past years, King has said that "black gay community leaders were jealous of the media attention he was drawing and angry [at him] for making it appear that black gay men were spreading the virus in women" (Kiritsy 2002, 2). King's inability to see the logic in this critique indicates the type of myopia present in his "mission," as he attends to his supposed "innocent" and lost black female subjects. However, as DL men are constantly referred to as gay in public discourse, it becomes more evident that the punitive gaze that is projected on to what he calls this "fraternity of invisible men" has dire consequences for black gay men and their relationship to the black community.

Within this discursive context, King's use of fraternity evokes a conversation about his consistent move to establish the DL as a peculiar cultural group. King's rhetoric in the press and on the *Oprah Winfrey* Show suggests that he feels compelled to combat the reductive impulse within the public to condense DLness to gayness; whereby, in most instances, he demonizes gay culture to create an authentic cultural narrative about the DL. Together, his body and his words produce an understanding of the DL that is narrowly racialized, gendered, sexualized, and classed. King constructs gay culture as white and feminine, while the DL is its antithesis. He ignores the heterogeneity within white gay culture, as well as the presence of a diverse black gay community. In previous conversations, he has evaded both communities in order to generate a legible yet unique characterization of DL men. In this commitment to painting the DL black, he allows the demonizing, deadly, and downright "wrong" acts of some men to be only the burden of black men.

Ironically, the often unspoken reduction of DL to gay is at the center of King's appeal to the public. King, through his rhetoric, reproduces, reifies, and recalls certain stereotypical presumptions most often inscribed upon homosexual bodies. In one moment in the episode, Oprah asks King if he still dates men and women. He responds with an emphatic: *"Date?!"* Oprah then inquires, "Not even have any kind of relationship beyond sex?"—as if she is surprised. King responds, "If I was gay, yes! If I was a gay man, I may wanna be in a relationship with another man . . . and play house. But when you on the DL, all you want to do is have sex. It's about gratification not orientation." King's insistence upon the centrality of sex and promiscuity among DL men reinforces the belief that equates gay sex with the spread of HIV/AIDS. As he attempts to set himself apart from mainstream gay America through disidentification and reliance on the myth of the domesticated gay man, he describes the DL in ways that are aligned with public imaginings of gays. King does not, or cannot, identify the ways in which marginalized bodies often experience different but similar projections as "deviance" that is seen at the core of minority communities. In addition, he conveniently forgets that men of color have always done "gay" differently. Thus, as he repels gayness, he misremembers the role of race in the construction of sexuality; but, rather, insists on remembering a gay self that is most legible by those in Oprah's audience. He misses an opportunity to truly educate or minister, demonstrating how even black gay men choose "discreet ways of being in the world." Instead, he essentializes both gay and DL men in terms of their sexual relations as a way to simplify the most complicated element in this DL puzzle: the (in)congruous relationship between a racialized masculinity and a normative queer sexuality. Rather than insist on the separation of the DL from a gay understanding, it would be more productive to recognize their (mis)shaping as an extension of historical narratives about marginalized people more generally.

Unfortunately, though every spectator has a different degree of familiarity with DL discourse, King's strategic placement of his narrative outside of contemporary gay history inadvertently reiterates and reinforces a narrow perception of the DL as being a manifestation of the thug in queer face. His positioning of DL men as being *so* distant from their gay counterparts, all the while traversing hetero-/homonormative boundaries, seems a somewhat dishonest rendering of social interaction. Do DL men, when seeking to locate discreet spaces to engage in same-sex desire, simply stumble upon existing homes of eroticism? While DL men are not gay men, they, indeed, do share similar sociocultural spaces. Yet King insists on separating them in order to provide the most unique narrative—one where the black and masculine can coexist. Unfortunately, like aforementioned media texts, he can only arrive at this possibility through the evocation of a thug-like figure. As the first physical embodiment and representative DL voice, King's portrayal of this population, no matter how problematic, is charged with making sense of what is predominantly a shadowed presence within press material. Rather than combat the more dangerous constructions of queerness, King often embraces "deviant" and thug-like narratives in hopes of authenticating his voice as quintessentially "down low." Interestingly, King's middle-class position is never highlighted in media texts or in his interview on the *Oprah Winfrey*

Show. I argue, as Martin Favor asserts, that King calls upon the authenticating narrative of the "folk" and the "working class" (1999, 4) to authenticate himself as not only black, but also properly masculine. However, his linear construction of what constitutes the masculine—"I had women and men all over the country" and "I don't date men"—is complicit with stereotypes that have, at once, been a part of both black male and gay male history. Thus, while King attempts to work himself out of what he sees as deviant sexuality (white gayness), he figures himself within another: thug blackness.

King's rhetorical move casts DL men out of what is often called the post-Stonewall moment, where the prevailing discussion surrounds sexual "orientation," by instead placing DL men in the pre-Stonewall era where queers of all colors were considered seekers of "gratification." This rhetorical move not only frames DL men as repressive and politically digressive, but also situates black men in a position that deems them socially backward.[27] As King marks discreet homoerotic experiences as inherently promiscuous, he flips the "down low" to simply "low-down." This assertion of the hypersexual DL man is flawed in two ways: first, it presumes that, as King states, *"All DL men want to do is have sex,"* and, second, that the absence of desire for committed male-male relationships necessitates random male-male sex acts. Oprah facilitates this move as she attempts to force King to embrace a gay identification, what Immanuel Kant calls a "categorical imperative."[28] While she is boggled by his refusal to label himself as gay, she is adamant about the impossibility of DL men embracing a "straight" identification. As a result of her discomfort with King's claim that "people look at gay men as less than men," Oprah attempts to counter his position with references by saying, "I see gay men as men." It is clear that she does not want to deal with the sexual uncertainty that seems inherent when sexual desires avoid definitive labels. Consequently, Oprah situates King's narrative within a gay paradigm, making sense of this "sexual underground," while simultaneously demonizing the population she means to defend. While King seems underdeveloped in his theories of DL culture—as he consistently frames his personal experience as collective—Oprah's naïveté about the realities of racialized gayness in America misinforms her viewing audience. Together, they embark on a similar journey to simplify a complex cultural network, rather than to unravel its complexities.

Unfortunately, it is not until the post-show discussion on cable network television's Oxygen channel that we gain access to more complicated notions of sexuality, disease, and the DL.[29] Indeed, this is made possible by the town-hall meeting format, which facilitates a more dialogic, interactive engagement. This post-show discussion allows for those who have been in the trenches, such as the executive director of the Black AIDS Institute, Phill Wilson, to attempt to undo the heavy-handed work of King. An example of this corrective work is when King, Oprah, and a college student are engaged in a battle of semantics—they disagree about whether DL men are "gay," "bisexual," or "straight." Rather than claim stakes in this battle, Wilson aptly intervenes: "People actually really don't live their lives in segments. People come in as complex individuals. . . . They bring their race stuff . . . their male stuff . . . and their homosexual stuff into the room—" Oprah interrupts, "That's interesting; my mind is still over there [as in 'left field']." While Oprah's interjection seems to discard Wilson's remarks, it was one of the more astute assertions in both her actual show and post-show. Wilson's interjection opens a space to discuss the intersectionality of race, gender, and sexuality, which pushes the envelope on King's misshaping of the DL as simply a black man's libido run amok.[30] Still, at no point during the course of the actual show or its post-show dialogue is there an explicit critique of the homogenous framing of the DL that is produced within King and Oprah's conversation. It appears that King offers an acceptable and digestible version of what he understands as "DL culture," while suggesting that DL men do not operate from a place of intersection, but dissection—compartmentalizing the sexual self from the gendered self and from the racial self. Consequently, he finds himself in a web of contradictions. Even if we accept King's construction of the DL as situational queer thuggery, it is nonetheless a conception clearly informed by race, gender, and sexuality. The interview itself illustrates King's own commitment to a certain type of racial masculinity, as well as many callbacks to the pleasures of his heterosexual adventures. Nonetheless, Oprah closes her conversation with King by saying, "Thank you, J.L., for the courage to speak out." Indeed, King speaks out, but his courage is questionable as he recites the fictions that continue to reify the narrow understandings of queer men and black people as always already having a propensity toward deviance.

On the Down Low/Low-Down: Construction of the "Double Li(e)fe"

The outcome of the *Oprah Winfrey Show* was predictable. The momentum of the DL as a product for public consumption accelerated as J. L. King was valorized as its "poster boy." A host of articles were written, several television shows employed the theme in an episode, and King's book, *On the*

Down Low: A Journey into the Lives of "Straight" Black Men Who Sleep with Men, instantaneously soared to the *New York Times* best-seller list and remained there for three consecutive months. Immediately after the book was released, I went to a Borders bookstore to purchase it. As expected, it was already sold out. At the third bookstore—located in a largely white subdivision of Chicago—I finally apprehended a copy. On my train ride home, I realized who had bought many of those copies: black female followers of the DL messiah. My choice to only spend a brief moment in my text looking closely at his book is symptomatic of my desire to not reinscribe the dangerous myths evident in King's version of the DL chronicles. Much of the book, however, was narrated in a condensed version on the *Oprah Winfrey Show*.

On the Down Low is a uniquely personal and prescriptive book, which takes us on a journey from King's bedroom of destruction where he is "found out," to his travels within the black church, all the way into his own theorizations about "DL types." The jacket copy for *On the Down Low* asserts that "he delivers the first frank and thorough investigation of life 'on the down low.'" While I agree that he is "frank," this book is not an investigation but rather a memoir. More importantly, this personal narrative masquerades as a generalized exploration, which is what, I believe, is the book's main problem. The style in which King moves from his own narrative to general readings about the DL as culture suggests that his experiences, or those he witnesses, are representative of the larger population. For example, as he narrates the tensions that arose in his married life, he states:

> I tried to make her think she was crazy when she caught me. I tried to make all our friends think she was overreacting. . . . I would complain, I turned the whole thing around to avoid taking responsibility. The bottom line is that I slept with men because that's what I liked—the same as all my down-low brothers. (2004, 50)

How can he speak for all DL men? Moreover, how can he conclude that his experience is identical to "all" DL men? This move illustrates the problem with his narrative choice. Rather than tell *his* story, he tries to tell *their* story. He affirms the critique posed by Sidonie Smith and Julia Weston in their book *Women, Autobiography, Theory: A Reader*, in which they state, "We are a postmodern society in which the disappearance of the unproblematic belief in the idea of true selves is everywhere compensated for, and camouflaged by, the multiplication of recitations of autobiographical narratives" (1998, 7). Somehow, through his autobiographical narrative, King is able to articulate a true DL self—though his figuring may not be applicable to the whole population. Not only is his move to speak for "all [his] DL brothers" an unfair shift, but it also presumes that all DL men hold the same value of male-male sex; he contradicts his claim that the DL necessitates a desire for both sexes. Nevertheless, it allows him room to construct a universal deviant, who is a "threat" not only to the heterosexual female reader, but to those who believe that DL men's male-male desire is temporal.

This previous example highlights what I argue is the first of four main tasks in his book: King's legitimation of himself as *the* authoritative voice on the DL subject. *On the Down Low* appears to take on four primary tasks: (1) It legitimates King's place as the "insider" in terms of his relationship to DL culture and DL men through confessionals and self-persecution (read: DL punishment); (2) it situates male-male sex by DL men within a moralistic discourse of lust and promiscuity; (3) it purposefully creates fear in its readers by rendering malicious acts by men and invoking the drama that propels a reader to keep going; and (4) it regenerates a discussion of HIV/ AIDS, though in a context of the DL, in order to call the black community's attention to its silence around issues of sexuality and disease.

In the introduction to *On the Down Low*, King bombards us with religious metaphors and language. As he writes and "reflects," King states, "My heart is heavy with the memory of leaving the arms of these women . . . to have sex with men," and he admits his remorse: "My soul is heavy with remembrances of all of the social gatherings I attended with my girlfriends . . . while secretly trying to hook up with other men at these events" (xiii). Here, his confessions almost sound like repentance for his "evildoing." As he invokes such religious rhetoric juxtaposed to his several sexually immoral "deadly" acts, he situates sex acts with men as being outside of the domain of "righteousness." In essence, "we are invited . . . to regard homosexuality [or homosexual sex] as indecent and/or obscene" (Watney 1989, 61). Though King participates in these acts, he attempts to redeem himself as he confesses, "Now that I give my sexual partners a choice—free will—I feel I am no longer living in sin" (75). Nonetheless, the men on whom he reports are sinners in need of punishment and religious reconciliation. This not only separates King from the "brotherhood" he claims to be a part of, but places him above them—a "reformed" DL brotha.

Why does King write this narrative if he is no longer "on the down low"? In his book, he claims that "this work was ordained by God" (xiv) and that "this work is also a testament to my love for the women who are and have been a part of my life" (xv). While such a "mission" is admirable in theory, the execution must also support such aims. As I look closely at his chapter "She Can't Compete with Him," the evidence of King's aim to create alarm in women is apparent. He opens with the following passage:

> They [women] feel that if they do their job properly in the bedroom their man will not have to stray. However, if your man sleeps with men, there is nothing sexually you can do that will make him stop. . . . If a man enjoys sex with a man, there's not a woman alive who can compete with that desire, because, it's simple, *she's not a man.* (47)

King engages in an act of competition between the woman and the "other" man. In this case, the "other" man is usually assigned the identification of gay. Thus, King instigates a homophobic response from his reader, while also stirring anger within women as he virtually deems her inadequate because of the potential of her "man [to] have sex with other men." King relies on the historical feeling of failure that women have internalized when their men cheat; except, in this case, he does not deem them as failing in their relationships, but unable to compete with male-male sex. In a sense, King replays a misogynist view of women's roles in society, as he measures their inability to compete by the absence of the phallus. Indirectly, King positions men, including himself, as always holding the penis and therefore possessing "power and control" (50). Yet, one must wonder, if the man's penis has so much power, why do DL men supposedly return to the vagina? Still, King's point here seems to be that women can never fully gain loyalty from their men who sleep with men. Thus, the penis is a threat not only to the health of these women, but also to the stability of their relationships.

On the Down Low is predominantly a text that circulates myths about men who have sex with men, while making sweeping statements that create fear in women. Nonetheless, King's book does attempt to regenerate a discussion of HIV/AIDS. Yet through the publication of *On the Down Low*, and its subsequent career within print media and television, he restores the energy given to thinking not only about DL men, but the role of gender in sexual negotiation. This is clear in his interview on the *Oprah Winfrey Show* where Phill Wilson encouraged the public to move outside the idea of the DL and focus on sexual behavior that could lead to HIV/AIDS transmission. However, King makes similar moves in his book, as he is self-conscious about his largely female audience:

> And most important, she must make it clear that she practices safe sex, and tell him that she wants to get tested together so that she can have peace of

mind and share intimacy more completely with him. For women who are married or in a long-term relationship where condoms are no longer being used, I recommend that they get tested, and ask their mate to get tested without accusing him of being on the DL. (72)

Here, in the middle of his book, King proposes a strategy for condom negotiation. Whether men are having an affair, on the DL, or IV drug users, this assists women in better positioning themselves in the sexual interplay, without the fear of emasculating their men or making false accusations. Yet I cannot ignore that this discussion happens within the context of a DL discourse; thus, HIV/AIDS is still being relegated to the DL man's body. While I have suggested that homosexual sex indirectly becomes marked as the agent of HIV/AIDS transmission while women become the repositories for disease, King's awareness of his audience warrants a discussion of how desire is policed. As we construct the DL in relation to HIV/AIDS, and as men who always already have female sex partners, King's female readers are inclined to become suspicious of their men's "DL status," as one woman referred to it. This surveillance technique, somewhat encouraged by King's rhetoric in and outside his book, creates an alarm for black women in that they feel as if they must not only be aware of their own sex acts, but even more aware of the sexual behavior of their male counterparts. Specifically, this rhetoric produces an attitude that somehow contracting HIV/AIDS from a man who has sex with men becomes more deadly than other forms of contraction. But as Phill Wilson reminds us in the after-show of the *Oprah Winfrey Show*, "The disease is no more nicer to you, no matter who you contract it from." Thus, King's strategy for women is most compelling outside this DL context and perhaps as a pedagogy that is helpful in all cultural situations.

On the Down Low operates as an autobiographical text that passes itself off as a form of critical research. While King's experiences may, indeed, be his own, the suggestion that he is engaged in research suggests some theoretical-methodological aim, which he does not outline. The average readers, however—whom he calls the "Shanequas and Dr. Shanequas,"[31] who understand "experience as a good teacher," or who may be less inclined to be as critical as I am here—will evaluate the narrative as authentic and new. On the other hand, one woman told me that King's book is "nothing but E. Lynn Harris with a little less of a flair." While her comment is somewhat flippant, it does highlight an interesting observation. Much like E. Lynn Harris's construction of men who engage in discreet homosexual/homoerotic relationships, King specifically shapes much of his DL narrative within middle-class black America.[32] While he acknowledges the range of men who may be on the DL, his cited examples—the "pastor," "corporate executive," "military man," and now J.L., spokesman and writer—belong within a middle-class paradigm. Indeed, this "picture of what a DL brother looks like" is more dangerous than the thug, who we envision as not only unclockable, but somehow undesirable in the long term. *On the Down Low*, then, not only attaches HIV/AIDS to DL men, but also locates its prevalence within middle-class black America. This is the greatest crisis of all. Black men, who are thought to uphold the "politics of respectability" as upstanding citizens, those who construct the ideals of black manhood, are now participating in deviant sexualities.

Return to Daddy: The Necessary Fiction of Crisis and the State of Black Affairs

Many television shows, articles, books, movies, and documentaries about the DL subject see themselves as doing critical work to better inform (and often entertain or excite) the broader public. In turn, the public is shown problematic media representations of not only black men, but of black male sexuality. Yet all engagements with this topic—because of its relative newness in the media—act as an awareness campaign. While these "missions" may have some potentially meaningful purpose, as Renato Rosaldo so aptly informs us, "benevolent intentions do not erase damaging effects" (1993, xii). As this chapter illustrates, media constructs linear narratives about DL men, while the public consumes images, imaginings, and stereotypes of not only black men but black people. Together, the presence of deviance, destruction, and death—as presented in mass media—constructs the necessary fiction of "crisis," which serves to alarm not only black women and the black community, but also state-sanctioned institutions whose mission is "protecting the health and safety of all Americans and for providing essential human services, especially for those people who are least able to help themselves."[33]

The damaging effects of such benevolent acts have never been more painfully apparent during the course of my research than when I entered a pharmacy funded by the Chicago Department of Health on Chicago's South Side. In January 2005 I stumbled upon a poster that I had first encountered in mid-2004 on the now-defunct website www.livingdownlow .com[34] as a J. L. King contribution to HIV safety.[35] This poster, an extension of all the discursive damage that King's political-intellectual immaturity has created, attempts to act as a preventative measure in the fight against HIV/AIDS in the black community through a focused initiative toward the

DL population. Indeed, King's work is not the only HIV/AIDS prevention material of this type. However, after his appearance on the *Oprah Winfrey Show* in April 2004, he was proclaimed the "DL poster boy." Therefore, his work and words were deemed "expert" and his DL gospel was understood as truth, leaving room for little scrutiny. Unfortunately, the mass hysteria that rippled among black women—this new "knowledge" about these diseased men living a "double life and double lie," as King espoused on *Oprah*—would encourage further policing of not only the black male body, but the black community as well. As the DL has become a perceived sociosexual pandemic within black America, it has created a broad concern among those within and outside of black communities. Consequently, community organizations, activists, and state-sanctioned institutions have begun taking action in order to "save black women."

The Centers for Disease Control and Prevention (CDC), the primary agent of HIV/AIDS prevention worldwide, is one organization that has made such commitments. The CDC—as the national public health institution that promotes "health and quality of life by preventing and controlling disease, injury, and disability"[36]—is the major distributor of information on HIV/AIDS. Every year they commission prevention materials, research, and resources that target potential "at-risk" populations. In 2004, as they became attentive to the concerns surrounding the DL, they commissioned what is now referred to as the "Down Low" poster, created by J. L. King.[37] This poster as well as other prevention materials are available for purchase on their website and also distributed to health agencies that may service DL men or those "affected and infected by them." Therefore, as I entered the public health facility, located in the heart of Chicago's historical "black mecca," it was clear that the state saw fit to begin its campaign here.

Together, this state-sanctioned "Down Low" poster and other media coverage on the DL not only attempt to regulate the black body, but also construct what Maurice Wallace has referred to as a "metapicture" of black men. The metapicture, a concept he borrows from media scholar W. J. T. Mitchell, is understood as "a piece of movable cultural apparatus, one which may serve a marginal role as illustrative device or a central role as a kind of summary image, what I have called a 'hypericon' that encapsulates an entire episteme, a theory of knowledge" (Mitchell 1994, 49). Wallace employs this concept in his book *Constructing the Black Masculine* to read the historical and contemporary imaging of black men within media contexts as a hypericonographic, but simultaneously villainized, subject (2002, 21). For my purposes, I employ the term "metapicture" to discuss how the DL as topic has now become a problematically iconographic figure in the discourse surrounding HIV/AIDS, particularly in the black community. Moreover, I am interested in how a certain metalanguage of race and (homo)sexuality, to borrow from Evelyn Higginbotham, operates to construct both a criminalizing and demonizing narrative of not only black DL men, but black people more generally. I argue that the focus by the media on the DL or HIV/AIDS as cultural apparatuses obscures the ways in which knowledge is being (re)produced about black people and sexual minorities. As journalist Duncan Osborne argues, "It is much easier . . . to blame the spread of HIV on these scary, thugged-out, black faggots—that is the subtext in these stories—than it is to grapple with the complicated epidemiology of HIV in America" (2004, 1). While Osborne's claim is astute, I would add that it is also easier to identify the "criminal" of HIV/AIDS in blackface, as black people have historically been situated within a narrative of savagery, disease, and dysfunctionality.

The CDC's newest poster is, at best, a replica of the dominant media discourses and is emblematic of Osborne's assertions. This poster pictures three black figures, two male and one female. The female, who is pregnant, is dressed in black while looking over her left shoulder and rolling her eyes at the scene behind her. Standing directly behind her is a man dressed in a black business suit, with a touch of white in his dress shirt, who touches her hip as he gazes toward the camera. In his rear—pun intended—is another black man, wearing sunglasses and dressed in a white suit (so-called hip-hop gear) with his left hand placed gently on the businessman's chest. Superimposed across all of their waists are the white words "Down Low." In addition, the caption, to which we are supposed to pay the most attention—located way down low—reads, "What you don't know can kill you . . . Get the facts. Get tested!" There are several layers here. Yet the symbolism is clear: the man in the white suit represents the DL man who penetrates the businessman, who penetrates the black woman, who is only able to penetrate them with her gaze. This image ironically mirrors what I have argued in this chapter to be the evolution of the DL in discourse. First, the discourse began with the homo-thug as the quintessential DL figure, then it moved into the middle class as the "down-low phenomenon," and finally toward the black woman (middle class and baby carrying) as the most threatened by these dangerous "vectors of contagion."

The power differential set up in this poster is quite interesting. Who is holding the power in this pose? The man in the suit—who gazes out at the camera as if to say, "I got this!"—has the power. Here, it seems, power is equated with not only economic mobility (as the man in the middle is middle-classed by position and aesthetic) and deadly secrecy (as his pose

2.2 "What You Don't Know Can Kill You . . ." HIV/AIDS prevention poster (2004).

seems to indicate an awareness of deceit). In addition, the caption—"What you don't know can kill you"—also suggests that the person in danger is the female figure, as she is the only one who "[doesn't] know." While I might agree with the premise that being tested regularly is a necessary step toward saving lives, the danger of HIV/AIDS is not exclusive to black females, but everyone. For, indeed, the two men may also be as unaware about their HIV status as the young woman. Nonetheless, her punitive gaze—like our understandings informed by contemporary DL rhetoric—charges these men with the crime of infection, even before we see any test results. Consequentially, this poster attaches a value to the life of the woman, while discarding the ambivalent circumstances behind her. Ultimately, what becomes apparent is that as long as we continue to lose individuals of our community at such disproportionate rates, we are all in danger of a racial and cultural genocide.

It is also possible to read this poster image as a racial allegory. The two figures in black—the supposed "straight couple"—are adorned that way to represent pure "blackness." While the thugged-out DL man, dressed in white, represents the way that homosexuality has historically been situated to contaminate blackness and is often seen as a white phenomenon. Consequently, the lettering for "Down Low," also in white, suggests that discreet male-male sex is what Eldridge Cleaver has called the "racial death-wish" (1999, 101). Hence, the black man becomes white the more he engages in homosexual behavior; in this context, he also writes his own death through same-sex relations, which always already equal death. Clearly, the man in the middle has not fully assimilated (as he still has his "girl"), but the white dress shirt may put him on his way. The DL man's gentle hand placement on the suited man's chest might even be a reach for his jacket, an attempt to expose his (undisclosed) whiteness. In this way, the white shirt underneath the black jacket recalls historic discourse that constructs practices of homosexuality as white "infections" within black society. This so-called disease, or "death-wish"—the homosexual presence—is ironically constructed as the main vector of contagion of HIV/AIDS within hegemonic discourses. Here, the logic of this mythology assists in further persecution of not only the "DL brotha," but all those who participate in same-sex relations. The two men, then, are constructed as active and voluntary agents in their own death, while the woman is purely a casualty.

The possibilities for this poster are multiple. However, the central theme seems to be quite apparent. Black men on the DL are a threat to heterosexual stability and are harmful to the health of black women, their children, and the black community. The punishment for this crime is enforced through two forms. First, when the woman glares at the scene behind her, the image of the two men, she draws our attention to not only their presence, but also their proximity. This consciousness, coupled with our own cultural anxieties, forces a punitive gaze from the viewer. Either way, we are aware that the actions in the poster are to be scrutinized, as they are dangerous and "low-down." More specifically, through the casting of the quintessential thug figure in an intentionally haunting pose, we can also see how this poster instigates a fear of discretion. Such an appeal prompts not only a critique of down-low subjectivity, but poses articulations of discretion as always already indicative of troublemaking, rather than a processes of survival for those who are heavily surveilled. In this way, the queer discreet subject is posed as a problem, while recovering heterosexual bliss is positioned as utopic and necessary. Hence, "What you don't know can kill you." This "you" is not remotely universal; this caption is preoccupied with the dis-ease of discretion, rather than the workings and acts evidentially linked to HIV/AIDS.

While all forms of prevention have their potential benefits, the drawback of this image is that it perpetuates the stereotype of black men as dysfunctional, irresponsible, and deadly. This image is as dangerous for the black community as it is while circulating as fodder for mainstream media's capitalization from black pain. As a state-sanctioned institution is willing to market this image as representative of its campaign against the spread of HIV/AIDS, it legitimates a misguided approach to HIV/AIDS prevention and research. Greg Millett and David Malebranche, in their aforementioned study, recommend that public health research and prevention shift focus from identifying "at-risk" groups to "risk" behaviors. Millet and Malebranche explain:

> The role of bisexually active black men in HIV transmission is a more complex issue than depictions of black men on the down-low as sexual predators and black women as uninformed victims. Future HIV research and programmatic activities must reflect this level of complexity by focusing on the sexual behaviors and sociocultural processes that facilitate HIV transmission between black men and women. (Millett et al. 2005, 57S)

Rather than focus on men who have sex with men, DL men, or even heterosexual women who have sex with men, they suggest identifying *how* people have sex rather than who they have it with. Some examples they give are that "black heterosexuals, more than any other racial or ethnic group, have more sexual partners . . . are more likely to have unprotected sex during anal sex than vaginal sex. . . . [B]lack women are more likely to report vaginal douching" (56S). All of these are sexual behaviors that are categorized as potentially placing people at higher risk for sexually transmitted diseases. This has great implications for not only the practice of public health but for public discourse. Whereas the media and public health have focused on the discreet practice of sexual identity by DL men as harboring and spreading disease, this approach moves us away from *who's* in the bedroom to what *happens* in the bedroom. Specifically, Millet and Malebranche urge an investigation of not only what happens but also of targeting the sociocultural parameter that may encourage unsafe and high-risk sexual behaviors. From this data, rather than moving to what I term "lifestyle" campaigns, we may need to develop better strategies of visual education. In essence, such prevention strategies such as the "Down Low" poster alarm the public, rather than challenge the sexual behaviors of those most affected by HIV/AIDS.

In his book *Welcome to the Jungle*, Kobena Mercer announces that "black people are somewhat immune from media-led panic around issues of HIV infection" (1994, 155). Indeed, the discursive scene above contradicts this claim in our contemporary moment. However, the DL has regenerated a form of "media-led panic," which tells us that there is still a search for a risk factor that can be blamed, rather than a solution to the sociocultural condition to prevent the disproportionate and saddening increase of AIDS among those Zora Neale Hurston called "the furthest down below." Such constructions of blame further deters proper attention toward funding for HIV/AIDS treatment, prevention, and cure. In addition, it facilitates a paralysis in the productive work that is being done toward such aims. As attention focuses on the seemingly untouchable "down-low" figure, rather than examining the sociocultural situations that produce a DL behavior, cultural-specific safe-sex messages and tutorials on sexual practice within marginal communities declines. Ultimately, change in sexual behavior is sacrificed for the sake of sexy subjects for public consumption.

I argue that what may be hindering black mobility and the establishment of a stronger political front is our commitment to a "respectability" politics. These self-regulating and self-policing politics, discussed by E. Frances White and others,[38] create unhealthy and unnecessary boundaries of blackness. As black people try to uphold "purity" and "morality," they seem more concerned about stigma than the material effects of pain and suffering among many black people—men and women living and dying with HIV/AIDS. This focus on stigma is what allows DL discourse to be a convenient distraction from significant interventions that could be made in terms of prevention, treatment, and the sustenance of the quality of life. For example, why is there so much attention on "closeted gay black men spreading AIDS" rather than encouraging "straight" people to get tested regularly? Quite simply, if ritual testing and treatment is incorporated in heterosexual culture, the spread of disease can be reduced. The surveillance of already stigmatized bodies will not directly impact heterosexual transmission of HIV or other diseases. Finally, rather than approaching queer sexuality as an anomaly in black America, we may be better served if we normalize queer presence through discourse and recognition—enabling a space to discuss men making responsible choices with the health of *all* sexual participants in mind. If we move the discourse outside the realm of homophobia and debates of "risk and blame," and into the realm of love and responsibility, we may be able to mobilize change.

The black community, which is saturated with masculinist tendencies— yet no more than white society—could use a black feminist sensibility in its consumption and reproduction of sexual narratives. As Patricia Hill Collins suggests in *Black Sexual Politics: African Americans, Gender, and the New Racism* (2004), a close examination of "structures of domination" and their effects on multiple communities within the black community could be a starting strategy to undo the repercussions of the many violent attacks made against the black body through media and other agents. Within this critical attention, a damaging construction of either black men or black women is a violence enacted upon all people, and regulations and rules mandated on black queer sexuality are threats to the possibilities of black heterosexuality. This co-constitutive perspective on oppression, with its transgressive reconfiguring of how we understand the interrelatedness of our marginalized subjectivities, could help us move toward better treatment of the multiple issues related to not only HIV/AIDS, but our (mis)understandings of sexuality more generally.

I wish to end with a paradox: the Down-Low Brotha. This caption, descriptor, and naming device has been pervasive within media and my life for years now. Yet its paradoxical quality is never questioned. As the DL has become the focus of media attention, it has been framed as not only a "risk" to black women or the "blame" for black women's increase in rates of HIV/AIDS, but also the necessary fiction that would facilitate a moral panic around black family and health crises. The black man, here, is discursively dysfunctional. But the coupling of "DL" with "Brotha" continues. Is this not a paradox? The term "brotha," in this context, seems inappropriate given the black community's disavowal of and unfamilial relationship toward queer men in general. Indeed, this tension is felt when a journalist such as Cynthia Tucker—in her March 14, 2004, *Atlanta Journal-Constitution* article—stated that "no group support or safe-sex counseling would do these young men as much good as broad acceptance of homosexuality" (8D). As the National Association of Black Journalists met in August 2005, frustration over black male representation arose, as Steven Gray noted that "we have missed the mark . . . by focusing on AIDS and demonizing black men" (Dodd 2005, 2C), which challenged the perception that everyone was on the anti-DL bandwagon, just as they were on the anti-AIDS platform. In another candid conversation, a woman told me: "The down low in media is the violence. Black men themselves aren't just messed up. The problem is the community—we have to find a way to embrace brothers, get them to love themselves, so they make less mistakes and cause less problems."[39]

Her words took me back to one of the only billboards I have seen that targeted DL men in Atlanta, Georgia,[40] which ironically was located just a few blocks from the Martin Luther King Jr. Center. The billboard—which featured two black men engaged in conversation, dressed in college apparel and casual slacks/jeans—had a caption, written like a personal letter, that read: *Brothers, Know We Love You—Just Protect Yourself and Others*. While this may seem ambiguous, in the "gay black mecca" the message is legible. For those potentially less familiar, the billboard also included the sponsoring health organization, which brought attention to its implicit, or explicit, meaning. However, rather than analyze the image, I wish to turn to the caption. This billboard, in my mind, moved the term "Down-Low Brotha" from a paradox to an orthodox. Here, the collective community spoke the words "We Love You." This one phrase, positioned for public consumption, removed a sense of blame and also urged responsibility in the name of love. Most significant, however, is that after the dash a call is made for black men to protect themselves (sexually) and others (meaning anyone). This reference includes, but is not limited to, heterosexual safety. The nonspecific appeal—the absence of any *one* direct sexual referent—allows space for transgressive preventative sexual politics. The billboard recognizes the multiple sexual possibilities for black men and has found a way to encourage safety on all fronts. While this outreach billboard is an alternative for HIV/AIDS prevention, it is also symbolic of an alternative needed within black "community" politics. As we move toward ending the rise of HIV/AIDS and facilitating better methods of addressing the issues of disease in black communities, we must find ways to generate an understanding of multiple sexualities within the context of love.

THREE

"Out" in the Club:
The Down Low, Hip-Hop, and the
Architexture of Black Masculinity

For whom is outness a historically available and affordable option? Is there an un-marked class character to the demand for universal "outness"? Who is represented by which use of the term, and who is excluded? For whom does the term present an impossible conflict between racial, ethnic, or religious affiliation and sexual politics? What kinds of policies are enabled by what kinds of usages and which are backgrounded or erased from view?

—Judith Butler, *Bodies that Matter: On the Discursive Limits of "Sex"*

DL offers a new-school remix of the old-school closet, an improvisation on the coming-out narrative that imagines a low-key way of being in the world.

—Jason King, "Remixing the Closet: The Down-Low Way of Knowledge"

As I was inundated with various articles, news stories, and magazines trans-lating this clandestine community of DL men, I became more interested in hearing their voices. Friends had told me of their "sightings of DL brothas" in the club and online, but I had never had conversations with these men with whom they mingled. My intrigue began one single night of being a wallflower on the club wall, as a thirty-something hard-body brushed up against me asking, "How you get down?" And my knee-jerk frown was quickly caught and transitioned into a smirk that welcomed a conversation revealing his articulation of himself as "being on the low" and looking for a "young, nice brother" like me. Our thirty-minute whispering along the wall—as it may have appeared to be a flirtatious exchange—was actually an informal interview, navigated by my intrigue at his refusal to say he was gay, his admission that this was his first time at an "alternative" spot, and the many questions he asked me in hopes of peeling back the mysteries of queer space. Over a year of ethnographic observation, I would interact with over forty DL men[1] and perform twenty formal interviews with those I had met at the Gate. As I began to sift through the narratives, the saliency of space, music, and the construct of hip-hop masculinity compelled a richer chapter. Thus, while many of the experiences with these men are chronicled through the ethnographic detail, in this chapter I focus on only two subjects, who speak to the complexity of this space. Many of the stories, left on the cutting-room floor, as it were, are carried into the next chapter, which follows men into the virtual world. I must also say that the two experiences distilled here share various representative elements—which speak to the utility of sexual discretion and the architecture, or *architexture*, of black masculinity. DL men—as they are often resistant to dominant narratives and doings of sexuality—write their way out of a largely hegemonic paradigm, entering into spaces and communities that have historically been a part of black male constructions of sexual identity.[2] DL men are new bodies dancing to an old song: the complex rhythms of sexual discretion.

This dance, both literal and metaphorical, is the focus of this chapter. Here, I am most interested in the ways that DL men negotiate their "private" identity within queer club space. I wish to move from the printed page to the stage, focusing on the black queer club space and DL men's participation within it. As DL presences in predominantly openly gay male spaces may sound contradictory, it unveils the significance of space in expressions of sexual desire. DL men's participation in a queer space, but with a commitment to discretion, questions the popular perception that one is "out" if he is in a gay club. DL presence within the Gate[3] reveals that black masculinity with its diverse textures uniquely enables the possibility for discreet sexual desire. In contrast to the previous chapter's rendering of problematic media aims, I am interested in understanding how and why certain discreet performances of sexual identity are privileged and what allows for their prevalence within certain spaces. Specifically, what arrangement or structuring of the "black masculine" makes DL presence possible, perhaps comfortable? This particular chapter explores DL men's travels within a traditionally or predominantly queer club space—where the diverse performances of a certain brand of masculine identity constitute and give credence to a DL positionality. In this club, I discover how "space . . . unleashes desire. It presents desire with a transparency which encourages it to surge forth in an attempt to lay claim to an apparently clear field" (Lefebvre 1991, 97).

In my fieldwork, the most "transparent" space has been the Gate, the home of queer black dance on Friday nights, on Chicago's Northwest Side. In this particular club space, DL men perform "straight" masculine identity, while they also engage in homoerotic desires. Following several men in this space, I was able to witness their desires for each other and desires for a cultural space where men could do what I later discuss as "coming in"—finding a style and texture in a space where they fit. Most illuminating and representative were the experiences of twenty-two-year-old "Shawn" and twenty-three-year-old "Tavares."[4] Of all the men I spoke with, Shawn was the first I saw at a gay club. I use his experiences to illuminate, complicate, and outline some of the contradictions and complexities that arise when a DL guy goes "out." Tavares, in contrast to Shawn, is a lifelong friend who had more recently told me of his desire for men. One night, when I mentioned to him that I was going to the Gate, he asked to join me. I chronicle his first experience in a predominantly male queer setting. Together, their narratives illuminate how what I designate later as the *architexture* of black masculinity can corroborate/collaborate with queer desire. These encounters prompted many questions: How do these men negotiate their commitment to a heteronormative understanding of self, while participating in homonormative social and sexual activities? What is it about DL subjectivity that allows for such possibilities? What is it about the structures and textures of the club space that invites these performers of discreet sexual identity?

Black Queer World-Making: Going Inside the Gate

Growing up in the 1980s and '90s, during a time when white queer politics were in your face and white queer images were dominant, my black queer world consisted of a ravaged imagination with no playground to explore and experiment. This understanding of black gay men as invisible or "quiet" continued with my collegiate experiences, as the predominant gay presence once again were white gay men. The potentiality of a black gay setting where men actually engaged homoerotic desire seemed at best foreign, at worst a fantasy never to be realized. It was not until my senior year in college that I learned that there were many people who had transformed my vivid imagination into a reality. Indeed, across the country and throughout the world, there existed spectacular spaces of black queer expression. In order to understand, experience, and enjoy my black queer self as a part of a living (rather than dormant) tradition, I would have to acknowledge what the critical performance scholar Dwight Conquergood knew well: "That sometimes—you do have to go there to know there."[5]

I first went to the Gate with my best friend, Aaron, after we came home for Christmas break in December 2000. As an undergraduate, I ventured into the white gay club scene under the racist "all black people look alike" mentality that marked the culture of so many white gay establishments, by using the ID of an upperclassman who was two shades darker than I. When I turned twenty-one, however, I was afforded open-door privileges to participate in whatever "adult" activity I desired. My visit to the Gate was my first official "black gay function." I remember asking folks in line, "Is it hot in there?" to which many applied in the affirmative. Many of the clubgoers were also lamenting the closing of the Incinerator, a black gay club that evidently had been the place to be "black and gay, and fabulous" prior to the Gate's arrival, according to one patron.

Interestingly, the Incinerator was a house club, which many argue lost its business to the "rise of hip-hop."[6] What was most significant about the Incinerator was its history as the only black gay club, seven days a week. The Gate, on the other hand, is gay once a week—becoming the Friday-night outlet for a large hip-hop queer mass. While those who attend the Gate have an option of listening to house or hip-hop, all of the club's advertisements and publicity seems to highlight its hip-hop appeal. Together, those who "kicked it" at the Gate partook in what Fiona Buckland, borrowing from Lauren Berlant and Michael Warner, describes as *queer world-making*[7]—"a conscious, active way of fashioning the self and the environment, cognitively and physically, through embodied social practices moving through and clustered in the city" (Buckland 2002, 19). While Buckland does not deny the possibility for a racialized subject to engage this practice, her research does not advance a theoretical application that accounts for racial subjectivity. During that Friday-night party, the Gate's patrons were definitely participating in an act of black queer world-making through their appropriation of a traditionally black heterosexual space and transformation of it into a space of and for queer desire.

Excited to be a part of this black queer world, Aaron and I entered the gates of the Gate. As we approached the cashier, we read a sign announcing, "ALTERNATIVE LIFESTYLE NIGHT," which also explained why there was a ten-dollar cover charge. We both looked at each other, astonished at the use of the terms "alternative" and "lifestyle," which clearly marked the space as not only queer, but temporarily non-heterosexual. This framing of our evening of fun suddenly became queer, in the sense of odd, as we had configured this opportunity as not an alternative, but an only option. Second, we were also appalled at what seemed to be an inflated price for clubbing. Both of us, having ventured to predominantly white clubs, had become accustomed to three to five dollars covers for entry. In response to this escalation in price, Aaron referred to the cover as a "rip-off," and I at that time called it a scandal. Later I learned otherwise. Todd, a manager at the Gate, told me that "for black club owners, there is a greater price to pay—for the possibilities of misbehaving and also to make up for the lack of money made through the consumption of alcohol and other club activities." Clearly, the prices for this queer party were the product of something that went beyond scandal and rip-off. It was an example of the way Chicago's system of racism shows its face in every part of black life. However, our sentiments, and those of many others I have talked to, reveal the ways that this customary practice toward black parties informs a (mis)understanding of the economics of queer world-making. As a result, the escalated costs of clubbing at the Gate, when compared to "white" establishments," almost always suggested an unethical and outrageous "lack of appreciation" for black patronage. Due to such high costs, in what seems to always be hard economic times for black people, many choose to stay at home or truly find "alternative" things to do. This, I know, has not only led to disgruntled patrons, but has also contributed to the historical demise of many black gay events in general. Despite the ten-dollar cover, we entered this space of queerdom hoping that what was inside was better than what we had witnessed thus far.

As we entered the Gate, we heard the thump of house music and observed many bodies, mostly men, moving across the dance floor, feeling the groove, standing along the wall; the place was charged with homoerotic energy and rhythmic impulses. Initially, we didn't acknowledge the dynamics of space as much as we were attentive to the music and the "type" of folk in each space. It was not until we entered the second room, the hip-hop room, that we made any real assessment of the differences in clientele on this night: we noticed that it was crowded and filled with a sort of "brute masculinity," as Aaron put it. Immediately, I thought of cavemen when he used this analogy, but I understood the gist of his commentary. Indeed, there was something rough and rugged about the way people moved in this space. In this first episode at the Gate, I only remember us exiting the room quickly, as we began to sweat profusely in the midst of those dancing and moving to DMX's infamous "y'all gon' make me lose my mind up in here."

Feeling that we were literally going to "lose our minds," we returned to the house room, where we felt more comfortable and at home. In retrospect, I am sure that Aaron may have felt out of place in his Kenneth Cole black slacks and fitted white shirt because most of the men in the hip-hop room were not dressed in similar attire. Instead, they were adorned in what had become known as hip-hop gear: loose low-riding jeans, big shirts, and baggy wear. I was wearing a similar ensemble to Aaron, a black shirt (somewhat fitted) and a pair of regular-fitting jeans. I felt a tinge out of place, as well. Nonetheless, our return to the house room made us aware of the great contrast between the two spaces. The house room welcomed us. This was most clear when the vocalist on the DJ's track began to sing, "Divas to the Dance Floor." Quickly, we took to the dance floor as if that were a cattle call to our middle-class, college-going, Kenneth Cole– and DKNY-wearing selves. We thought we were divas—the cream of the crop. But more than this, we felt that we were "free" to express that part of ourselves that we had repressed for so long. This song initiated our move into black gay culture, showing us what we loved most about it: the fabulous music, the fabulous people, the fabulous DRAMA!

Fiona Buckland marks this act of being "fabulous" as a quintessential gay cultural performance sensation. Indeed, it is an essential component of black gay life, as it is in white gay cultural productions. However, the Gate, as a space that contained both house and hip-hop music, seemed to occupy two distinct modes of expression. While the house room and music were "fabulous," it was clear that the hip-hop room and music were deemed "cool." If one simply observed the house room, where one witnesses voguers in high fashion from DKNY to Prada, dancers wearing traditional Kenneth Cole, and the classic tight shirt/tight jeans models, he or she would recognize it as a place where "I'm fabulous and I don't care what you think" is the general sentiment. Whereas the predominant look in the hip-hop room was more uniform—demonstrating people's desire or consciousness of specific fashion trends traditionally associated with hip-hop music and its consumers. This is not to suggest that fabulousness and coolness are determined by fashion. However, clothes are one way that individuals in space can display both their individuality and conformity. Although this binary description may imply otherwise, it is important to note that I am not claiming that hip-hoppers and house-heads, as they are often called, don't share space or blur the lines. Yet, for this project, the distinctions between the two spaces are important as they reflect a larger dominant shift/divide in the black gay cultural experience at this historical moment. Therefore, the dynamics of the hip-hop room as a space that lends access to down-low positionality is of utmost interest. Indeed, this space circulates contradictory messages that supersede traditional boundaries of gender and sexuality, where men negotiate their relationship to and between masculine bravado and black queer culture.

This odd congruence, between hip-hop and queer desire, has "coolness" at its nexus. Here, I wish to discuss coolness as a more general expression, which Marlene Kim Connor in *What Is Cool?: Understanding Black Manhood in America* (2003) understands as a guiding ethic on how to dress, behave, and interact with approval from a largely black and male spectatorship.

Coolness is a theory in practice—an embodied rubric that regulates and monitors what is and is not acceptable among black men under and outside of white surveillance. While I argue that coolness is not a uniquely black expression, it is a modern descriptor for a historical tactic. Most importantly, coolness acts as a way of survival, a coping stance/pose that black men utilize, in order to make do with what they do or do not have (Majors and Billson 1992, 4–5). Coolness is a performative utterance and action, whereby men define themselves within and against traditional standards. Indeed, like all performances, it changes depending on those involved, dimensions of space/place, and who is reading and interpreting the scene of action.

The Gate's hip-hop room seemed to spill over with coolness. Our quick entrance and exit, a sign of discomfort, was probably a resistance to such odd congruency. Queerness and coolness rarely are coupled in traditional black rhetoric. More pointedly, hip-hop as the impetus or interlocutor for queer desire is foreign to circulating mythologies of sexuality. Indeed, everything we had learned in our experiences about hip-hop and gayness said that "ne'er the twain shall meet." In addition, our tradition of queer experience included white men, techno music, and "fabulous" apparel. Naturally, the Gate's ability to forge a relationship between hip-hop and queerness was fascinating, but also triggered feelings of discomfort. We were queer indeed, but we were not hip-hoppers; we preferred house (more honestly read: techno) music, and we wanted to be fabulous rather than cool.

Indeed, the dynamic duo, hip-hop and queer space (or coolness and queerness), are incongruous at surface level, but a deeper examination can explain this coupling. Historically, hip-hop culture and music have gone against the grain of traditional American music and style—often critiquing dominant structures and modifying other musical forms. Likewise, queerness has also disrupted normative tales of sexuality, restructuring the perceived composition of our society and generally challenging normative sociosexual rules and regulations. Together, they seem to make a "fabulous" pair. These two world-making apparatuses disrupt norms, interrogate new ground, and encourage exploration outside the domains of normativity. Ultimately, the relationship between hip-hop and black queer expression is a sort of meeting of two queers. Thus, hip-hop music's use as a medium for homoerotic engagements is not odd, but almost anticipatory. Furthermore, the Gate as a predominantly black establishment would naturally welcome black forms of musical and cultural expression—its patrons are young black men and women who often are consumers of hip-hop in other contexts. And young postmodern black queer subjects are often most inclined to situate sexual identity as only one part of the self, rather than the most privileged point of identification.[8] Whereas white queer subjects may often construct a more peculiar culture, black queer subjects often appropriate traditional black (often heterosexual/sexist) mediums of entertainment for queer use. While this appropriation does, in fact, mark the black queer subject as unique from dominant structures, in these terms black gays can recognize both parts of the self, concomitantly. To follow this line of thought is to understand that black queer participation and enjoyment in hip-hop is congruent with black life—where hip-hop often operates as the nexus between the black and the queer. This reality corroborates the theoretical shift in the academy that understands the black subject as multiple, rather than monolithic. In a world that compartmentalizes different parts of the self (i.e., sexuality from black forms of expression), the black queer male/female subject understands that his/her being in the world is informed by all parts. Therefore, hip-hop is as much a part of queer world-making, as queer world-making is a part of the history of hip-hop.

Indeed, black queer world-making is a way of making history in a society where black experiences of same-sex desire and interaction are too often underrepresented and underappreciated. Hip-hop at the Gate provides a unique experience for black queer subjects to embrace such desires while maintaining an allegiance to macro-cultural forms of expressions. The (un)conscious moving and making of a black queer world constructs a black queer history that is dynamic, though often "down low." The Gate is one place that participates in a black queer world-making in Chicago, where it uniquely creates a conversation between seemingly distant, but clearly familiar, cultural expressions. Black men like Robert, a DL man whom I met five months earlier during an ethnographic observation, illustrates the value of a space like the Gate, where he said he could "feel the body of another man's without feeling ashamed."[9] Nonetheless, he acknowledged the peculiarity of this space while also recognizing the inability for this exchange in other circumstances. Robert marked the key cultural difference between this queer world and the "other" when he told me that in the Gate "there is no need for hiding and hushing." Indeed, the Gate provides such a space where black gay/queer men can express same-sex desire with little or no disgrace. In this sense, black queer world-making is as much about constructing a history as it is building a "home." As Chandan Reddy informs us, home is always a "contradictory location that is open and hybrid" (1997, 367), much like the hip-hop space at the Gate—which blends hip-hop and queer roots on the route to non-normative desire and pleasure.

The Gate, in its rerouting of queer desire and pleasure into social space, constructs a home where a subject can "have his/her cake and eat it too," so to speak. The black queer subject can live in the space of hip-hop, engaging traditional black (read: black heterosexual) musical forms and cultural styles, while also engaging in queer desire. This space, home, "is open and hybrid." As the domestic home has often afforded very little opportunity for black queers to enjoy and celebrate their desire, the Gate offers an opportunity for them to challenge such a limited understanding of home, constructing a temporal "pleasure zone." While the relationship between hip-hop and queerdom presents an enthralling question, of most interest here is how black queer subjects utilize hip-hop in queer space. Particularly, how does hip-hop serve as an interlocutor between discreet performances of sexual identity and explicit engagements of queer desire? How specifically, do DL men utilize queer space, navigating their desire for discretion and the pleasure of homoerotic engagement? How do these men literally dance down low, while simultaneously remixing the closet? To gain any critical understanding of this process, we must go "in da club."

"In Da Club": Homoerotic Activity in a Heteronormative Playground

It is about 12:45 a.m. on a cold, below-zero February morning on Chicago's Northwest Side. I stand in front of what once was a site of industrialization—a dark brick building with a one-story front and its raised back—now a structure that contains often contradictory architectures of homo- and heteronormative performances. The Gate is a parade of contrast. The physical appearances and fashion "looks" are definitely diverse and dynamic. As I stand in a line of approximately seventy-five people outside of the club, the "straight" bouncer yells, "Have your IDs ready." I scope the never-ending processional, where there are black men and women of all ages, a few whites and Latinos, a couple of drag queens in pumps, and some folks who appear "to have gotten the night mixed up." After twenty minutes of us taking in the scene, the line begins to move. I am elated because my arms are getting goose bumps, as I am only dressed in a blue polo shirt and loose-fitting blue jeans. Seeing that I don't have much meat on my bones, this "cool" attire was probably a bad choice for this processional in the middle of a Chicago winter. Troubled by the tingling sensation in my fingers and concerned that my elbows will begin to ash, I proceed forward in the line, as a young woman who is adorned in FUBU fashions (that's For Us By Us) passes me and hands the big six-foot-four bouncer her VIP pass. This, to my dismay, allows her to bypass the parade. I hear disgruntled patrons in line expressing their frustration, while my shivering body tells me that I should've been with Miss VIP. Before long, I enter the corridor that leads to the actual club. Plastered on the wall still hangs a sign that announces, "ALTERNATIVE LIFESTYLE NIGHT." Near this sign is another that reads: "After 1:00 a.m., the cover is $12.00." "Hell no!" scream some of the folk standing in line as they read the sign. I, of course, pay the cover, unsure about what is so special about the 1:00 a.m. hour, but knowing that there is a rich queer world waiting inside.

Bodies of all ages, sizes, shapes, colors, and fragrances fill the "house" space. I walk past a bar to witness bodies divided across the dance floor by wooden beams in a twenty-by-forty-foot space of sensuality and sexuality. Indeed, this house was divided, clearly quartering off one "type" from the "others." There is a section of men over thirty in one quarter, voguers in another, and the other half contains men and a few women who are under thirty, uninhibited in how they move and groove—who may often be conceived as the liberal or "queeny" types.[10] Both DL men and traditionally "masculine" gay men often read themselves against the latter category. Effeminate men—or the "queens"—are the characters in this dance space who are most often positioned as artificial, fake, or not "real men." Here, the "sissy," "fag," or "punk" is understood as being a pretender or impersonator. These assessments assume that for men, masculinity trumps femininity, denying the possibility for both gendered norms to exist in one body, or more importantly for their development or appearance to be disordered. Not only do such claims allow "masculine" men to deem their performance as natural, but they also reaffirm that gender is a "stylized repetition of acts" (Butler 1999, 270). Interestingly, such claims of inauthenticity could be made for any masculine performance—noting that all gender performances are impersonations.[11] If one accepts RuPaul's oft-cited claim that "we are born and the rest is drag," then all men in queer space are practicing the art of impersonation. Yet this does not situate any one gender as more real or authentic than any other. Still, the prevalence of men in the hip-hop room illustrates which performances are valorized as being most authentic. While the macho bravado or most "thugged-out" images are often deemed as most "real" or "authentic," there are clearly competing versions of what is, or ought to be, the black masculine. However, in the Gate it seems that one particular narrative has won out but has not completely taken over.

While there may be debate over who belongs at the Gate or within which quarter of space, the convening of black queer men for sociosexual engagement is an electric gathering. In the Gate's house room, black men perform gayness and blackness simultaneously. And while there may be shame in the shadows, the rhythms control the character of this space—filling it with pride and celebration. Typically, I join the crowd of men under thirty, where we move to the sound of the urban drumbeat, industrial scratches, gospel riffs, and the rare remixes of rhythm-and-blues songs together. We dance to house music, which seems to release the body from some of its constrictive impulses, exploring its multiple meanings and possibilities. Those who don't wish to dance stand against the wall, smiling, frowning, talking, drinking, and sometimes even singing. These bodies often exchange space, switching between being a dancer and a wallflower. However, many who feel the "groove" remain in their sweat and swing, living on the dance floor. Unfortunately, this house would not be my home today. As I walk past another bar, I follow a crowd into another space, located in the back of this warehouse, the hip-hop room.

The hip-hop space is a strong contrast to the house room. As I push my way through the crowd, I gently brush up against hard muscle, soft and sometimes sweaty flesh, noticing the many costumes of those who inhabit this humid and frenetic space. As I navigate through the crowd, I hear a familiar rhythm and walk up a short flight of stairs onto a passageway above the dance floor, a location where many seem to settle. The new hit by Eminem's protégé 50 Cent—"In Da Club"—is blaring from the speakers:

> *You can find me in da club,*
> *With a bottle full of bub*
> *But, mama, I got the X [ecstasy]*
> *If you into taking drugs.*
> *I'm into having sex,*
> *I ain't into making love.*
> *So come give me a hug—if you into getting rubbed.*

I become entangled in these lyrics and wonder about their function in this space of desire and dancing. Surveying the action, from what Michel de Certeau has called the "God View,"[12] my critical ethnographic instincts are overactive. Everything is present, alive, right in front of me, above me, and even behind me. The vulnerability I experienced was the result of overstimulation—where the heightened action within the space left me available for unwarranted touching, pushing, and shoving. My body, as it absorbed so much of the vibrant action in the club space, was the receptor of much uninvited, and often unwelcomed, energy. And I wonder, "Why is it here, from this scape, that I typically encounter men on the DL?" Many men I have spoken with have described this point of view as "safe" or the place where they just "chill." This is a unique vantage point as it sets you apart (creating vulnerability), while giving you the scopographic power (providing control with the gaze). As one DL man told me, "I can see all the pickings from here." I would contend that while the God view is a point "which transforms the city's complexity into readability" (de Certeau 1984, 124), it is also a location of power and control. This balcony-like passageway allows the viewer to observe action from afar and potentially locate those whose gestural schemas, and/or "sex appeal," are in line with their ideals. The traveler in this queer world can be a bit more selective about who piques his queer desires. From this spectatorial location, the voyeur has control and is almost unavailable for direct physical interaction. Often when I approach random "strangers" to inquire as to their reason for choosing the hip-hop room or the Gate club, they often cut the conversation short or disregard my attempt to converse.[13] These moments have heightened my awareness as to the navigating powers of the ethnographer—as a trickster-traveler who has to work for access into whatever community with which he/she works.

As I stand at the God view, I am so aware of what is happening in this queer world. This consciousness can be partially attributed to my vantage point, but also to the words of the rap song—the way that the lyrics seem to match the action on and off the dance floor. We were in the club, there were some "bub" (champagne) drinkers, and there was body language that suggested, "I wanna have sex" and not "I wanna make love." Meanwhile, I am doing what I call the sway dance—moving from side to side to the rhythms but not really exerting much energy. I look up and around as the crowd shakes, jiggles, and gets down. This space, though filled with many different bodies and forms of bodily expressions, has a somewhat homogeneous character stamped with a certain "look" or "pose." This aesthetic is discussed in Thomas DeFrantz's "The Black Beat Made Visible," where he suggests that "it is the tightness of the body that speaks most to a hip hop dance. . . . These dances are fundamentally concerned with controlling the body, holding it taut, and making it work in a fragmented manner" (2004, 75). While DeFrantz is discussing early hip-hop dance history, the age of break-dancing and pop-locking, similar trends remain in clubs like the Gate. In these dance spaces, the performers limit their movement rather than find multiple ways to flex the muscles and navigate through space. The dancing seems more contained to a specific location, with little mobility, yet much diversity. Though informed by some of the ritualistic expressions of hip-hop in popular culture, each body tells its own story.

As I look above me, below me, and beside me, I observe physical and facial expressions that recall childhood experiences of "mackin'" and "hollerin'." These type of poses and approaches were popular when I was a young boy growing up on Chicago's South Side. Men would often stand, in a neutral position, allowing their eyes to do much of the talking. Then, as they approached the person with whom they had interest, they would quickly perform this "tight" and often "tough guy" posturing. This performance was often accented by a hand on the groin, an expressionless face almost always absent of any hint of a smile, a cool slouch in the shoulders, and the classic concaveness in the chest. A similar aesthetic appreciation is present in the Gate. Interestingly, however, the presence of women in this space is hardly felt. Yet the "mackin'" and "hollerin'" styles of performance are projected on to bodies of the same sex. There is the dancing male/butch-femme binary and its ideological counterpart, heterosexual male/female pairing. Still, it is striking how the style of dress and dance characteristics are consistent, as to suggest that everyone had received a similar cultural memo for the evening. In this space, the dress code is in—and it's called hip-hop fashions (anything produced by fashion gurus like Nelly, P. Diddy, and Russell Simmons). Bodies move slowly and stiffly, with little exaggeration. These are men who through the image of the "thug" or "homey" make the masculine man (or woman) come alive.

> My flow, my show brought me the dough
> That bought me all my fancy things
> My crib, my cars, my pools, my jewels
> Look, nigga, I done came up and I ain't change.

As this bridge plays, I become more excited and decide to come out of my standstill and catch the groove. As I step down from the passageway onto the dance floor, to my surprise I see Shawn. This twenty-two-year-old college student classifies himself as being on the DL and previously vowed that he would never "be caught dead in one of those sissy clubs." It was with even greater surprise that Shawn acknowledges me and proceeds to take my hand and place it on his groin. This was the first time he had ever made such a move, but the time and space encouraged him to lose many of his inhibitions and insecurities. When I later asked Shawn about the incident, particularly the level of comfort he displayed, he insisted that it was due to the alcohol and apologetically said, "I guess I'm becomin' a little bit too comfortable." This statement prompted a longer historical explanation:

> I wasn't always that comfortable. For real. I mean, me and my guy—my best friend—the first time we went to the club in D.C., we practically hid. We wore our hats so far down over our faces; the most you probably could see was my

smile and his goatee. We wore real big clothes to conceal our identities. . . .
Now I don't know who would have known me in D.C., being that I was from
the west suburbs of Chicago.

This admission, clearly marking Shawn's evolution from being very discreet
to less discreet in his participation in club life, is informative. While it illuminates a certain level of "comfort," it could potentially suggest that Shawn
has "come into himself." However, this comfort within the space of the
club does not speak to his behavior in company outside of the club. In fact,
I observed that Shawn's anxiety over how his fraternity, friends at school,
and family would respond to his presence became an almost overwhelming
concern. Specifically, he articulated a concern for his reputation among his
"brotherhood" as the "pretty-boy ladies' man"—a title that clearly informed
Shawn's general performance of masculinity. The most striking image in
this narrative is the costume for concealment, the utilization of presumable
hip-hop gear to mask identity. Shawn was astutely aware of the value of
clothes in the regulation and monitoring of what is properly masculine. In a
sense, Shawn and his friends' clothing are the material masks for their queer
desire. On the one hand, his cap is a signifier of hip-hop, while, on the other
hand, it is also a sign of Shawn's desire to both not see as well as be seen. All
at once, hip-hop is the corroborator and the concealer of queer desire.

The more one understands the cultural work of hip-hop, within and outside black queer environments, the less surprising it becomes that DL men
patronize the Gate. A couple of weeks prior to the incident with Shawn, a
guy standing at the bar had approached me by saying, "I'm here with my
girl and her gay friend, but I get down too."[14] After this admission and my
mild response, he proceeded to rub my leg. I suppose the wordless realm of
physicality was being used to clarify the meaning of potentially ambiguous
language.[15] I slowly smiled, grabbed my drink, and continued back to the
dance floor. He attempted to follow. After talking with other gay men who
frequented the Gate, I discovered this is not abnormal. Often these spaces
allowed for DL men to express desire that would otherwise be neglected and
kept dormant. However, as queer space somewhat de-stigmatizes queer sexuality, men could feel less stigmatized by their participation in homoerotic/
homosexual behavior.

Likewise, Shawn was able to not only be present at the Gate, but also to
activate his sexual desires without the fear of losing his "masculine" card. My
astonishment over Shawn's presence at the Gate and his behavior therein
was related to his adamant insistence that his identity was "private," a term

that connotes a keen sense of discretion. Typically, the men I had encountered previously would not be seen in an announced "gay" or "alternative" night at any club. Since this encounter, I have seen Shawn at one other "gay" club that offered a hip-hop fix. In a later interview, he told me: "I can't stand house music—hip-hop is where it's at!"[16] It became clear that his ability to perform a hip-hop masculinity was part of the impetus for his participation in this particular "alternative" Friday night at the Gate.

50 Cent continues:

> *I'm that cat by the bar toasting to the good life*
> *You that faggot-ass nigga trying to pull me back right?*

The last line invokes audience participation. As I deepen the groove of my sway dance, gay men and women shout: "Faggot-ass nigga." Actually, they shout the whole line, but it is this part of the phrase that throws me. It seems contradictory for these queers of color to engage in such a chant. I turn to a friend, giving him a look of shock and disheartenment, and he says, "It's just like the way we use 'nigga' by itself." But why would those who, like myself, have endured being called "faggot, sissy, punk" rearticulate such problematic rhetoric? Why would Shawn, or DL men in general, seemingly draw pleasure from this chant of hate and homophobia? As people threw their hands in the air, almost marching to construct a chorus-like concentric circle of "faggot-ass nigga," something told me that this was "cool."

This performance of heterosexism seemed to work in collaboration with a larger desire to be "cool." The queer subjects who yelled "faggot-ass nigga" could feel a part of a larger black masculine sphere—one that usually excluded them. In this masculine imaginary, the way to often affirm one's normality is through the participation in homophobic or sexist acts. When one takes possession of the "faggot" or the "nigga," it reduces the legitimacy of such ascriptions being made upon the speaker's body. In this way, the utterance of the profane empowers the speaker/chanter, affirming his status as appropriately masculine. This chanting moment was emblematic of the "cooling" of the hip-hop room, while also illuminating the ways in which one type of masculinity seems to pose itself as *the* cool. These so-called performances of heterogender (read: heterosexism) position the hip-hop space as the greater of the two rooms. It is within the hip-hop room that the "real men" reside. Traditional hetero-masculine behavior and codes deemed this space as "hot." This behavior, though highly problematic, suggests, as Robert Farris Thompson does in his aptly titled classic essay "An Aesthetic of the Cool" (1966), that hot is always balanced by cool. Whereas Thompson is speaking to the literal hotness of bodies, I employ "hot" to refer to contemporary black vernacular, where this adjective signifies the best place to be, the spot, and the atmosphere that is most enlivened. Indeed, the men in the hip-hop room understand this room as such, while often the "room of sissies," as one patron referred to the house room, was seen as a place less desired—"really gay," so to speak.

I also read this instance of hip-hop heterosexual rage in queer face to be a moment where gay men can temporarily "de-queer" themselves. I argue that such a chant may work as a way to set these men apart from the "others" in the space. It is a strategy to disavow one brand of masculinity, while embracing another. In this conceptualization, the "others" who are outside of the traditionally masculine—those ascribed titles such as "femmes," "bottoms," "punks"—are marked as inferior, less than those who carry traditional masculine codes and behaviors. Shawn explained the every Friday-night 50 Cent chorus by saying, "A faggot is a punk—it's not about what he does in the bedroom; it's what he doesn't do." His perspective suggests that the ability to spout this sexual epithet is about condemning the feminine male. In addition, Shawn's comment also ridicules those who perform the non-dominant role during sex.[17] Hence, his comment about "what he does not do" signifies a discomfort not with being the non-dominant sex partner, but those who perform a style of masculinity that signals this sexual preference. Of course, Shawn doesn't consider this style masculine, which begs the question, "Is there a way to masculinize, or even affirm, bottoms in this world of queer world-making?"

For Shawn, I guess not. Shawn's perspective further accentuates the ways in which "femininity is always already devalued in patriarchal societies, those associated with the feminine are also viewed as inferior" (Johnson 2003, 69). There is no room for femininity in the domain of the masculine. A man is considered either masculine/feminine; the different styles of masculinity often remain unaccounted for or unrecognized. Of course, femininity is the less ideal performance of gender, making the distinction between who is properly masculine and who is not. Much of these understandings of gender are residual hegemonic perspectives that almost always uses the effete or feminine to describe the "gay," setting straight men apart from those who are identified as "gay." This act of devaluation of some gay male bodies is modified in the Gate, as some "masculine" gay men can at once feel "straight," while DL men can affirm their allegiance to heterosexuality (read: heteronormativity) through a harsh critique of those who perform queerness and manliness differently. Furthermore, it allows some men to carve a space for the cool, creating a necessary hierarchy of masculine performances within the Gate.

It would be dishonest to ignore the ways in which "faggot-ass nigga" is somewhat of an inside joke. All of those who participate in the "alternative" night at the Gate are aware of their appetite for those of the same sex. Thus, the utterance of the chant also brings with it a reminder that the space is a queer, or "faggot," terrain. In some ways, the mass chant announces, "We are black faggots, but look who's in possession of these words now." In this sense, my friend's comparative analysis between the chanted phrase and the vernacular use of "nigga" is an apt one. Black queer men reappropriate these terms, turn them on their head, and thereby reduce the power of the term in constructing their identities. However, I would suggest this analysis is less applicable for men on the DL, as they often disidentify with traditional identifications of (homo)sexuality in everyday life.

I spend critical time in this chapter on this moment of hip-hop heterosexist and homophobic chanting because it exposes what I believe is the true pleasure of this queer zone, for black gay men and DL men alike. In this space, performances of gender and sexuality are in flux—men are able to be queer, while also acting straight, or even straight while acting queer. Patrons of the Gate are able to realize the treasure of performance that many of us scholars take as given: "Performance is a means by which people reflect on their current conditions, define and/or reinvent themselves and their social world, and either reinforce, resist, or subvert prevailing social orders" (Drewal 1991, 9). The Gate offers an occasion where black queer men can attain pleasure through the stimulation created by the multiple valences within the hip-hop space. In this unique space of queer world-making, these men can "reinforce, resist, [accept], or subvert" dominant modes of gender and sexuality. While black men can identify and perform their queer desire (resist/subvert), they can still participate in the rituals of patriarchy (reinforce/accept). At the Gate, or any queer world-making space for that matter, bodies "produce paradoxical effects which cannot be understood if one tries to force them into a dichotomy of resistance or submission" (Bourdieu 1991, 94). This may be the queerest characteristic of this space—where heterogender, hip-hop, and homoeroticism are married through music and dance.

This queer possibility is what Katrina Hazard-Donald misses when she addresses hip-hop's dance as a form that "encourages a public (and private) male bonding" through the disbursement of male bodies, moving and communicating through space (1996, 229). Her discussion is not only heterocentric, but it also denies the possibility for queer potential in the spaces where black men gather in the name of hip-hop. Instead, she attempts to frame these "male-bonding" episodes as purely platonic and historically traditional, only significant because of the ability for black men to proclaim a sense of brotherhood. She ignores what Eve Kosofsky Sedgwick has informed us is the homoerotic potential of all male-bonding circumstances. Sedgwick, when examining what she calls "homosociality," reevaluates the often assumed impossibility for the homosocial to become homoerotic. In *Between Men: English Literature and Male Homosocial Desire*, Sedgwick attempts to demonstrate the "unbrokedness of a continuum between homosocial and homosexual" (1985, 1)—bringing forth a significant discussion of desire's presence in what could be called "male spaces." A discussion about such possibilities has been almost absent in the commentary of those who write about the homosocial domain of hip-hop. My discussion here attempts to expand beyond acknowledging the potential of space in constructing and producing desire, but rather how the Gate, as a unique space, opens doors for a specific desire by a particular group of men. Moreover, this chapter illuminates the many ways that hip-hop is employed for queer use. In the hip-hop space, all black queer men can participate and feel "normal," almost un-queer, as the culture of the space encourages homoerotic desires for each subject, as he dances in the largely heteronormative playground.

"In Da House": Bringing Hip-Hop Home

Though my fascination is with the hip-hop space at the Gate, specific performances in the house room are germane to the understanding of masculinity in space. In this section, I map and examine the ways in which hip-hop masculinity travels. Particularly, I look closely at a peculiar moment where a DL man engaged in desire in the house space, though operating under the rubric and rhythm of hip-hop. In short, I am interested in how some men perform "cool" in a space that is often understood as being "fabulous" and filled with "faggotry." Throughout my research, for instance, I have found that some men embrace, appreciate, and even express attraction for the "feminine," while simultaneously subscribing to a hegemonic masculinity themselves.

Indeed, I was surprised when Tavares, my childhood friend of almost sixteen years who was always known as "*the* ladies' man," volunteered to join me on a Friday-night venture to the Gate. Tavares was a twenty-two-year-old young man, often in and out of his mother's home in the south suburbs of Chicago. Since the mid-1990s, I observed many black families moving because of gentrification—from the ghettoes of the city into the south suburbs of Chicago—a migration that often had damaging and debilitating effects on minority children, for the sake of middle-upper- and middle-class progress. While this transition was often understood as a mobilizing act by the city for black people, it often facilitated in bringing about greater segregation in the city and schools, while also displacing many poor blacks from their inner-city relatives.[18] I often attributed Tavares's discomfort in his suburban home to his nostalgia for the South Side of Chicago, where most of his friends and family dwell. Unfortunately, on one of his many hiatuses from his mother's home, Tavares began a new hobby of living with, as he said, "big girls who love me" and "serving" marijuana in the neighborhood. Unfortunately, the latter occupation landed Tavares in a Cook County correctional facility, where I would spend much time visiting him and ensuring that he had the support and resources necessary for physical and mental survival. A month after serving time, he came to stay with me for almost two weeks. This visit offered me a fruitful opportunity to not only get reacquainted with my "brother in spirit," but also to listen deeply to his many experiences. Sleeping in my bed, chatting on my computer, rummaging through my videos, and surveying my books, Tavares learned things about me that I had never disclosed to him during our childhood. The first thing he learned was that I love Whitney Houston; the second, that I am gay. The latter bonded us in ways indescribable, while the former simply occasioned weird looks from him.

Tavares's presence in my intimate, so-called private space opened a door to vulnerable, valuable, and very enlightening dialogue. Tavares's entrance into my personal space opened my eyes to what it feels like to be "exposed." Though I was very open with my sexuality, my politics, and my home, it was still awkward to see and experience Tavares making certain evaluations and judgments on my "private" materials—I often felt under investigation. Sometimes he would rummage through my *Advocate* magazines—with queer subtexts in its covers—turning his nose up or simply making an uncomfortable sound. In addition, he would ask questions about the *how* of male-male sex as if he had no clue or was repulsed by the idea. To avoid these conversations, I began to remove these materials during his visit or make them less visible. I quickly realized that my anxieties over his inquisitions were incomparable to the type he felt in terms of his discretions and choices he might make as he attempted to stay "down low." It was these intimate moments that always reminded me that the ethnographic walk is a privileged one—a journey that requires attention to *how* we gather information before being concerned with *what* we gather. On the fragile plain of conversation with Tavares and other men, it has often been difficult to generate more intimate, deeper discussions. Though we were friends of many years, my new role as an ethnographer seemed to create some distance between us. However, our already-established closeness made it possible to turn potential feelings of exposure into moments where the subject could exhale and release many inhibitions.

The potential rewards of such an approach was made most obvious when, on the second night he stayed at my home, Tavares witnessed my "going-out ritual." This included talking on the phone to find out every friend who would be at the Gate, while simultaneously choosing something "hot" to wear. I am sure that this element of preparation made it clear that I was not going to a "straight" club. When I finished on the phone, I ironed my clothes, took a shower, and then I announced that I was leaving. Before I could even ask if he needed anything, Tavares said that he wanted to go with me. I asked him, "Why?" He responded, "What am I going to do, sit here at the computer and listen to Whitney?" I said, "You know where I'm going, right? I'm going to a gay club." He said, unaffected and unflinchingly, "I know."

Tavares's willingness to go to the Gate registered as a queer idea, but not queer in the sexual sense. It was queer because it became an instance when a heterosexual man was doing "straight" differently and defiantly. In this moment, Tavares showed me that his understanding of himself as a man was not contingent upon the disavowal of the effete or homosexual but the ability to not be preoccupied with my sexuality or overdetermine what his participation would signify. His ability to accept my queerness continued when I had to pick up Dedrick, my partner at the time. Together, they shared jokes and bonded—usually through various forms of making fun of me and my idiosyncratic ways. Interestingly, their greatest point of connection was around musical tastes—from Eminem to Do or Die. At the time, I sat silently and took in this moment with great interest. This act of male bonding reaffirmed what I have articulated earlier about the many transgressive possibilities for hip-hop, on and beyond the dance floor. I was most excited to see Tavares and Dedrick in action in the hip-hop room at the Gate. Admittedly, there was a theory being tested—a theory that was proven to be incorrect. In my early trials in the field, I learned quickly not to anticipate outcomes because they almost always turned out differently from what I expected.

When we arrived at the Gate, I paid the whopping thirty-six dollars for all of our admissions, since it was after 1:00 a.m. Moving through the customary procedures, we entered the Gate, and I asked Tavares if he wanted to take his hoodie to the coat check, as it would probably be too hot in the club. He refused. We continued into the Gate, whose energy and tone were pretty standard. It was much more crowded than at visits mentioned earlier. This night the dance floor had no empty spaces, the walls were crowded with people, and there were even lines for the washroom. It was a perfect night to feed the potential anxieties felt by my straight buddy from childhood. In such a crowd, one's body was always touching other bodies; one was constantly being looked up and down. Everyone from drag queens to drunks were attempting to make contact with Tavares. Appropriately, I quickly dashed toward the hip-hop room—an area where I was sure that Tavares would feel most comfortable. Immediately, Dedrick and I hit the dance floor. Tavares stood back against the wall observing the scene, while reggae beats played loud and strong. Quickly, the reggae turned to rap, and Tavares briefly joined us, doing a dance similar to my sway dance—a default move for music with a steady beat and for people who don't want to get too carried away. After a couple of hit songs, Dedrick and I continued dancing, but Tavares went off to the sidelines of the dance floor and simply stood in front of the speaker.

After being engrossed in a moment of dancing with Dedrick, I looked over and realized that in the midst of the large crowd, Tavares had disappeared. I panicked. I assumed that he was looking for me, as Dedrick and I had slightly shifted on the dance floor. I walked up to the "God view," peering out onto the dance floor, but he was not there. I moved to the balcony level, thinking that he might have given himself a personal tour of the hip-hop room. He was nowhere to be found. Maybe he went to the restroom. I walked through the crowd and cut to the front of the line, gazing into the restroom for Tavares. Just as I was about to return to the hip-hop room, Dedrick came and informed me that Tavares was watching the voguers. What? This was the last place I would have expected to find this "ladies' man." Nonetheless, I found Tavares standing, almost entranced, as the voguers waved, flipped, and dropped to the infamous "Ha!"—a musical piece that has historical reverence in the ball culture of black queer life.[19] I asked him, "You like that?" He replied, "It's funny—they crazy—but it's entertaining as hell." His fascination shocked me. Looking at his hooded face, I knew that Tavares's interests had shifted from entertainment to erotic pleasure. He watched the voguers with the same visual pleasure that he had watched all of the "tight females" who used to get off the Third and King Drive bus during our childhood. It was this look of desire that Tavares possessed as he gazed upon the "femme-queens" and the "girls up in pumps." He watched them for the remainder of the evening.

It was not until a later conversation at my home that I understood this erotic impulse that seemed to guide Tavares's desire for femme bodies. Tavares was in my room, at my computer—while I lay in my bed—and he told me that he had "a thing for femme cats." At first, I was preoccupied by the inversion of typical animalistic description of men as "dogs" flipped in this context to "cats." More interesting and informative, however, was how such an appreciation for the feminine disrupted and discounted the assumption that DL men only have interest in the masculine. Here, Tavares gave value and recognition to a desire for something outside of the masculine, showing a moment where his masculinity and heterosexuality were not contingent upon his object choice being a masculine subject. It is for this reason that Tavares's experiences in the house room become most appropriate in this discussion of hip-hop.

I argue that though Tavares prefers a feminine subject of desire, his interests are still in line with a certain heterosexual privileging system. Tavares, as a DL man, maintains his heterosexuality through his pursuit of a surrogate female figure. His relationships with "femme cats"—who are often understood as an androgynous male and/or transgendered female—allow him to still imagine himself inside the dominant matrix of sexuality, as these figures are often referred to and often refer to themselves as women.[20] Like those in the hip-hop space discussed earlier, Tavares attempted to undo his queerness through his participation in what can be understood as un-queer acts. It is no coincidence, then, that when Tavares described the femme cats he had seen and "hollered at" elsewhere, he emphasized the female characteristics as being "so real . . . I mean just like a woman's." This thinking reveals the ways in which any feminine/female body acts as a fill-in for the birth-assigned female with which Tavares was most familiar. Still, he cannot deny that he is engaging in queer acts with those who identify themselves in queer ways. This is most apparent when he articulated his same-sex desire in the somewhat ambiguous phrase that he was "feelin' that way toward another dude." Though he may relish the femininity of his sexual object-choice, he is always aware that it is a "dude." It seems, however, that he feels less threatened by his own desires when he imagines and acknowledges those with whom he shares interests as females or femme cats. In this sense, Don Kulick's ethnographic analysis of Brazilian travestis' desire for "straight men" is relevant and instructive for this case study: "Not only is desire meaningful only in relation to difference, it is also what *produces* difference—a male is a man *because* he desires a woman; a travesti can feel like a woman *to the extent that* she desires a man and is desired by him in return" (1998, 126).

The "production of difference" is what triggers Tavares's attraction toward "dudes" as being "all good." The difference, rather than sameness, attracts him to feminine subjects; whereas the queer world around him seems to endorse a more homonormative relationship.[21] Consequently, Tavares stands as somewhat of a queer queer, who reconfigures queer desire as heterosexual. As long as the subject of his desire speaks "woman" through performance and pose, he is comfortable and content. This female performance legitimates his desire, marking it as authentically "straight" and "more normal," as he put it. Such desire for normality, normalcy, and normativity seems to be the anchor for expressions of desire in these spaces, where masculinity seems so fragile, contingent, and contained to hetero-patriarchal ideals.

In addition to his ability to establish his heteronormativity through desire choice, Tavares also continued to position himself within hip-hop masculinity by enacting a gendered performance that has its roots in hip-hop culture. He stood rigid, with his hoodie covering and concealing his face, periodically moving to the beat. As he talked with those who passed by who fit his preferred image, he carried himself in a manner that bespoke "coolness" and positioned him as in charge and in control. I even noticed that his voice deepened and hardened in a manner similar to that of young boys courting young girls over the telephone. As he engaged with feminine objects of desire, through his performance of the heterogender, he was able to mark his place in this space of queer desire. Tavares, like many men on the DL, could only come to embrace homoerotic desire through the performance of heterosexuality, or heteronormativity. Together, Tavares and Shawn tell us two different stories about DL desire, disrupting any mainstream, monolithic notion of the performances of discreet sexuality. They serve as examples of the ways in which space "unleashes desire"—forcing them to find ways to compensate for the force-fitting pressure to submit to hegemonic masculinity. Their experiences in the club space accentuate and reiterate the ways in which sexuality is greatly informed by the constant constructs and constraints of a black masculine architecture.

Something in the Architexture:
Heterotopia, Masculinity, and Homoeroticism

For this construction of black male identity, we can thank many cultural architects who include Eldridge Cleaver, Amiri Baraka, Louis Farrakhan, Dr. Dre, and 50 Cent.[22] In these constructions of black masculinity, queer desire and performance are suspect, stigmatized, and incompatible with certain notions of blackness. Additionally, we can be grateful to white

supremacist capitalist patriarchy, which demands and rewards a certain performance of masculinity for black men in America to gain some access to
agency and power.[23] On the one hand, the Gate, in its homage to hip-hop,
destabilizes the "queerness" of this space and shapes a heteronormative imaginary with a queer subtext. On the other hand, the Gate uses hip-hop to
facilitate, encourage, and even legitimate queer desire. Indeed, something
strange occurs in the invocation of hip-hop in queer spaces. This presence
of the "strange" reminds me of how my mother would respond to abnormal occurrences within our house by screaming, "I swear there is something in the water!" Likewise, I am professing that there is something in the
architexture.

Clearly, I am not the first to connect architecture, as a material form, to
ideology within a given culture. In fact, this relationship was discussed as
early as 1847 in author-architect's George Wightwick's writings on the body
and architecture:

> A building is a body or a "carcass," lettered over with beauty of diction, with
> poetic illustration, and with the charms of rhetoric. . . . [W]hat the skin is to
> the body, the hair to the head, the eye-brows and lashes to the eyes, and the
> lips to the mouth—such is the marble casing to the walls, the cornice to the
> facade, the pediment and the architecture to the windows, and the porch to
> the door. (1847, 37)

What is most important in Wightwick's discussion of architecture is his focus on the body and space as interdependent. The body is as important as
space; each part of the body and space requires the other. In Wightwick's
construction, body and space form a dialectic rather than a dichotomy.
While Wightwick's discussions seem to get at the dialectic between space
and human behavior, I argue that "architecture" as a term does not get us
there or sufficiently explain what is happening. In this project, I am as much
interested in how certain spaces invite DL men's participation, as I am interested in the interior issues that allow DL men to find liberation, tension, or
satisfaction in the Gate. While many would refer to both as "architecture," I
want to employ a more appropriate term: *architexture*. While "architecture"
alone accounts for physical space, the addition of "texture" tells us more
about the "feeling" of space—the expansive cultural fabric that dwells in
specific sites of queer production. "Architexture" is a term that describes the
dialectic between the interior and exterior manifestations of masculinity. In
Maurice Wallace's *Constructing the Black Masculine* (2002), he argues that in
order to understand the construction of the black masculine, we must con-

sider the architectural structures in which it resides and also those structural foundations around which it is built. To this end, I utilize the term "architexture" to describe the contours of black masculinity with regards to spatial characteristics and cultural dimensions.

Architexture, as a material structure and a meaning-making apparatus, is a productive point of entry for my discussion of DL men in the hip-hop room of the Gate. At the Gate, there seems to be a constant thread of masculinity that impacts the music and the men. As a performer-witness at the Gate, I have experienced the impact of certain commitments to masculinity, while also participating in its construction and reinforcement. Between my first visit to the Gate and my subsequent journeys, I have learned that there are many codes, characteristics, and necessities in order to gain greater access into men's lives. The Gate's physical space assists in the masculine characteristic of the club. The industrial and working-class motif in addition to the separation of house and hip-hop into separate rooms signify the value and visible difference between two worlds. The industrial features are in alignment with the black masculine subjects in the space, and their character concurs with the cultural fabric of the Gate's patrons. "Architexture" seems most applicable, then, as a term that best accounts for this strong relationship between the physical space that helps shape what is possible and the internal presence that helps dancing subjects to make sense of what is possible.

It was only through a concerted effort to understand *how* men *do* the DL—a rehearsal of sorts—that I was able to refine and often reproduce the style of masculinity being produced in and outside the club space. At the Gate, either you follow the rules of hip-hop, or you are deemed outside the realm of normality. The Gate houses a brand of masculinity that reifies, reproduces, and rewards Shawn's and Tavares's heteronormative ideals, making it a space more open for DL presence and participation. Todd Boyd has called this gendered performance "the desire to be hard," which is much like "cool" in its somewhat visual posturing often associated with gangsta culture that is most often conveyed through style and image (2004, 70). The Gate, through its patrons' dress and gestural style—and its architectural design's sterility and staleness—promotes and projects a sense of the "hard." As the music fills the space with a hard sound in order to narrate a hard ideal, it prompts "hard, tight dancing," to which those who find queer performance difficult can engage in with less anxiety.

It is DL men's physical presence in the queer club, as seen in the previous chapter, that much of media has latched on to, as they stake claim to an "out" DL subject. In actuality, most men at the Gate are not "coming out" but participating in a sort of "comin' in." They have arrived in a queer space that welcomes them but does not require them to become an official member. The Gate is a black home they can come into, where the relatives understand the fullness of diversity, liberalness, and transgressiveness, and are most honest about different forms of desire. The discursive demand that one must be "out" to participate in gay activities ignores that all gay activity does not take place in public, and that participation does not always guarantee membership.

Indeed, DL men are out in the club in the sense that they are a part of a queer world-making moment. However, outside of this club space, they live very discreet lives, void of public displays of pleasure and desire for those of the same sex. Shawn referred to his life outside the club as "being out in the real world." When men would mark this difference in this way, I would often reply, "Is the club space not the 'real world'?" During our conversations, I was often aware of how Shawn and others dichotomized the queer world and his everyday heteronormative performance of identity. These admissions clearly gesture toward the ways in which the Gate allows DL men to imagine themselves in a sort of utopia (but not quite). This pleasure, attained through a queer world-making experience, may be the answer to the problematic question "Why are they in a gay club if they are not gay?"

This "utopia, but not quite" pleasure is what Foucault has referred to as a state of *heterotopia*. Heterotopias, unlike utopias, are real places. In his public lecture "Of Other Spaces," Foucault uses the mirror as an example:

> The mirror functions as a heterotopia in this respect: it makes this place that I occupy at the moment when I look at myself in the glass at once absolutely real, connected with all the space that surrounds it, and absolutely unreal, since in order to be perceived it has to pass through this virtual point which is over there. (1987, 24)

Here, I find the difference between the real and the unreal, heterotopia and utopia, to be contingent upon time. As Foucault makes clear, "The heterotopia begins to function at full capacity when men arrive at a sort of absolute break with their traditional time" (26). While the subject appears to be in the mirror, everything that he experiences is real; but once he exits the mirror, he is no longer in the mirror, and his image and its surroundings have a different meaning. The image that he acquired in the mirror is gone, and he is left with the everyday imagining of himself rather than the situational, specific look of the mirror.

For Foucault, then, heterotopias are spaces where people temporally reside. These spaces allow individuals to lose sense of time and to picture themselves and their world in ways that mark time as inconsequential. For DL men, the club is one of many potential heterotopias. Queer spaces that allow DL men to live queerly—though constrained by time—allows them to explore often unavailable, or inconvenient, possibilities. Unlike a heterotopia, a utopia is without material grounding, potentially timeless, and available only to the imagination. While Foucault uses an abstract space to speak to the possibilities of heterotopias, his material examples provide clearer understanding: "theatre, cinema, garden, cemetery, prison." Each of these spaces serves a specific purpose, allowing its residents to go to a different world for a specific period of time. The Gate's hip-hop room is a heterotopic space. Though Foucault omitted the club in his original theorization, its characteristics definitely fit within his paradigm. As DL men travel to spaces like the black queer club, they enact desires that are often foreign to heteronormative understandings of manhood. As they participate in queer world-making, they are engaging with heterotopic sites.

As heterotopias break with the ordinary, everyday life, they serve as monitors of our social conditions. For example, the necessity for the creation of queer dance spaces in general alerts us to the lack of queer social sites, places where queer men and women can act erotically without scrutiny. Because most clubs embrace a heteronormative understanding of what is acceptable, queer men and women must develop their own spaces. In essence, queer world-making is a way of creating a heterotopia. The Gate's hip-hop room offers those who are sexually marginalized but who have specific cultural roots to "have their cake and eat it too." Particularly, it offers black queer men an opportunity to take traces of the everyday and mix them with the extraordinary to create a scene where they can make their erotic imaginings real. The Gate, in its use of hip-hop and its preference for a certain texture of masculinity, is a unique place—where contradiction seems to fuel its energy and erotic possibilities. Here, black men can imagine themselves within and outside of societal ideals—mapping their own reality, making real what only seemed imaginable.

Heterotopias are sites structured in privilege. The Gate allows men the privilege to engage in, enjoy, or perform same-sex desire. Hence, they are similar to "safe spaces." Like heterotopias, the Gate "always presuppose[s] a system of opening and closing that both isolates and makes them penetrable" (Foucault 1986, 26). Thus, for DL men, the Gate has as many real risks as rewards. However, because of its "curious exclusions" (26), the risks are limited and its rewards multiple.[24] Indeed, Judith Butler's rhetorical questions at the outset of this chapter are apropos as racialized queers often cannot afford or desire to be "out." Thus, the closet as a threshold apparatus does not fully illustrate the ways in which the patrons of the Gate work through their sexuality. Black queer people have always done queer differently. Symbolically, the Gate, unlike the closet, is not a place of residence but a place for possibilities to be explored. The Gate is a heterotopic playground whose architexture allows its patrons to explore and enjoy temporal pleasure—through its conjoining of oft-thought disparate traditions. In a sense, rather than being a container for sexuality, the DL act as a frame (or fence)—through which men can better imagine and articulate sexuality on their own terms, privileging sexual discretion anchored in a traditionally masculine framework.

In this chapter, I have attempted to highlight one complicated space that exhibits black queers "making do" within a heteronormative society and cultural tradition. As media and other intellectual endeavors pursue this topic, it is important that they listen deeply and "down low," and be attentive to sociohistorical circumstances of black men and the histories connected to the spaces in which these men put their bodies on the line. As Aaron Betsky informs us, "Queer space is not one place: it is an act of appropriating the modern world for the continual act of self-construction . . . Queer space queers reality to produce a space to live" (1997, 193). Whether it is on a phone chat line or on the Internet, as discussed in the next chapter, or in the hip-hop section of a black gay club, DL men and many black gay men search for spaces where they can imagine a world that allows them to "just be." In this sense, "to be" is engaged in a politics of "becoming"—a black queer world-making—where one's positionality can shift without scrutiny but with understanding.

A few years ago, the Gate's Friday-night party came to a sudden end.[25] As I sit at my desk, reimagining the space of the Gate and the many possibilities within, I am drawn back to the underground dance scenes in Isaac Julien's film *Looking for Langston* (1988). I return to a masterful moment when he flashes back to a historic scene in which black men are gathered in a discreet space to party and partake in homoerotic desires. Some stand with drinks, some chat, and some dance with each other—all feeling the pulse of the erotic and the pleasure of this rare opportunity. Dressed in period suits and clothes, drinking and tasting the finest things, these men engage in desire on their own terms, in their own way, somewhere "down low" and outside the radar of heteronormative gazes. This moment in film mirrors so much of what I saw at the Gate. Black men and black queer men engaging in desire and using space, style, and music to guide their performances. The Gate is no contemporary coincidence; it is a space that resurrects an older, rich tradition. It is a retelling of black queer men, cautiously and creatively, dancing desire. It is an illustration of black queer performance happening outside the closet, but inside the Gate.

FOUR

Goin' Down Low: Virtual Space and the Performance of Masculine Sincerity

Communities are to be distinguished, not by their falsity/genuineness, but by the style in which they are imagined.

—Benedict Anderson, *Imagined Communities: Reflections on the Origin and Spread of Nationalism*

The "grain" of the voice is not—or is not merely—its timbre; the significance it opens cannot be better defined, indeed, than by the very friction between the music and something else, which something else is the particular language. . . .

—Roland Barthes, *Image, Music, Text*

When you on the [phone chat] line, you can tell who real masculine or who a real sissy. . . . Same thing on the Internet, if you listen between the lines, you can tell who out there and who ain't. . . .

—Anonymous caller[1]

The black gay club is not the only site where men can "unleash [queer] desire." In this chapter, I examine the performance of the black masculine by men within virtual spaces—a phone chat line and a popular website designed for men who have sex with men. This chapter shifts focus from how masculinity is read by examining bodily signifiers to the strict interpretations of the aural and visual. By employing Roland Barthes's metaphorical reference to the "grain of voice," while also giving it literal significance in how we understand communicative acts, I uncover how the voice is read, constructed, manipulated, and reproduced in two distinct spaces frequented by DL men. In essence, I am interested in how DL men represent themselves in spaces where their voice is the primary mode of communication (phone chat line), while also being attentive to how they render their voice and others as "masculine" in cyberspace (the website for male-male interests called Steve4Steve). In some ways, the Internet as a site of anonymity for DL men is not surprising. However, if telephone historian John Brooks's claim is true that the "telephone is our nerve end to society" (1976, 9), then the unwritten values of this space in queer cultural production are worth investigation.

Historically, ethnography has been understood as an act of entering a certain physical space while collecting data, conducting interviews, and rendering the scene though a "writing of culture." This tradition has limited the scope of ethnography's possibilities to reach beyond physical space and move into virtual spaces. Specifically, one of the most under-researched terrains is the telephone lines. This mechanism of verbal communication has often been pitted outside the imaginable realms of ethnographic research:

> When one speaks of working *in* the field, or *going* in the field, one draws
> on mental images of a distinct place with an inside and outside, reached by
> practices of physical movement. These mental images focus and constrain
> definitions. For example, they make it strange to say that an anthropologist
> in his or her office talking on the phone is doing fieldwork—even if what is
> actually happening is the disciplined, interactive collection of ethnographic
> data. (Clifford 2002, 54–55)

Consequently, this chapter offers a critique of studies that focus on actual physical space, as well as view Internet exchanges as the sole virtual site of male-male discreet encounters. While this chapter is interested in the operations of traditional virtual spaces populated by DL men in Chicago, the most innovative contribution is its examination of how the phone chat line acts as a more economical alternative for many to find erotic predilections and to legitimate their own commitments to black masculinity. The phone chat line's existence and excitement, evident through its large use, speaks volumes about the economic disparities of many black men, specifically, and working-class people, more generally. In the select spaces explored in this chapter, many decisions are made exclusively upon the texture and "grain" of the voice, be it the actual speech of the subject or the language used to describe himself or his personal sexual desires within a brief profile. I argue that these judgments are made based upon what Barthes refers to as the "something else"—a somewhat enigmatic equation that draws upon subjective experience and knowledge of the machinations of specific spaces.

As I travel through the Bi-Blade (the "public" phone chat line) and Steve4Steve (an Internet site), the determinant of the authentically masculine and therefore desirable is often what I refer to as "masculine sincerity." While "sincerity" has been used by John L. Jackson in *Real Black: Adventures in Racial Sincerity* (2005) to discuss alternatives to authenticity, I utilize this concept to describe how men decipher between the making and the faking of gender performance. This distinction is highlighted in Victor Turner's examination of identity performances, where he attempts to move beyond the limited idea of performance as fakery to view it as a process of "makery" (1982, 93). While Turner's perspective has great merit within interrogations of performance, certain engagements within virtual space challenge Turner's move for a more generous understanding of human behavior. The virtual spaces I investigate allow for the possibility for what is made in these spaces to be seen as real, as much as they can be understood as fake. Nonetheless, I am most interested in how individuals utilize certain codes to at least appear sincere or to present themselves as properly masculine. In these spaces, performance can be understood as both makery and fakery. Nonetheless, even the contrived performances are creating meanings as they construct an understanding of what it means to "do the down low" in virtual space—a "making do" with black masculine ideals and queer desire. In many ways, these spaces illuminate the nuance of sexual discretion, revealing its makeshift creativity and the subtle ways that traditional lessons of the masculine perfect tacit performances.

This ability for language to be understood as distinctively "masculine" or "DL" in virtual space, and its reproduction by those who travel in the virtual spaces, are key to this chapter. As a result, this chapter travels new terrain by being attentive to the by-products of racialized language and racial epistemology in constructing the meaning and purpose of space. Through an examination of discourse created by those who disidentify with gay, bisexual, or any other traditional categories, it makes real the notion of "queer linguistics." Whereas other scholars have investigated "gay English" or gay spaces of cultural production (Baker 2005; Leap 1996, 1999; Ringer 1994), this chapter uses the DL as an exemplar of *queer* linguistic and cultural production.[2] Don Kulick and others have argued that queer linguistics have little to no utility, by citing such categorization as a misnaming because "the only language ever investigated . . . is language used by those the researcher identifies as lesbian, gay, bisexual, or transgendered" (1998, 66). While I agree this has been a dangerous move on the part of such scholars, I wish to not throw the baby out with the bathwater. Though the academic tradition may have relegated queer linguistics to gay and lesbian linguistics, my research attempts to depart from this ritual. This project affirms and challenges the claims of Kulick and others by suggesting that there is a real significance and importance to employing queer in the academic discussion of language. In the spaces explored in this chapter, I locate a black queer world-making, which expands the historical category of queer to not only include racialized subjects, but also speaks to multiple sexualities outside of what previous studies have often included and even what Kulick's polemic seems to suggest "queer" contains.

Black Queer World-Making: Part II

As an undergraduate at Cornell College in Mount Vernon, Iowa, I struggled to locate black queer experiences. It was in this quest for blackness that I began to utilize the "party line," as it has historically been called—a free phone chatting system that allowed black men who have sex with other men to hold private and public conversations. I discovered this network of black men while in Chicago when friends of mine would call in to taunt others who frequented the line. For example, my friend Rob would call in and play the fire-and-brimstone minister who thought "all fags are goin' to hell!" When he would hang up, he would say to me and other friends who witnessed his charade, "Chile, I upset the building today!" Or my friend Milan would call in and act as the "big queeny bottom who was looking for a big dick top" to fuck her. He was probably the most extreme. However, most times, the line was a way that these "kids"—and we were young— would find ways to commune with others like us when our parents were asleep or had gone to work. Unlike more common phone chat lines, in this space individuals could actually maintain conversations as if in virtual "family" rooms—sharing their everyday experiences, expressing their desired interests in other callers, or simply taunting others who inhabited the space.

It was not by any coincidence that while frustrated with the cacophony of whiteness in Iowa—which I constantly consumed, engaged with, participated in, and contested—I went back to this pastime. In the rural white plains, I often yearned for traces of blackness either on television, among the few other black folks on campus, on trips to Iowa City, or in my ventures to Chicago's black gay club scene. However, when those experiences were not available, the phone chat line officially called the BeeHive was my haven.[3] Using my dorm room phone, I would dial in and "gag" with several other young black gay men.[4] Whereas in Chicago this call was free, in Iowa it was long distance and quite costly. Evidently,, I joined many other "homesick" college students—using our college account access codes—to pay for our taste of black gayness. Indeed, it often proved to be worth it. The BeeHive had three distinct features: (1) a caller could obtain a mailbox, where he could attach a greeting that would indicate his intentions and where other callers could leave messages; (2) a caller could enter one of nine "private" rooms—where a maximum of twelve callers could reside—and decide which conversations he wanted to join; and (3) a caller, after entering the room, could announce his interest in another caller and prompt him to press the same numeric digit to create their own private room (often, in jest, many would follow them). Indeed, the boundary of public/private was blurred in the BeeHive.

Typically, I would enter a room quietly to find out updates about Chicago's black gay life. Of course, this "information system" was limited in its ability to tell all, but the size of the "known" young black gay community always seemed relatively small. Interestingly, these private rooms were crowded with those who loved to gossip and tell their "business." From time to time, there would be highly political conversations—such as "coming out," the black church and gay persecution, and my favorite, "How can you tell a bottom from a top?" The latter was an ongoing weekly conversation. I often found myself annoyed by the essentialist underpinnings of the discourse and would move to another room where the conversation was more to my liking. Truthfully, I was satisfied to hear the voice of black urban gay Chicagoans, in their various textures and tones; particularly, the cultural vernacular from which I was estranged in Mount Vernon, Iowa.

The voices of these men were refreshing and often, for my pleasure, erotic. This would explain why the BeeHive, for my few years at Cornell College, became a channel through which I expressed sexual desire for black men—through phone sex. Here, I could express my homoerotic longings for black men without actually *being* there. I could imagine my body engaging with another brown body, being aroused by the verbal nuances that I found most desirable during sex. Most importantly, I could make active what was dormant—the sexual part of my sexuality. The BeeHive released me from the white community of Iowa, as well as the perspective of queerness as almost always white men performing sex/sexuality. In this space, I was allowed to partake in a black queer parlance, as black men gathered in hopes of co-articulating sexuality on their terms through "gagging," dialogue, reading, and erotic demonstrations through phone sex.

Years later this site became central to my research on DL men. While I am sure there were DL men on the "line" in previous years, though they did not refer to themselves under that nomenclature, something told me that this space was still sweltering with discretion. After all, my friends and I were somewhat DL as we would convene on the "line," as a substitute for an outlet to actually commune in any particular physical space. My return to this virtual space, however, was the result of a conversation with Charles, a thirty-five-year-old man I had met at the Gate. In our conversations, he indicated that his first sexual experiences were simply "sexual fantasy" through phone sex on the "PL," a new name for the party line.[5] The striking resemblance between "PL" and "DL" notwithstanding, the phone chat line was still an active agent in the construction of black homoerotic/homosexual experiences. Though Charles refused to engage in ongoing conversations, his narrated experience revealed that the party line had retained its popularity. In addition, his narrative suggested that the phone chat line may have been a more "private" and pragmatic forum for DL men than the club space, as meeting grounds for those men who desired relations with men. The phone number of the PL was passed on by word of mouth—much like the snowballing process I used to locate DL men—while its specific codes, navigations, and other tactics were learned through practice and trial and error. As I returned to the line after a long hiatus, I needed to learn the party line's recent nuances, since as with most modern modes of communication, there were some technological advancements.

The most obvious and significant change was the creation of an actual private one-on-one chatting area called "CB." Evidently, this is a riff on CB radio, which is a mode of short-distance radio communication often utilized by truck drivers or constant travelers, whereby they can have one-on-one conversations with other travelers or contact local emergency facilities. The phone chat line's CB space allowed local callers to communicate and participate in interactive and interpersonal communication. In this space, callers create personal profiles where they describe themselves, articulate their interests, and include whatever information they feel necessary for listeners to hear. In addition, they can screen the profiles of other callers and leave messages demonstrating interest. If so inclined, participants can leave messages for each other, request a one-on-one private chat, or block/skip undesirable callers who have shown interest in their profile. According to Charles, this was the space where he would dwell in search of perspective partners for his "phone-bone" experiences. Accordingly, as I adventured to perform my ethnographic research, the dynamics of this space seemed most appropriate for serious consideration in gaining access to the backstage performances of men who preferred a "discreet way of being in the world." As anticipated, this space provided fertile ground for my critical inquiry, bursting with contradictions, admissions contrary to my expectations, as well as identifying another space where black and queer could reside not in tension but in tandem.

Everybody's on Top: The Construction of a "Masculine" Community

One of my first observations about the CB space was that being sexually dominant—a "top"—was a metonym for "masculine," and its use instigated a distinct cultural climate among callers. In August 2002, when I first called the party line for research, there was a popular addendum used in the profiles of those who professed to be "on the down low": "Top brotha right here." It appeared that everyone was on top, a top, or liked to "fuck." While, indeed, there were several callers who performed the non-dominant role in sex—those who identified themselves as a "bottom," "submissive," or "versatile"—the predominant DL caller identified as a "DL Top" or a "Top Brotha."[6] This affirmation attested to what Roger Lancaster learned in his ethnographic explorations in Nicaragua, as the unequal distribution of stigma that is contingent upon the role played in sex (1992, 241). In the CB space, the prevalence of "top" men changed the texture and tone of masculinity on the line. For example, the preoccupation of callers with certain masculine tropes created a space where gay men and DL men desired to appear as masculine and "normal" as possible. When reviewing a profile of young man named Maalik, this became most apparent:

> [Deep voice, dark guttural tone, often hard to understand] Yeah . . . you got dis DL, bisexual nigga right here on the souf [South Side of Chicago] . . . I know y'all prolly tired of hearin' dat shit—shit, 'cause I am too. . . . I'm saying [voice gets deeper], but that's the truth with me . . . man . . . I don't like feminin niggas at all . . . not attracted to feminin niggas [voice gets higher]. I only hang with straight niggas . . . [more emphatic, slightly higher]. And if I can't bring you around my homies . . . [more fluid in tone, back to the beginning tone]. Looking to hang out with a nigga. I work, go to school, shit like that, looking to hang with a nigga, see what you look like. If somethin happen, it happens. Only into tight guys—people be confused [slows down and mumbles] 'bout what is fine. That's what I'm looking for . . .[7]

Maalik is clearly both aware and unaware of his performance of the properly masculine. On the one hand, he is conscious of the desired vocal and verbal rules necessary to establish himself as DL, while also unconsciously shifting vocal tones, inflections, and fluidity. Like most gender performances, there is always slippage. In this case, the slippage in and out of a deep "Barry White" voice was much more apparent than was common—either he was not well-rehearsed or had limited experience on the chat line. Considering his assessment that callers were "tired" of hearing self-proclamations of DLness, the former is probably more accurate. His assessment of callers' attitudes toward the DL title demonstrates a familiarity with the space, as well as the popularity of evocations of being "on the DL." Generally, the mastery of deep tonality, with consistent and convincing character, is the standard for those announcing themselves as a "DL brotha" or a "brotha on the down low." Though Maalik does not serve as example of this "passing" talent, he does exhibit his knowledge of the value of a certain type of masculine performance. In essence, to Maalik, his cool performance on the PL was an indicator of his sexual position. Maalik, in his commitment to the masculine texture/tone and the (non)reliability of his voice to sit in for his body, is emblematic of an investment that many men have in the black masculine schema.

When Frantz Fanon exclaimed, "I am fixed" (1952, 116), as he theorized the function of the "epidermal schema," I believe that he was not only seeing the white gaze inscribing images upon the black male body, but also the black male inscribing those images upon himself. He was imagining a historical moment like the present, wherein there was a dangerous sedimentation of the "black masculine" schema—when certain stereotypes are seemingly embraced, internalized, and rarely rewritten or complicated. Unlike Fanon's narrative, the men in the CB attest to the fixedness of not only a racial identity, but also sexuality and class. In this space, there is a consistent strain within the performances of not only an idealized masculine bravado and voice, but also a commitment to gender normativity, or normalcy. Here, voice and verbal cues work together to inscribe these men with masculine meanings, allowing those who converse or listen to these men's profiles to imagine a body that exudes proper masculinity and the desired sexual role. This is the "particular language" that Barthes signals in the chapter's epigraph—the "something else" that produces a meaning beyond the content of the message. Most importantly, after callers are acclimated to the space, they learn the language necessary to produce their desired outcomes.

This was a top-privileged space with little room for so-called "sissies" or "femme bottoms." The disavowal of all that was effeminate positioned DL men, and some gay men, as possessing "normal" gender characteristics. Those who performed the active role in sexual intercourse, or at least verbally claimed they did, were less stigmatized than the presumable feminine "bottom." Ironically, to label oneself a "top" had a certain aural acceptance not given to the passive participant in sexual intercourse. The hearing of "top" affirmed a masculinity that could pass in the more pedestrian crossings of black life—down the street, in the supermarket, and in the company of family and friends. As a result, the proclamation of being a top or DL top seemingly became the pass into being embraced as authentically masculine. The predominance of callers who proclaimed the dominant role in sex demonstrated its use-value. Nonetheless, the pervasiveness of so-called "tops" perplexed my ethnographic ears as there had to be "bottoms" for them to engage in sexual intercourse. If most of these men supposedly preferred other DL men, there must exist a contingency of men who are "bottoms" during sexual intercourse. The absence of these bodies from the CB space spoke not only to a commitment to a certain type of masculinity, but also to how the management of sexual roles gained appeal and provided callers with authenticity and authority. Undoubtedly, there was some dishonesty in what sexual roles callers played. Yet, as a caller told me, "you would never know until you get them in the sack." In other words, the proclamation that one is a "top" does not necessarily match the actual role performed during sexual intercourse. Nonetheless, in this marketplace of queer desire, tops were literally on top and bottoms were, indeed, subordinate. Everybody wanted to be understood as being on top, and no one desired to be on the bottom.

I quickly realized that much of what I would learn about the down low would be gathered from being attentive to how callers described themselves and the type of codes that were inscribed in their chat-line profiles. Unlike my experiences in the black gay club, the collection of ethnographic material would be generated from a type of participant-observation that often did not require classic formal interviews. In addition, I realized that the overt interviewing process, in the case of populations that refuse attention or prefer discretion, is limited in its utility in telling "what's really going on." This was most clear as I realized that CB was an agenda-driven space, where callers had clear goals and specific modes of acquiring their desired outcomes. For this reason, I knew it would be a challenge to set up personal conversations. Callers were primarily in CB for erotic "hookups"—be it phone sex or what was often understood as a "meet and greet." Seeing that I was ethically unable to do either and was utilizing CB for research purposes, my interests in the everyday lives of DL men could only be satisfied through close attention to what was being said and not being said in personal profiles, as well as responses by those who showed interest in me as a potential object of desire. Unlike the club, the patron who is standing alone and open to conversation, or at least flirtation, was hard to find. However, it was definitely productive to do some "deep listening"—as Dwight Conquergood had taught me to do, which for him meant being as concerned with presence as with absence.[8] Thus, this chapter attempts to not only unveil the relationship between space, discretion, and constructions of masculinity, but also to illustrate the centrality of rules and regulatory agents in what is often thought of as "private space."[9] The marking of this space as private was central to participants' ability to establish certain styles of "masculinity" as acceptable, as well as demarcate who is authentically DL and who is not. Such boundaries construct a space where DL men can feel more comfortable and where black gay men can find innovative ways to write themselves into heteronormative gendered ideals.[10]

This cultural congruency between DL men and black gay men somewhat explains why the negation of the "other" (in this case the femme and "out" gay man) was a common practice. Whether black and gay or DL, the more masculine caller was elevated to a position of power and desire. For example, one caller's profile described himself as a "cool DL nigga on the line, looking for another DL nigga," while also stating clearly that "no queens, no sissies, only DL brothas" were of interest. His mode of validating his own masculine persona only happens through the denigration of more effeminate men. While it appears that for him "DL" means everything non-feminine and non-identifiably queer, when I asked what was meant by "DL" in his profile, he responded, "I can't believe you hit me up with that shit, but DL is whatever it mean to you. What you think it is, that's what it is. . . . It's whatever it means to you." For this caller, "it" is a fixed sexual identity that should be common sense for those who are, indeed, DL. It was clear through the caller's tone that he was annoyed at my inquiry, as if I was insulting him by asking such questions. As he repeated, "It's whatever it means to you," it became clear that I was deemed a trespasser who was outside of his "community." My lack of knowledge situated me as a "sissy" or "queen"—as my inquiry seemed uninformed.

Though I understood what definition of DL was circulating in the CB space, my ethnographic naïveté was deemed not only ridiculous, but inappropriately feminine. In addition, I was quickly dismissed as a potential candidate of interest for the caller's conversation or as a potential "meet and greet." My perceived lack of knowledge resulted in the caller pressing the number four, which would skip to the "next guy." Evidently, I did not possess the standard knowledge or the masculine ideal that permeated the CB space. Shawn, the DL guy who tried to place my hand on his groin in the Gate club, relayed a story where he experienced rejection in the CB space of the party line. He described an instance where he felt as if his "DL card" was snatched when he did not fulfill the vocal, or performative, expectations of other DL callers. A college student from a middle-class background, Shawn refused to disguise his voice to ensure his passing into "straightness," or what was commonly understood as masculine. Thus, he was often dismissed as being "gay" or a "punk." It is Shawn's reaction to always being "suspect" or queered in his middle-classness that I believe fueled much of Shawn's antagonisms with many men who were openly and unapologetically queer.

While the repudiation of the so-called "out brotha" was common, it more importantly elucidates the arbitrary judgments made within this space. Shawn's hypercritical opinions of the effeminate men, like many men who choose more discreet ways of being, exhibits his own discomfort with being emasculated and his unease with those who articulated a conscious gay identity. The further distance that DL men position themselves from everyday queers, the closer they move toward normalcy. On this chat line, a masculine memo is distributed with specific instructions; yet various individuals often lose or have their "cards" taken away. DLness is often used to measure masculinity and masks the plurality within this particular community. In addition, those who describe themselves as being DL and those who prefer a discreet way of being in the world seek men who claim to possess those visible markers of masculinity often located within hetero-gendered bodies.[11]

As a result of the overwhelming number of callers who make such demands for masculinity, the space is homogenized in ways that resemble historical treatments of race as a category. Many have tried to fix, or bracket off, the category of blackness in order to signify sameness among a community of people. Yet this artificial production of sameness neglects the diversity among black people. Still, many try to fit into this limit-filled box. The same is true in the case of the DL—many regulate to affirm their own truth, while ignoring the "other" voices within their communities. Consequently, many men fix themselves to fit certain masculine ideals. While these regulatory practices create imaginative cohesion, Judith Butler reminds us that they more accurately "invoke the heterosexual norm through the exclusion of contestatory possibilities" (1996, 109). In this case, those who understand black sexuality as private, and therefore to only be performed in properly masculine ways, exclude those who feel otherwise. Thus, less masculine men are relegated to the quiet of the bedroom, while also quieted in the waves of the party line. This creates the illusion of homogeneity within the CB space, wherein DL becomes synonymous with "top" and acts as an index for accepted and proper masculinity. Regardless, the absence of aural bottoms, or queeny tops, does not mean they do not exist. Rather, it demonstrates the powerful economy of the top within this black queer world.

While sexual labels and positions are central to how DL men framed themselves as masculine, other attributes were offered as validation of gender-sexual authenticity in the CB space. Often callers made references to not only the structural build of their body, such as "muscular" or "thick," but also drew explicit attention to their physical endowment. Such statements like "Big Dick Top," "8 inches thick and round," and "hard dick looking for a bubble butt" were used like keywords in callers' profiles. While this was not the language employed by all callers, the commonality of these phrases is indicative of the ways in which a sense of community was created through what Rusty Barrett refers to as a "homo-genius" language. Using the work of Saussure, Barrett discusses how communities build a language where ideal speakers reflect the language and language structure of his/her society (1997, 182). In "CB Land," as one caller referred to it, a predominance of a certain type of language has constructed a cultural situation where voice and self-description verify the status/role of individuals within the community. In addition, it equips callers with the ability to locate themselves within the DL community and to dismiss those who are impostors, or "fags." Along these lines, there was a concerted effort among men to eliminate interest from callers who were understood as undesirable. The catchphrase "No Fats, No Femmes" could be found in many profiles. In line with dominant historical privileging of certain bodies, this tendency illustrates a need to see oneself as what one is not. While initially the coupling of "femme" and "fat" seemed highly arbitrary, its logic becomes apparent when recognizing the construction of overweight and feminine bodies as non-normative ideals. This move by DL men to pit themselves against the "fat and femme" allows themselves to write themselves into what R. W. Connell calls "hegemonic masculinity" (1995, 64).

The extreme nature to which these masculine ideals were privileged was made most evident when my childhood friend Tavares revealed that there was a strong economy in "meetin' and greetin'." He referred to this act as "paper-chasin'." In other words, he had been paid to meet up with someone and engage in some type of sexual act. While I am certain that there were many who profited from their participation on the line, DL men seemed to have an overwhelming appeal to patrons hiring for sexual acts. Tavares—like many men I spoke with—made it very clear that this sexual-capital exchange was not about pleasure when he shared that "getting my dick sucked is getting my dick sucked. And if somebody gonna pay me to suck my dick . . . shit . . ." He later indicated that it was enjoyable, but mostly because he needed the money. On the one hand, Tavares attempted to at-tribute his same-sex experiences on the PL to a matter of profit; while, on the other hand, he admitted feeling genuine sexual excitement from his various patrons. The tension illustrated by these two statements is clearly a product of stigma. As mentioned in previous chapters, DL men are sexual-passing subjects who navigate between the stigma of (queer) sexuality and their ac-tual desire for same-sex relations. In this example, Tavares in some ways fits within this formula, but I would like to suggest he also gestures toward how capital may push desire under dire financial constraint.

The profiteering component of this stigma for working-class men like Tavares offers another way to survive economic hardships and unfortunate circumstances.[12] Unlike many DL men on the chat line, Tavares had a very broad "hookups" list. From single DL men, married men, transvestites or MTF transgendered, openly gay men, and various physical types, he engaged in sexual activities in exchange for money and/or housing and food.[13] In a recent conversation with a group of gay men, they admitted to "putting up and feeding so-called straight men" in exchange for some "good sex or just for good charity." While the sex exchange was consistent with my previous findings, the charity factor was confounding. After several conversations, as well as further one-on-one talks with Tavares, I realized that they were buy-ing masculinity. Many gay men had such strong desire for the "masculine" that they would not only allow many DL ("straight" or "trade boys") free rein in their homes, but would also pay these discreet men to receive oral sex from them.[14] In a gathering of black gay men at my home, one man stated, "Fags love a thug—they want a *man*, not any man!" This sentiment highlights the surplus value of the DL brand of masculinity, exemplifying how hegemonic masculinity is not only privileged among DL men, but black gay men as well.

While black gay and DL men seem to be highly invested in certain styles of masculinity, after the DL became fodder for public discourse, there ap-peared a tension within the virtual space. As the demonizing inscriptions upon the black male body were being consumed, criticism and concern were as pervasive among black gay men as among black women and the larger black community. For example, one gay caller who called himself BD told me, "These men are dishonest. . . . They use us, go back to their wives, and potentially spread disease with and without knowledge." While this remark seems to gesture toward envy for the priority given to the female partner, it more importantly identifies a defense for black women. Nonetheless, his biggest contentions were that "*these* men were not comfortable in their skin" and "confused." These "internal issues," as BD called them, were unacceptable. Like the media and its thirsty consumers described in chapter 2, BD ignores the many pressures and presences within black men's lives. In fact, he later admitted: "It took me about eight years to tell anyone what I was doin', but I did it." As he attempts to commend himself, he unconsciously empathizes with many DL men's sociocultural positions as fathers, brothers, sons, friends, and workers. Unfortunately, his sentiment like many others corroborated with popular opinions noted in previous chapters where the DL was made synonymous with immorality and disease.

My knowledge that gay men had a different relationship to marginalization created expectations that their opinions would differ from popular discourse. However, I found that many black gay men had also found their "criminal" in the DL body. While I don't mean to suggest an intentionality in the criminalizing tendencies of gay men, I do wish to denote the amount of pleasure exhibited in gay men's ability to deflect negative attention from themselves. In addition, their focus on the duping and disease aspects of the so-called "DL lifestyle" evokes an "us versus them" construction. This framework allows gay men to remove themselves from being *the* queer threat—posturing as a figure who is the queer friend who not only defends morality, but black (heterosexual) health. In essence, it seems that openly gay men—who have historically been constructed as "bottoms" within this spatial context—are now inverting that legacy. In other words, they are positioning themselves in a privileged location of hierarchy through a moral queer versus immoral queer dichotomy, as they criticize DL men on the basis of issues of dishonesty and disease. In this sense, they reposition themselves on the top of black sexual discourses—becoming the proper example of male-male desire.

Consequently, the reputation of DL men within the CB space was often challenged by gay men. Callers would either announce their desire not to be contacted by "confused brothas" or "DL men," or they would simply enact BD's strategy of "skipping to the next caller." Yet the frustration expressed in the CB was not just a product of arbitrary power play. There had been several news reports that cautioned callers that "straight" men were using the line as a vehicle to attack "queers." While I was engaging in research, an ex-lover of someone I was dating was robbed and brutally murdered during a "meet and greet" with two allegedly DL men. This series of events not only created a "disgust" for DL men, but also a fear of "homosexual panic" being enacted against openly black gay men by those who were then called "closeted fags." Intuitively, many men who typically identified as DL callers not only qualified their understanding of themselves of DL, but also created profiles that implied that the term was an abused one. While many refuse to change their way of being, in terms of discretion they tailor their profiles to only attract callers who can tolerate or understand their positionality. For example, one caller publicized this profile:

> You got a brotha that's frustrated as hell [pause]. . . . Me and this nigga sup- posed to have an understanding and shit—I'm married, and this the first time I decided to hang with him . . . him and his guys . . . but he wanna front me off, and he tells these mf's I'm confused, that I'm tryin' to live two lives. I love my girl, love being with her, but like dippin' with a nigga too. Then . . . this nigga friends start comin' at me . . . this motherfucker wasn't even sayin' shit. . . . I ain't with that whole scene [deep sigh]. So. . . . I'm looking for an- other nigga . . . once we have an understanding, we have an understanding. . . . *Ain't no breaking the law.*

This profile narrative illustrates one of the ways that many men situate them- selves as DL, while responding to the popular critiques of the way they move within the world. In this case, the caller clearly describes himself as traveling between men and women—marking his heterosexual relationships as most significant, while his queer relations are simply sexual.[15] Unapologetically, the caller signals surveyors of his profile that he has a clear frustration with the public sexual visibility that he witnessed in a recent encounter. This act of storytelling made other callers aware of his unwillingness to submit to popular calls to visibility or for the quick shift from discretion to disclosure. Indeed, he outlines the "drama" of the situation—he articulates a desire to reduce the possibilities of both visibility and criticism. Important for this discussion, he illustrates the tension that I pinpoint between some black gay men and DL men, in terms of the different expectations for sexual comfort or outness. The man who took him among his friends had a different com- fort level with his queer sexuality and denied the caller his own choice in making his sexuality a public conversation. Finally, the caller's final move to incite issues of "breaking the law" illuminates how a desired discreet posi- tion can be a binding agreement between men. The calling out of his sexual- ity by the openly gay man, ridiculing his "confusion" and participation in a double life, denied the DL caller the ability to narrate, or not narrate, his own sexual pleasures.

While this example serves to elucidate the tensions between men in CB space, it also speaks to its various risks. Particularly, it highlights how DL men's commitment to discretion can be challenged and questioned. The CB space, which was often referred to as a "cool" space connoting a sense of safety, now becomes a place of "drama" and potential danger. Rather than the laudatory remarks I would receive from DL men in the beginning of the research, I now heard: "The line has too many fags." This declaration is not as much homophobic as it is a recognition of the difference in approaches to sexual (in)visibility by DL and gay men. It may be for this reason that many men with whom I spoke moved to the Internet for their homoerotic experiences. Indeed, this is not the sole reason. Yet the Internet does supply more ways for an individual to engage in fantasy, while monitoring and maintaining their discreet positionality.

DL Virtuality: Anonymity, Quasi-Visibility, and Steve4Steve

While there has been substantial research on gay men on the Internet (Nakamura 1995; Shaw 1997; Campbell 2004; Baker 2005), little work has explored how black gay men navigate their identity within the virtual world. Moreover, the discussion of DL men in Internet chat rooms is often thought to be a paradox. For example, the infamous *New York Times* article "Double Lives on the Down Low" (Denizet-Lewis 2003) frames black cyberspaces as an anomaly—rare places where dangerous things happen. Similar to perceptions of DL men at the Gate, the presence of their actual image in cyberspace seems to be contradictory to their assumed tenets of "discretion." This narrow construction of what DL can include is popular within and outside the community of men themselves. However, these findings negate the faith and trust that some men have in Internet spaces that are largely exclusive. In addition, many take for granted the possibilities for virtual interactants to hide their identity, as well as information that may endanger their anonymity. This section of the chapter charts new territory as it travels within a space called Steve4Steve, a national Internet site, often frequented by men with whom I speak. While nationally this site is predominantly white, black and Latino men uniquely pervade this space in Chicago. This rarity possibly speaks to the limited networks for men of color in engaging in homoerotic pursuits, as much as to the fact that many queer spaces exclude men of color (Nero 2005). While in a city like New York there is a history of black and Latino queer social networks, the need for such virtual spaces in Chicago is greater.[16]

While anonymity has often been concluded as being the central feature needed for travel into virtual space by men who desire men (Reid 1996; Danet 1998), this finding is somewhat incomplete. I argue, like John Edward Campbell in his book *Getting It on Online: Cyberspace, Gay Male Sexuality, and Embodied Identity* (2004), that several components are at work, as he explains:

> I contend that such anonymity alone is not sufficient to foster feelings of safety in the case of queer erotic exploration. Rather, I would suggest that it is the more complex convergence of online anonymity, shared presumptions of both a particular gender and sexual identity, the policing of these presumptions, as well as communal efforts to exclude hostile discourses, that has, for queer interactants, made these channels hospitable spaces for queer exploration. (55)

While anonymity may be a key component of the pleasure gained in cyberspace, these other factors seem complementary. In addition to Campbell's assertions about what makes queer virtual space desirable, it is impossible to exclude racial identification from the formula of "hospitality." Particularly in the spaces where DL men reside, it is imperative to understand the interworkings of race, gender, class, and sexuality—as various categories become salient within cyberspace, in terms of representation and navigation. This became most clear for me when an interactant in Steve4Steve said that he preferred this site because he saw "real black men." This comment has all the inflections of racial and gender authenticity. The marking of "real black men" demonstrates the ways in which the architexture of black masculinity always already conjoins blackness with a gendered identity. Thus, it is virtually impossible to understand what black men do within virtual spaces without paying attention to the intersections of their multiple identities. Within no time, it became clear that black male bodies adjudicated themselves in particularly ways, while equally being assessed by those who were not black, but powerfully present online.

Steve4Steve is a traditional cyberspace site that highlights the significance of intersecting identities, where individuals communicate via internal messages, while opting to have external face-to-face interaction at a later point. As is common with most virtual sites of interpersonal communication, each interactant can create a profile to inform other individuals of their physical, mental, and sexual characteristics. However, the site is peculiar in its required information: "You *must* include in your profile: age, height, weight, waist size, body type, hair color, body hair, ethnicity, and what your sexual desires are (i.e., 1-on-1 sex, relationship, friendships, misc. fetishes, etc.)." The fact that these fields are required, forces interactants to appeal to the physical-erotic eye. In addition to these required fields, there are also "optional" components such as a personal profile, professional information, substance-consumption habits (smoking/drinking/drugs), as well as what sexual features (role, "dick size," HIV status, etc.). Finally, the last "optional" field is the personal/private photo. For many DL men, it is ideal that this latter component is optional. However, most men with whom I spoke did post some type of image: either an actual picture of themselves, a nude photo that shows their genitalia, or an image that would speak to their masculine schema (i.e., Tupac Shakur, a Jeep, or a scene from an urban neighborhood). Regardless, the option to select an image of choice allows for what I refer to as "quasi-visibility"—to be seen and unseen—a feature that accommodates the predominant desire to only present part of the self.[17] This choice not only represents a move toward anonymity, but also a strategy to avoid folks from "getting it twisted," as one man stated. In other words, no one can be confused about the aims of the interactant, attaching themselves in ways beyond the sexual-physical. Here, the medium is indeed the message.

I began my research on Steve4Steve by reading through thousands of profiles, locating trends and tropes within the descriptions, desires, and other disclosed details. Particularly, I was interested in profiles that explicitly used the term "DL," as this suggested a certain consciousness about what one may include in the personal narrative. I found that men from all racial, cultural, and class backgrounds employed "DL" to signify a certain level of discretion and masculinity.[18] While this was not a corpus study, where I examined the quantitative frequency of certain linguistic terms within profiles and what they may mean, I was interested in the consistent narratives that were being publicized by DL men on this site. Indeed, there were certain trends in how men would situate themselves and their sexual desires. For the men who had literally expressed a DL positionality in their profile, there was limited information offered about their personal lives. One interactant, whose screen name was DLChicago76, included all physical components of himself but omitted any information that would potentially allude to his professional background. In other words, though his profile stated "5' 9", 145, 32w, swimmer's build" as his physical description, the other optional components were excluded. In this way, the interactant could draw attention to not only his physical description, but also the provocative picture of his penis. This profile was intended to appeal to a certain viewer, one who was solely interested in a sexual experience. Likewise, many profiles include nude pictures of the interactant, which served as a stand-in for the conventional headshots. Such illustrations would include everything from upper torso shots to actual images of the genitalia, as well as photographs of men engaging in particular sex acts. This choice, for the nude photograph to stand in for the actual face, reduces the interactant to his sexual function and constructs the DL positionality as one solely concerned with sex. Indeed, the common practice of this stand-in effect can create a misunderstanding of DL culture and the full-scale objectives within cyberspace. While there are several men for whom sex is a priority, the absence of these men's faces in the space is more of a conscious choice to avoid recognition. As DL men attempt to regulate and monitor their visibility, like DLChicag076 they recognize "my body is enough."

The dominant mythology—of DL men's investment in discretion and acting as a somewhat disembodied subject, through the absence of actual identifiable images of the self—is sometimes challenged in Steve4Steve profiles. Many men who travel within the site choose to publicize photos of their face and/or their body for others to review. When I first saw the profile of an interactant called DL_Blackboi with an identifiable headshot— but limited descriptive information—I was surprised. Up until this point, I assumed that this would be outside the DL protocol, especially since I understood discretion to be at the core of DL men's everyday praxis. Thus, to see a clear shot of this man's face on this queer site was, at best, shocking. After several discoveries of similar profiles, I realized something significant. Many men did not feel inclined to hide their images because the likelihood of exposure was rare. Indeed, the other men who resided in this space shared the common desire for male-male experiences. Furthermore, men like DL_Blackboi reduced the opportunity of discovery by including limited information for other interactants, or possible viewers, to identify who they are, where they work, and other potentially threatening information. Lastly, such choices of visibility speak to the diversity within the enclave of DL men who travel within the space, as some are more discreet than others.[19] As in all "communities," there are a range of investments—some more extremely discreet about their sexual desires than others. The few men who do expose their faces attest to how the DL is often evoked to simply signify the presence of the masculine, indicate their navigation of sexuality outside specifically queer-oriented spaces, or as a description of how they move within the world in terms of privileging a private livelihood. These men, in line with David Ziller's book *Photographing the Self*, understand "auto-photography" as a "method of nonverbal communication which provides a frozen image with a message" (1990, 70). Likewise, in Steve4Steve the self-photograph and the attached written text act as a sort of advertisement—the selling of the masculine, or ideal, sexual subjectivity.

Rather or not DL men select to make public their face or body, many men like DLChicag076 will often omit certain information and write their profile narratives to regulate who will pursue their interest. For example, DLsmooth1977 indicated that he was a "discreet brother interested in only the same." This statement attempts to bracket off who is, and who is not, eligible for the interactant's interest. In essence, the publicly visible black gay man is an undesirable candidate for many men's sexual pursuits—what Murray Healy has called the "I am what I want" theory at work (1996, 63). In order to ensure interest for other interactants with similar interests, men in Steve4Steve often identify the characteristics that potential mates must possess. However, I argue that this desire for men who are like the interactant is not only about a desire for more masculine men, but also a way to feel more "straight." Tyrone, an avid Steve4Steve user, told me the following:

> I want somebody I can go out to the bar with, play pool, and no one ever knows we are more than buddies. When I talk to these guys on here [Steve 4Steve], I am always cautious about meeting. We are not going to meet without talking on the phone. [Pause.] I need to know they are cool like me . . . that they can be out and about and they don't wear their business on their outside.

Tyrone's sentiments are common, as they reflect a concern for appearances and external affirmation outside of cyberspace. Though many men meet without prerequisite phone calls, Tyrone insisted that he has these conversations with all of his "hookups." This need for aural affirmation of masculinity not only reveals the dependency on vocal qualities, but also how Tyrone and others use the telephone as a second opinion. Tyrone admitted that once he has telephone conversations with men, there is much he can tell from just talking to someone. Among the many characteristics that he listed as being potentially unveiled in the Internet plus telephone conversation combo were "whether a brotha is really masculine," "if he uses gay language," "if he [is] a top or bottom," "if he is a liar," and "if he is a sendoff."[20] Of course, all of these guarantees are not guarantees at all. However, Tyrone's faith in his deciphering abilities not only speaks to his experience at doing the "hookup"—for almost two years—but also his investment in certain masculine codes and conduct as an index for heteronormative gender performance and sincerity. As Tim Edwards has eloquently articulated in *Men in the Mirror*, "For some, this intense masculinization of gay culture represent[s] a triumph of sexual expression and political opposition to heterosexual ideology, whilst for others it mean[s] attempted conformity to oppressive stereotypes of sexual attractiveness and practice" (1999, 108).

For Tyrone, and men who have similar standards, the Internet image and profile is never enough—further investigation is almost always necessary and a better guarantor of their gender-sexual ideals.

In order to more fully understand DL men's interactions within the Steve4Steve site, I created a personal profile for DownLow_25 that announced myself as a researcher who was interested in speaking confidentially with DL men:

> Brotha here wanna talk to DL men only. Trying to get the real deal on the Down Low. Media's not doing a good job and these so-called experts ain't tellin' the story right. I am not interested in your name, or anything that you are not comfortable sharing. But I am writing a book—I need to gather life stories of DL men who use the Internet and/or phone chat lines. If you wouldn't mind filling out a short questionnaire, e-mail me at: downlow1_2006 @yahoo.com.

My construction of the profile was informed by my awareness of key tensions that could be created between me, the "out" ethnographer, and them, discreet men. In essence, my crafting of a specific voice was designed to open a window of discourse through which DL men could see my transparency and personal commitment to their discretion. As men began to respond, many men expressed concerns about the confidentiality of their everyday lives and identity, fueled by the questionnaire's many questions. Therefore, after consultation with some of the men I interviewed previously, I recreated a questionnaire that allowed Steve4Steve interactants to determine the quantity and content they wished to share. In scenes of discretion, narrow and direct questions disable room for discreet choice. Knowing I was able to follow up with some men via instant messenger (chatting in real time) or over the telephone, I used the questionnaire as a text that would provide further explication for their doings inside and outside of the space. Additionally, I also assured their confidentiality by asking them not to tell me any information that they felt was potentially too specific to who they were (such as name and place of employment). After I had provided comfort, like the other men with whom I spoke, they signed a consent form—which allowed me to use their narrative in a published work and/or performance.

When I first posted my profile, I received several messages from openly gay men that expressed concern for my research outcomes. They often stated that they doubted my ability to get DL men to speak to me—not only because I was a researcher, but because, as one interactant said, "there ain't no real DL men online—they in the streets." While much of the DL population is inaccessible, as they perform sexuality behind the doors of surveillance, many do travel in cyberspace. As illustrated earlier, there are different levels of trust of the machine, various interpretations of "risks," and multiple commitments to different degrees of discretion. Therefore, I would retort (or not respond and just think), "I think you are wrong." This was definitely a statement of faith, as the first few times I left my profile online, I only received one response. As I spoke with another friend who does similar research, I was advised to change my profile image. Initially, it was a blank profile box with "No Photo" inscribed in it. I believed that my screen name Downlow_25 would attract enough attention, that interactants would be compelled to read my profile. After I realized, by the lack of responses, that this lack of an image was not enticing—particularly for a site that was constructed for its users to scroll and screen photos—I quickly updated my Steve4Steve profile. Using the front cover of Scott Poulson-Bryant's book *Hung: A Meditation on the Measure of Black Men in America* (2005), I not only gave free advertisement to this provocative and poignant book, but attempted to attract those who believe "I am what I want." Poulson-Bryant's cover shows a black man's upper torso with the word "HUNG" in bold print and vertically centered, while a measuring tape is diagonally stretched across his chest. The picture, I knew, was not only sexually suggestive, but a prototypical image for those who often understand themselves to be DL, as well as those who desire DL men. This experience of online rejection, or "no hits," gave me great insight as to why it is often necessary for DL men to utilize an actual photograph. It was probably less about a willingness to expose images of the self, or parts of the self, and more about eliciting cyber appeal. After I added a profile image, responses began to swarm in immediately.

While several men commented on how "tight" or "hot" I was, not realizing my virtual image was a cover of a book, about fifty men showed interest in answering the questionnaire. After e-mailing the survey to their accounts, about twenty-five men returned the questionnaire. The participants ranged in age from twenty-three to forty years of age. They were all black men, who came from various class and social backgrounds, and who indicated similar but distinct reasons for their Steve4Steve pursuits. Many men noted that the Internet provided a private space to express desire for other men, while also offering a venue where they could explore fantasies that were unavailable in their everyday life. There were three primary findings within the questionnaires: how DL men navigate within Steve4Steve, how the cyber-space experience relates to everyday life, and how they interpret their own performances of DLness and those of other interactants.

As DL men travel within Steve4Steve, they create their own interpretation of the space. Consequently, they construct strategies to navigate within various sites. When narrating how he moves within Steve4Steve, Get_Down25 had this to say:

> Honestly I don't approach guys, if I see someone attractive online I will speak and if they want to hold a conversation that's cool . . . but most of them nig-gas online be trying too hard to be hard. You can tell a lot from a picture . . . but how the fuck you "DL" and you got your picture posted on a fag website? How the hell you can be a "THUG" but your eyebrows thin and [you] got a bunch of Vaseline on your lips . . . some bullshit.

This statement is quite loaded with contradiction. For example, he predicates his move to converse with other interactants on being "attractive," but yet criticizes so-called DL men whose pictures appear on a "fag website." Later in the questionnaire, he states that one of his greatest fears is other interactants "being someone else than the person on the pic." This not-withstanding, the pejorative description of Steve4Steve as a "fag website" is ironic, as he travels daily within this space. Is he also a "fag" because of his virtual explorations and sexual desire for men? Furthermore, other than visual representation, how would he know if other interactants have thin eyebrows and Vaseline on their lips? It seems that he is committed to dis-counting the visual as a medium of representation, while using it for his own production of knowledge.

Nonetheless, chat rooms are historically sites where the textual and vis-ual meet to constitute meaning. Get_Down25 attempts to disconnect the two, in hope of authenticating his DLness. Like many other DL men I have encountered, he creates a virtual impossibility—reducing the opportunity for interactants to make some visual assessments before actual face-to-face interaction. In terms of his own individual practice online, this extraction of photographic images is unrealistic and non-ideal. Thus, his move to discount the visual is more of a rhetorical move rather than an actual ex-pression of his perspective. This desire to express an authentic DL persona through what one says publicly is common among men online. It benefits Get_Down25, and DL men more generally, to appear uncomfortable with queer visibility and "fags," even when these may be appealing features of looking online. Here he attempts to use a rhetorical strategy of disidentification as a way of "proving" his DLness in conversation with others (including me, the researcher) through the construction of a certain narrative. While there may be some reservations to making one's photographic image public, it is still a key feature on the Steve4Steve site. In many cases, it appears that the danger of the risk of exposure is reduced by the fact that this is a space exclusively for "fags," or a predominantly queer site.[21]

The role of cyberspace in reducing risk factors was never more apparent than in the responses given by DL_MarriedBiGuy. This married thirty-six-year-old professional in the entertainment industry and father of three children provided succinct but illuminating insight. One of the most intuitive statements that DL_MarriedBiGuy made was that "the internet allows me first and foremost anonymity. I can screen others who are in my situation and therefore I feel in control." DL_MarriedBiGuy highlights two features that many men share as essential to Steve4Steve: the feeling of anonymity and an ability to "screen" potential interactants of interest. For interactants like DL_MarriedBiGuy, who do not make their images public, they often understand their role in cyberspace as privileged. As objectifying agents, rather than objects being desired, they have the option of selecting with whom they will interact. Of course, this limits the options for meeting those who announce "no pic, no chat," but increases their authority within Steve4Steve as dictators of their own virtual experiences. Another reason for DL men's comfort may be analogous to many gay clubs, where it can be assumed that the interactants in this space practice male-male desire. As David Shaw explains, it seems that "the reason one goes to a gay bar [is for] common solace and excitement in the fact that it is one of the few places in society where by their mere presence all patrons can be assumed to be gay" (1997, 137). Though this may not be the case in a time where there is more gay-straight interaction in queer clubs, as seen in the previous chapter, there seems to be greater assurance in queer cyberspace sites. By this, I mean that sites like Steve4Steve require many intricate preliminary tasks such as creating personal profiles and constructing a coherent and attractive virtual identity—which will often discourage an "outsider" from becoming an interactant.[22] Indeed, constructing everyday or virtual identities is hard work. Rather for the sake of investigation, or to engage in secret male-male desire, the construction and/or maintenance of a profile identity can be an arduous process.

DL_MarriedBiGuy is a testament to this labor. Of all the men who responded to the survey, he seemed to really use the "additional comments" section as a space for catharsis:

I am a married man who at the age of 10 had my first sexual experience. It was with a relative 10 years older than I who was of the same sex. It was rape. I did not know that at the time . . . because I thought it felt good. I have tried to deny my true self by marrying and having children. What I didn't understand is that I would have been gay had I not been raped at an early age or not. I think I tried for years to blame it on that occurrence, but now I know I am a Gay man, who has chosen to hide behind a wife and children, as I was expected to do. I am miserable most every day and the only thing that keeps me going is the love I feel for my children and the love they feel for me. I will continue to have encounters with other men, probably for the rest of life. Why? Because the children I have helped bring into this world are much more important than my own needs.

Throughout his questionnaire response, he identified his married status eight times. Yet it was not until the closing "additional comments" that he expounded upon the value of his marital relationship in his sexual experiences with men. Interestingly, his expansion on the pressures of marriage excavated not only the significance of his children, but also horrific memories of his childhood. Like three other men who answered the survey, he marked the genesis of his male-male sexual experiences at molestation. The most profound element of DL_MarriedBiGuy's response was how he admits that his self-reflexivity allowed him to identify a different origin for his homoerotic pleasure within sociocultural factors, rather than his moment of sexual trauma. Furthermore, he suggests that his marriage was initially about "covering" what he understood as the result of rape, but later evolved into his escape from identifying as a "gay man." In other words, he refuses a gay identity because it seems impossible to be an avowedly "straight" man and embrace a queer identity label. However, the tension he locates between identifying as "gay" and being a "married man" highlights an interesting conundrum. Can there be a conversation of male-male desire without an invocation of accepting a gay identity claim? What forces DL_Married-BiGuy to make a rhetorical leap to an embraced gay identity rather than understanding himself as a man who desires men, but who also has a strong commitment to his family and certain patriarchal ideals? It seems that this rhetorical move is an indicator of the ways that the centrality of choosing an identity, or the rhetoric of outness, has penetrated public constructions of proper sexual identity. In the dominant narrative of family, there is no room for gay men who are married, or married men who prefer male-male desire.[23] With this in mind, DL_MarriedBiGuy continually recognized his marital relationship and emphasized, "I always practice safe sex! I have [a] wife and children to care about . . . make sure they are protected against my improprieties." Like many DL men, no matter how comfortable or content DL_MarriedBiGuy appears with his sexual desires, he is stricken with a sort of moral anxiety—which always encourages a degree of self-punishment within his rhetoric. Indeed, "being DL is like a hard job."

While some men do demonstrate remorse, when they are traveling between two different partners, many men are more concerned about the "risks." Indeed, the issues raised throughout this chapter are concerns at various points for different men. However, men like Mad_DLBody21 seem hyperaware of their risk of exposure or "being found out." He shared one narrative that reveals his somewhat hyperconsciousness about exposure possibilities:

> My first experience was at the gym and to this day I'm not big on going to the gym. Why? Because my girl came to me and said her friend['s] boyfriend was being hit on by men at the gym so I stop[ped] so she was not thinking the same about me.

Prior to this admission, Mad_DLBody21 admitted that he received oral sex in the bathroom of the gym and that it was exciting to be "watched by another guy." Yet his guilt was not about these homoerotic pleasures, but the potential of his "girl" being suspicious of him and scrutinizing his masculinity. As Mad_DLBody21 is clearly aware of the most dominant definition of the DL—men who travel between men and women secretly—while embracing this term, he tries to avoid being implicated in the common definition used to connote his discreet positionality. Rather, Mad_DLBody21 attempts to circumnavigate the possibility of personal and public humiliation, by opting for more intimate environments. Indeed, the Internet is a much "safer" site of homoerotic exploration. For Mad_DLBody21, the benefit of Steve4Steve is "if you hook up over the internet I never have to see you again." Unlike the gym, where men frequently return, his involvement with other interactants in cyberspace is contingent upon his own choice. Once again Mad_DLBody21 exhibits a concern for visibility, as he assumes that this endangers his primary relationship with his girlfriend. For many men, this site allows for selective choices, as well as eliminates the possibility of discovery, as the community of interactants is comprised of individuals whose public persona is different than their personal profiles and/or personality.

Authenticating the Impossible: Changing Times and the Impact of HIV/AIDS

As I concluded my explorations on the BeeHive and Steve4Steve, this disconnect between the everyday persona and the personal profiles was becoming most apparent. New descriptions and new details became common within personal profiles—information that conjoined the personal/everyday and the private/public virtual images. The most noticeable presence was that of the discourse around HIV/AIDS that became central to both sites of virtuality. On the phone chat line, comments like "A nigga is looking for healthy brothas—no sick brothas—clean brothas wanted" or "Why dudes on here be lyin' about their shit . . . if you got AIDS or whatever, just say something, so I can be on my way" were commonplace in my travels through the aural channels of the BeeHive. Similarly, such attitudes were visible on Steve4Steve. Virtual interactants began to post, as a part of their profiles, such addenda as "HIV Negative as of 3/4/06" or "I'm Clean"—as indicators of evidence and knowledge of their sexual health. While initially such admissions can appear transgressive and potentially groundbreaking in terms of safe-sex and testing awareness, the truth is that these admissions are discriminatory measures within both spaces. Indeed, they indicate a fear and awareness of sexually transmitted diseases. Nonetheless, the presence of these as "taglines" within individual profiles acts as a practice of boundary-making. Through the self-marking being "clean and disease-free," individuals not only announce their own health status but indicate that these are expected attributes for potential sexual partners. Such requirements draw a discursive line around individual profiles—pretending to be accurate statements of fact, which are actually admissions that deserve scrutiny. Since this is the beginning of a trend within both spaces, it is difficult to predict what effect this will have on the communicative exchange between individual callers and interactants.

Nonetheless, these profiles that assert HIV-negativity situate certain callers and interactants as possessing a purity, or cleanliness, that seems impossible for the openly gay individual. In these spaces, as DL men enact this rhetoric of "cleanliness," they assign impurity to others outside of their discrete community. As Mary Douglas notes, "Rituals of purity and impurity create unity of experience" (2002, 2). Thus, as DL men separate themselves from their HIV-positive same-sex-desiring callers and interactants, they inadvertently construct a unified identity not only around DLness, but HIV status. However, HIV status here has more significance than health. This regulatory announcement—claims to purity—rewards the performance of a certain style of gendered sexuality with a somewhat arbitrary outcome. The attempt to equate DLness with being HIV-negative is not only a tactic to divorce it from popular discourse, but also to divorce DL men from the affected/infected gay community. Here, in some ways, DLness prevents the infection of HIV. Indeed, this is never more apparent than when my black gay friends share instances in which they have met and sexually engaged with DL men. Many have shared that when they inquired about the status of a potential sexual partner, the response was something akin to "Look at me—do I look like I am sick man . . . ?"[24] This belief in a certain style of masculinity preventing disease transmission is quite hazardous in a time when we know that sexual behavior, not orientation, is at the core of sexual health. Indeed, this may have some impact on the perpetuation of disease, as individuals engage in hazardous acts under the "all DL men are safe" rule. While this idea of safety is not always present, it does have rhetorical value in spaces where "risks" are at the epicenter of cultural communication. The evocation of HIV-negativity as a trait specific to DL men enacts Goffman's apt theory that "before a difference can matter much it must be conceptualized collectively by the society as a whole" (1963, 123). Safety, in this case, is contingent upon a gendered sexuality that promotes a sense of normalcy—that which can only be possessed through the de-stigmatization provided by the properly masculine. In other words, DL men can affirm their own presence within virtual space as safe as an act of increasing their collective attraction value, as well as their ability to affect cultural shifts. The always already HIV-negative DL body can separate himself and his understanding of the self from the impure gay male body.

This new trend in profiles within the BeeHive and Steve4Steve accented how DL men responded to the cultural attacks mentioned in earlier chapters, especially in light of being named as the HIV/AIDS culprits in the black community. In essence, DL men reify their position as ideal through reinforcing the mythology that with masculinity comes safety (in terms of sexual health and personal identity). They invert the logic of same-sex relations as "dangerous," as they remove the gaze through highlighting an accomplishment in masculinity. Though such attempts to take the virtual focus from the DL elsewhere are pervasive, the stigma of same-sex desire flows within and outside this terrain with even greater momentum. Though DL men may reconfigure certain narratives, they are always pitted against public discourse. As they find strategic ways to displace myths, or suspend them, their taboo desire is writ large with questions and scrutiny.

Such hyper-scrutiny and surveillance require masculine sincerity. This chapter has illustrated DL men's investments in particularly framing their gendered selves, through the performance of critical negotiations of black masculinity and sexuality in virtual spaces. While it is almost impossible for DL men to deem themselves authentic, authenticity becomes a means through which some men articulate the sincerity of their masculine performances. Indeed, DL moves to de-queer the self are as much about gender as they are about moving away from the realms of cultural suspicion. In many ways, DL men are passing subjects—attempting to move into a realm where they are less suspect. This ritual of de-queering the self to outrun suspicion or exposure reinforces the "need" for a sincere and sedimented masculinity—which is later translated as "passing for straight." The next chapter attempts to historicize, contextualize, and theorize the sexual-passing subject as not only the antecedent to DL men, but also as having great utility for understanding the logics of racialized gender and sexual negotiation.

FIVE

The Pages Are Ridden with Discretion: Pedagogy of the Pass and Present

I know that in writing the following pages I am divulging the greatest secret of my life, the secret which for some years I have guarded far more carefully than any of my earthly possessions; and it is a curious study to me to analyze the motives which prompt me to do it.

—James Weldon Johnson, *The Autobiography of an Ex-Colored Man*

Codes always expose their own sense of camouflage, and they call attention to the ways they seek to "pass" by denying their own passing, so that any unmasking of the code places the subject . . . at the level of the invader, the one who ruptures a fragile transparency that then needs to be reconstituted in exile.

—José Quiroga, *Tropics of Desire: Interventions from Queer Latino America*

Visibility is a trap.

—Michel Foucault, *Discipline and Punish: Birth of the Prison*

From the Middle Passage to the slave quarters, the experiences of freedmen and freedwomen living under white surveillance, to the experiences of full citizens trapped in the confines of racism and its many injustices, black people have kept many secrets. They have hidden their religion, beliefs, thoughts, and, ultimately, their spirits.[1] In a sense, black mobility in America has always been predicated upon the agreement to maintain codes. Black people, under the surveillance of whiteness and white people, were often compelled to keep private those things they considered precious and in need of protection from those who potentially served as threatening forces to their humanity. Secrecy has often been a part of how those who live "furthest down below" attempt to make sense of, and make do with, how those in power establish and maintain control.[2] For this reason, most of the secrets of the marginalized are related to identity, community, and interior struggles. Passing has always been an available option to keep "down low" those secrets that, if exposed, could threaten the stability of more "respectable" images. Passing, as an act of creating and maintaining codes, attempts to steer attention away from stigmatizing characteristics, which are often delegated arbiters of the racial "other's" fate within a racist society.[3]

The DL subject resides at the intersection of sexual regimes of power, navigating between racialized identity and sexual desire. Indeed, these men who commonly identify as "straight" or do not identify with traditional sexual descriptors are what I call "sexual passers." The anxiety over this enigmatic positionality creates popular discourse and public rhetoric that frames the DL man as a problematic figure. The common (mis)conception of DL men is that their primary concern is self-gratification and individual mobility, while they allegedly discard the "dis-ease" they cause those within their community. Indeed, as José Quiroga aptly suggests in the epigraph above, as popular discourse attempts to unmask the sexual passer, it constructs a nefarious invader. Such simplistic, yet popular, claims are informed by the history and historical understanding of the racial-passing subject. Like the DL subject, the racially passing subject was often accused of being a "trickster" or solely concerned with the welfare of the self. To better understand the doings of the "DL brotha"—beyond deviance and dis-ease—we must review the lineage of misunderstanding about the racial passer in order to revise contemporary readings of what I call sexual passing. This performance, like racial passing, is the act of being framed or framing oneself as "straight" while being (an)other.

While much of this book has focused on the cultural pedagogy of the media and its misframing of the DL and sexual discretion, literature has also been a great location for the sexually discreet/discrete. Hidden in the texts of history and contemporary novels have been stories that have taught us the tenets of sexual discretion. However, much like the media, the lessons learned from literature are limited. Nonetheless, forging a conversation between the historic construction of passing and the contemporary representation of passing in literature and the press creates an opportunity to explore the subject from a historical perspective. This chapter is interested in how the frame of passing may assist in a fuller understanding of the DL subject and the mechanism of sexual discretion. Through an engagement with literature, we can locate the presence of the clandestine in texts, even before the subject of black sexuality entered popular public media discourse.

It is instructive, then, to examine the relationship between the historical racial-passing subject and those who pass within the realms of the sexual. This chapter turns to the archives of such historic performances and uncovers the parallels between historic and contemporary passing novels and performances in order to demonstrate the ways in which the privilege given to the (in)visibility of identity categories has created a complicated trap that explodes and confounds us. I contend that the legacy of racial binary thinking—"you are black or white"—informs how we understand sexuality in this contemporary moment—"you are either gay or straight." Such binary thinking reduces and simplifies the complexities of our racial and sexual lives. Moreover, this logic works to construct those who affix stable or fixed categories to their bodies as more "normal" than the "unstable" and unfixed passing subjects. Performance theory has shown us that "liminality and the phenomena of liminality dissolve all factual and commonsense systems" (Turner 1988, 25). Likewise, the passing subject—as she or he traverses the liminal spaces of race and sexuality—exposes the faulty logic of stability as a given. The DL subject disidentifies with what is traditionally labeled gay or bisexual, in order to maintain his role as a respectable citizen, a "real" man. Moreover, those who passed as white subverted the social arbiters of who was and was not "white," demonstrating the unreliability of phenotypical features to determine racial belonging. Indeed, these figures recalibrate our understanding of racial-sexual categories as stable and fixed. Nonetheless, as noted above, communities remain committed to constructing cohesive narratives that produce feelings of clarity. Yet racial- and sexual-passing figures within literature and everyday life unveil the fallaciousness of this logic, as literary and embodied performances disrupt the logic of fixed identities.

After rereading the passing novel and passing performance histories, this chapter examines E. Lynn Harris's contemporary novel *Any Way the Wind Blows* (2001) through the frame of sexual passing. I introduce sexual passing as a nomenclature for a particular performance of identity and as a specific genre/form of writing, but duly acknowledge the importance of recognizing other categories in the construction of the self. Like E. Patrick Johnson, Dwight McBride, and Philip Brian Harper,[4] I recognize the co-constitutive workings of identities, while understanding the oscillation of their centrality within a literary work. As Harris was the foremost writer addressing issues of black discreet sexuality in novel form, he drew tropes from historical passing narratives as he constructed various representations of DL men for a large public.[5] The historical construction of the racial-passing subject (read: also sexualized, gendered, and classed) foreshadows the DL subject who is now popularized in literature but was also ever present in previous eras.

When reading *Any Way the Wind Blows*, the operational similarities be-tween the historic color line and the contemporary sexual line become most evident. Whereas what Robyn Wiegman refers to as "economies of visibil-ity" (1995, 4) became the measuring system by which the racialized subject was judged and ascribed meaning, this system is now active in assessing the sexual subject. Paradoxically, the very system that depends on the visual produces impostors and impersonators in the art of racial and sexual dis-cernment. Today cultural expectations in regards to a subject's sexuality are heavily dependent on that which is visible—leaving many disappointed when what is visually available deceives them. Often it is this impulse that marks DL men as impostors and impersonators. Indeed, as Marlon Ross informs us, "the logic of race and the logic of sexuality (dangerously) bolster each other" (2005, 4).

Finally, I will illustrate the ways that such fallacious logic has moved from within the voice of literary texts and resurfaced in contemporary media via DL discourse. Our contemporary views of sexuality, seemingly closely aligned with modernist perspectives on race, signify a deaf cultural ear toward the multiplicity that is most apparent in postmodern America. As I examine a two-part segment in *Essence* magazine entitled "Passing for Straight" and "Deadly Deception," I identify how these articles reinstitute the anxiety of "passing" within the sexual realm. Most importantly, what is central to this analysis are anxieties that are rooted in the presence of sex-ual uncertainty. Here, fixed notions of identity paralyze critical thought and reproduce the very identities that are deemed problematic. Through recog-nizing the continuum of the "one-drop" rule on sexual terms, I locate how media discourses perpetuate the system that disallows for the recognition, performance, and normality of a "bisexual." In this case, the DL is a direct descendant of decades of commitment to racial fixity, whereby sexuality is a predetermined and "commonsense" category.

While both the black and white press provide cautionary and criminal-izing tales of the DL man "passing for straight," they reinscribe the racist sexual imagery that reduces black men to deviants rather than diverse and complicated subjects. Societal blindness to the union of racist and homo-phobic ideologies has produced, as Patricia Hill Collins makes clear in *Black Sexual Politics*, a community of people who "miss the mark" and do not realize that "too much is at stake for Black antiracist projects to ignore sexuality and its connections to oppressions of race, class, gender" (2004, 114). Consequently, more and more black male images that frame sexual passers as men of "deception" and "disease" are circulated and blindly le-gitimated under the guise of saving and sanitizing the race. This chapter cautions against such moves, urging us to adjust our critical eyes to reexamine our understanding of the modes and motives behind sexual passing. To this end, we can move from views of discreet black male sexuality as an ahistorical phenomenon by learning from history, rather than through literary lessons from E. Lynn Harris, thereby establishing a more sophisticated assessment of this explosion of sexual ambiguity within the public sphere.

Passing Literature and the Genealogy of Sexual Passing

No other texts have complicated, dealt with, and exposed the secrets of race, gender, sexuality, and class performances so specifically as the texts now known as passing novels. Passing novels and novellas typically illustrate the complicated lives of individuals of mixed-race ancestry who passed for white during a period when one drop of "negro" blood was thought to contaminate and corrupt the bloodline of white Americans. Mostly written between the late nineteenth and early twentieth century, novels such as Jessi Redmon Fauset's *Plum Bum* (1929), Charles W. Chestnutt's *House Behind the Cedars* (1900), and Nella Larsen's *Quicksand* (1928) and *Passing* (1929), and countless others explored the passing phenomenon.[6] While earlier narratives of passing often punished the passer on the basis of racial treason, these texts seem to complicate issues of passing. The aforementioned texts upend traditional passing narratives, by not only inadvertently critiquing the arbitrariness of the color line, but also revealing how one can perform within and outside of the system as a tool of survival.

Joining this critical lineage is James Weldon Johnson's *The Autobiography of an Ex-Colored Man*. Originally published in 1912 and republished in 1927, *Autobiography* stands as one of the most celebrated passing novels of its time. This novel offers a unique self-consciousness and self-reflexivity that is driven by the auto-ethnographic impulse that carries the protagonist's narrative. This novel, like Harris's *Any Way the Wind Blows*, allows us to be witnesses to the inner thoughts of the passer. This ability to see the passer navigate under various conditions enables a more generative reading of passing as a complex act that involves more than just the passer—but the spectator, societal constraints, and the dynamics of space. For a moment, I would like to use this novel to illuminate some important parallels that I have discovered in Johnson's narration of racial passing and Harris's structuring of sexual passing.

Autobiography begins with the ex-colored man's lament about the burden of secrecy and ends with a final chapter in which he fully discloses his secret to his fiancée—telling her that he is a light-skinned mulatto who has "passed" as white. This disclosure causes her hands to become cold, as she becomes transfixed with his body, demonstrating her fear over the seemingly instantaneous shift of the familiar to the foreign. In response, the narrator becomes self-conscious—as if he was "growing black and thick-featured, and crimp-haired" (204)—a visceral effect that has its roots in an awareness of cultural stereotypes, as well as minstrel leftovers from previous eras.[7] The ex-colored man's fiancée's external and internal repulsion is a symbolic summation of white imaginings of the "Negro" that sends her into a period of isolation, which, in turn, propels the narrator to become an "ex-colored" man. However, the narrator only becomes "ex-colored" through a post-confession performance, whereby he commits himself to a life as "white" rather than as mulatto and/or "Negro." With this act, he successfully reduces his and his future wife's anxiety over the race question. His turn to whiteness, and her ability to see his whiteness, is made symbolic through a piano selection—the manifestation of a more consonant love that leads to matrimony and the birth of their children.

Unlike other scholars, I argue that this escape from the "label of inferiority" is enabled through the manifestation of the "interracial" marriage and family, which concludes the novel.[8] I believe that this somewhat strategic move acts as not only the affirmation of his coming into whiteness, but also his journey into full American manhood and heterosexuality. Though his wife dies at the close of the novel, his commitment to his children and their welfare becomes his justification for his choosing to remain white. However, his constant refrain concerning the "inconveniences of being a Negro" suggest otherwise. As he characterizes, critiques, and even sometimes condemns "Negro life," it seems clear that the narrator attempts to escape the tragic narrative that seems to accompany the twentieth-century mulatto figure in literature and life—death, or absence of belonging. Key to the ex-colored man's act of moving into whiteness is how the narrator allows the audience to decide his racial fate—he never denies his racial past per se, but allows the misleading dependency on visuality to serve him. In a racist America, where those features that appear as optical guarantees mark him as white, he is insured a certain degree of mobility for himself and his family.

Such negotiations of racial identity may, at first, seem significantly disparate from my project. However, when one reads the "secret" within the *Autobiography* more closely, one can see, as Siobhan Somerville has noted in *Queering the Color Line: Race and the Invention of Homosexuality in American Culture*, that this passing narrative is about anxieties that are "at once racial and sexual" (2000, 125). The secret of the narrator's racial history poses problems for the fiancée because it (1) exposes that she loved a man who was not white and (2) admits that she was involved in an interracial (read: taboo) relationship. The *Autobiography* is not only about choosing to be properly white, but also sexually normal.[9] It is clear that both the narrator and his wife wished to avoid being queered, or marked as abnormal—even if that meant passing out of "Negroness" or ending the relationship with the Negro altogether. Such negotiations are akin to contemporary narratives describing the down-low dilemma, whereby the female partner and the DL brotha are engaged in similar trials, attempting to avoid being sexually and racially marked by either passing or admonishing the act of passing. This adverse reaction to "outsiderness" encourages racial and sexual subjects to "pass" out of any categories of abnormality, or "deviance," as it is often referred to. *Autobiography* is one of the few passing novels that understands "passing for white as a result . . . of cultural alienation and divided racial loyalties" (Fabi 2001, 100). *Autobiography* uniquely removes passing from a solely racial move to a performance from multiple positionalities. James Weldon Johnson recognized what Erving Goffman would later teach in *Stigma: Notes on the Management of a Spoiled Identity*, as *Autobiography* represents passing as a move away from all forms of stigma for the sustenance and/or achievement of status, as well as the right to remain "normal" (1963, 125). To avoid being marked abnormal or stigmatized, one must employ multiple methods of passing across multiple lines that not only include race, but also involve gender, class, and sexuality. In essence, all passing subjects—for the sake of status and normality—must remain "down low."

Various investments in linear narratives of racial and sexual identity, particularly claims of authenticity, have created an academic and social conversation where the passer is always operating within a "one-drop rule" system, where they never can inhabit multiple identities at once but must choose between "the true and the false." Such conventions are obvious in both novels, where specific characters insist that the narrator choose an identity, as well as by critics who impose the same imperative through their readings of the texts. Often within literary texts and by the reading audience, the racially/sexually passing subject is expected to choose his/her marginal identity over whiteness, in adherence with both the social and legal laws of the given period. It is because of these acts that I conclude that blackness had, and often still has, a *surplus value* that upstages the significance and weight of other factors in the construction of the self. Unfortunately, the one-drop rule that had been forced upon black people pre- and post-slavery has now become a more broad-reaching racial narrative—a way of keeping racial identity in check. For example, though Tiger Woods publicly proclaimed his own racial identity of "Caublin-asian"—to speak to his "Caucasian, Black, Indian, American, Asian" back-grounds—he is still recognized as a "black golfer." This type of sociocultural regulation, based on one drop of African blood, uniquely keeps people to-gether and divided, all at once. Where, on the one hand, people can gather around a certain sense of solidarity; on the other, they are divided by the blatant disregard for diverse presences within the community.

Though passing novels are often about mixedness, rather than dealing with both black and white, gay and straight, or even the in-between, the passer is almost always reduced to only having an either/or option. This literary formula provides for a simplistic understanding of the passer's cir-cumstance. The force-fitting pressure of making a racial choice, of following the one-drop rule, demands that we ignore the presence of the both/and racial reality in the lives of many who "pass." Such requests illustrate not only the sociopolitical climate of the moment, but also the dilemma with which many passers are faced. *Autobiography*, as a racial-passing novel, and *Any Way the Wind Blows*, as a sexual-passing novel, are only two examples of literary representations of the everyday enactments of such complex decision-making. Nonetheless, they serve as strong examples of the compel-ling parallels between the operations of racial and sexual hierarchies.

Where *Autobiography*'s narrator seeks sexual normalization through the coherency and consistency of race, the central protagonist in Harris's *Any Way the Wind Blows* seems more concerned with racial normalization through a cohesive and consistent understanding of sexual identity. Similar connections have been made more indirectly by such scholars as Debo-rah McDowell (2007) and Mae Henderson (2001) in their introductions to such classic passing novels as Nella Larsen's *Passing*, where they suggest that passing novels are almost always as sexual as they are racial. In their re-reading of these "classic" passing novels, they acknowledge the sexual secret hidden between the lines of fiction and illustrate how a traditional focus on race is both a result of history and critical inattention.

Acknowledging the absence of such "alternative" views of passing nov-els, several other scholars have began to do more explicit interrogations of the role of categories other than race in the construction of self. For exam-ple, in the edited anthology *Passing: Identity and Interpretation in Sexuality, Race, and Religion*, Maria Carla Sanchez and Linda Schlossberg insist on the inclusion of other categories such as religion, sexuality, and class in our discussion of passing. Furthermore, Sanchez and Schlossberg critique the centrality of the logic of visibility, or "occularcentricity," as they suggest that generally "we trust that our ability to see and read carries with it a certain degree of epistemological certainty" (2001, 1). Cultural critic and scholar Jeffrey Weeks, in *Inventing Moralities: Sexual Values in an Age of Uncertainty*, warns us that though we are witnesses to the flux and flexibility of identity "in a world of constant change people apparently need fixed points, points of alignment" (1995, 33). The inability to let go of this quest for fixity, coherence, and constancy has often produced critical work that misses the full picture of any one passing novel, as certain writings illuminate the very problem of this genre—the centrality of the (in)visible.

Harris attempts to conjure the role of the "invisible" in his earlier book *Invisible Life* (1994)—a novel that deals with the discreet sexual world of a central male protagonist. In *Any Way the Wind Blows*, he similarly creates a dialogue with the notion of "ex" (e.g., "ex-colored") to demonstrate what happens as black queer men are pulled out from "down low." Indeed, sexuality and our interpretations of sexuality are informed by embodiment and individual and collective understandings of sexual categories. To best understand the mark or appropriation of "ex" or specific dis-identifications with certain common identity terms, it is necessary to recognize the multiple levels of influence that other identity loyalties may have in our selection of social positions. When seen from this perspective, the ex-colored man's move away from blackness is the inverse of Harris's protagonist Basil's mark of "ex-straightness." Whereas the ex-colored man was privileged with white skin and had an interactive role in his ex-relationship to "Negroness," Basil is almost stamped with a scarlet letter and has limited control over his identity after being seen "having sex with another man." In Johnson's ex-colored man's era, a move outside of blackness was greeted with certain luxuries, while Basil's mark of "ex-straight" in the contemporary moment ruptures and shatters his expected sexual role, as well as his masculine definition. Thus, it is no coincidence, but rather representative of the respective eras, that the ex-colored man's "true" identity comes through an interpersonal confession to his fiancée, whereas Basil is discovered and exposed by his. This difference affirms Corinne Blackmer's belief that the "vast majority of African Americans under Plessey could not (or chose not to) 'pass for white,' whereas the vast majority of lesbians and gays do pass for, and are assumed to be (unless declared otherwise), heterosexual" (1995, 4). Nonetheless, both passing characters in *Autobiography* and *Any Way the Wind Blows* have the potential of returning to their initial categories of race and sexuality. Both characters, like Nella Larsen's Clare Kendry, are "always stepping on the edge of danger" (Larsen 2002, 143). Yet at the close of *Autobiography*, Johnson allows the ex-colored man to transition into safety and security through a white identity, while Harris in *Any Way the Wind Blows* constructs the passing figure Basil as always oscillating between sexual normalcy and sexual nuisance. Together, these novels assist in narrating the disparate, distinct, yet interconnected histories of passing in terms of race and sexuality. Forging a conversation between the two also illuminates the separate but similar traces that are involved in racial- and sexual-passing performances and public perception of such complex cultural moves.

The Ending of Ex-Colored, the Beginning of the Ex-Straight Man

E. Lynn Harris's *Any Way the Wind Blows* serves as an exemplary text for my engagement with the imbrications of race, gender, class, and sexuality among DL men and within contemporary writings on the subject. *Any Way the Wind Blows* is the final novel of Harris's trilogy of texts that chronicles the complicated life of Basil Henderson, the "terminal bisexual" man who passes as "straight."[10] The primary literary strategy used to prevent Basil's life from being marked as "tragic" is the emphasis placed on his development and his stellar performance of what Fiona Buckland (2002) would call his "heterogender"—the constant commitment to patriarchal norms and heterosexuality.[11] This gendered performance has become popularly associated with the DL male—the man who wears his masculinity on his sleeve, in his stride, and his privileged choice of (female) love-object—though such commitments are never guaranteed.

Any Way the Wind Blows is the first novel to explicitly explore the discord and disconnect between black masculinity and queer sexual desire. Its basic premise is most significant as its publication coincided with the popularization of the DL in the media.[12] In this 2001 novel, Harris's call upon the DL is no act of coincidence, but rather an appropriation of what was then a black colloquialism and newly established "sexual identity" for those who kept sexual acts outside the radar of the larger public. While Harris's usage of the term DL is a testament to his awareness of it being in vogue, his invocation of the DL is also a sign of his own imagining of discreet black male sexuality and its possibilities.[13] The effects of such imaging and imagining became most apparent when, in the same year of *Any Way the Wind Blow's* release, several women approached me in a panic over what they had read about these "closeted" black men. One woman, who was carrying *Any Way the Wind Blows* around at a conference I attended in Seattle, told me that her central concerns were with "deception," "disease," and the possibilities that "the DL was spreadin'." The connection she made between what she had encountered in these novels and "newspaper material perused in the Seattle airport" alerted me to the type of pedagogy that these books performed for all of Harris's readers, particularly for black women. Harris's novels were instructional manuals—uncovering the secrets of characters, while passing as a window into clandestine queer relationships of black men.

The outraged but fearful woman's elaborate rant had a quality very much like that of the wife in Johnson's *Autobiography*. Though the woman had no contact with a DL man, she crafted graphic illusions and imaginings of "an encounter," registering her anxiety over queer sexuality. In Johnson's *Autobiography*, the wife's anxiety is triggered by the narrator's confession of his bi-raciality; similarly, in Harris's *Any Way the Wind Blows*, Basil Henderson's bisexuality becomes the source of anxiety. In his novels, Harris creates male and female characters who express anxiety over homosexuality and/ or bisexuality. The creation of characters who react in this manner to sexuality, I argue, is Harris's way of manipulating his mostly female black readership to respond in a similar way. I do not believe that it is a coincidence, for example, that *Any Way the Wind Blows* was released during the same period as the emergence of what is now referred to as the "DL phenomenon."[14] Accordingly, Harris's influence and impact on the popular understanding of black bisexual performance, particularly the DL, are evident in the references made to his novel in popular texts and public discourse. Thus, Harris became the voice of precedence and prominence when discussing the evolution of how many men and women learn about black male discreet performances, especially the "DL phenomenon."

In *Any Way the Wind Blows*, the sexual-passing subject is Basil Henderson, an ex–football star turned sports management consultant. The novel begins a year after the foiling of Basil's marriage to Broadway actor turned pop-diva Yancey Braxton, after he confesses that he is sexually attracted to both men and women. Coincidentally, both Basil and Yancey relocate to New York, where their paths cross again when Basil realizes that Yancey has released a song titled "Any Way the Wind Blows." The song, about a woman who says good-bye to a man that she finds "in the arms of another man," is a smash hit. With the increasing popularity of the song, Yancey tries to make her mark in the music business, while Basil attempts to maintain his sports-consulting reputation. His occupational integrity is constantly being threatened by the distribution of his ex-fiancée's song, when anonymous informants (read: people he has done wrong, who want revenge) and his new young "trick," Bartholomew Jerome Dunbar (aka "Bart"), make him aware of their knowledge of his connection to the song. Basil, like most who attempt to manage stigma, attempts to navigate between his "private" sexual practice and his public image.

Like the ex-colored man, Basil witnesses his own transfiguration, as he is never able to "purely" be that which he once was—bisexual and "unclockable"—now that so many are aware of his passing performance. Basil experiences the classic passer reality, where regardless of the performance that he (the passer) would like people to see, he is always subject to an interpretive gaze. These interpretations, often informed by multiple ideologies, will often deem the performance inadequate or incomplete. Yet Basil is unlike the ex-colored man, as he is condemned for enacting a blatant deception and consequently is framed and (re)configured as a deviant sexual "other." Basil is "found out." This critical tension positions Basil as not only what Goffman refers to as "discreditable," but discredited—the former infers the possibility for loss of status and the latter insists that such loss has taken place. Nonetheless, Basil's character shows us that as much as his "disguise" is not permanent, neither is his discrediting. When he moves outside of certain social circles and spaces, he is able to renew his chosen anonymity and retain his sexual discretion. And as he locates trusting bedfellows in both genders, it is clear that for every suspicious spectator, there are many who find his performance of gender and sexuality inconspicuous and authentic.

When writing *Any Way the Wind Blows*, Harris had established an anticipatory and faithful following of readers who are often cited as saying that his novels are "fun and easy to read."[15] Indeed, there is a significant pleasure in reading and watching the unraveling of secrets held by Harris's male protagonists and their counterparts. But in a sociopolitical climate of so-called sexual crisis, what is most important here is how his work acts as a form of pedagogy that warns and informs the public of what was once referred to as the "dreadful bisexual."[16] Initially, the discourse had no detailed or nuanced explanations of the DL subject; therefore, the public was left to draw their own conclusions. As the primary voice of representation for DL men, these novels read as if they are "authentic" narratives of DL experience and what Harris's website frames as "cautionary tales." I argue that through his simplistic passing formula, Harris constructs more of a panic novel that passes for informative, stirs controversy, and creates various forms of alarm in the black public sphere.[17] Because of Harris's influence on the public's view and perception of the DL, it is necessary to critically examine how he (re)constructs the passing subject.

Any Way the Wind Blows picks up where *Autobiography* leaves off; the queer character is framed in heteronormative bliss. The novel begins with

Basil engaged in "pulse-popping sex" with a woman who Harris later establishes as the character who wants to be Basil's "baby's momma."[18] After his moment with the "baby's momma" figure, Basil confesses to the reader that he plans to continue his bisexual excursions—a journey that those who have followed the Harris trilogy anticipate. Basil, the passer, is engaged in an act of "duping" while avid readers of Harris's books are aware of his game. This narrative structuring evokes what Amy Robinson has called the classic passing novel framework—a triangle: "the passer, the dupe, and the representative of the in-group" (1994, 719). In *Any Way the Wind Blows*, and most of Harris's novels, there are three consistent figures: the passing sexual character, the naive believer(s) of the passer's identity as performed, and queer men who are involved with the duper or are aware of what Basil refers to as his "switching."[19] Harris's sexual-passing novels use the "switch" to move his narratives forward and create heightened drama and conflict around Basil's moving in and out of sexual normalcy.

Although Harris frames the DL subject as almost always conscious of his "duping," his awareness is never connected to other characters' perception or readership. I argue that such a construction is at best misleading; at worst, it fuels the cultural anxieties among women around this topic. As almost all characters in the novel are unaware of Basil's acts outside of heterosexuality, except those to whom he confesses, readers are left to believe that there is no room for the passer's pass to fail. However, as I have become an E. Lynn Harris reader, I know this invincibility is what keeps a reader attracted to and angry at the central characters. As one reader told me, "It's unreal." Indeed, it seems odd that there is never a successful "spoiling" of the passer's identity. Hence, *Any Way the Wind Blows* becomes a passing novel that includes other aspects of identity, but overemphasizes sexuality by suggesting that sexual passing is easy, an unconsidered choice, and attempted with all disregard to questions of ethics or personal consequence. Consequently, the reader often loses sight of the ways in which constructs of race, gender, and class create circumstances where sexual passing might be an act of survival or subversion of hegemonic sexuality. Moreover, Harris's imaginings mirror racial-passing histories where the passer is often understood as individualistic, void of a moral compass. I am interested in not only how Harris's books resemble racial-passing novels, but also the way they employ the tropes of those texts. Though entertaining, his novels perpetuate a cycle of imaginative violence from which he monetarily profits, while potentially damaging public understanding of the sociopolitical circumstances of black men and queer sexuality. While passing as an activity may captivate audiences through its social gymnastics, a unilateral focus on one identity position ignores the macro-cultural conditions that provoke and perpetuate the desire to pass.

In *Any Way the Wind Blows*, Basil is always attempting to make sense of a world, or at least a social situation, that repudiates him for his sexual desire and the unforgivable secreting of his sexual actions. Still, he finds resolution through the disavowal of his discursively disdained identity—silencing what he knows to be a part of himself, to live and survive in a world that seems to only value him most when he chooses one part over an(other). In this context, Basil is unable to embrace both of his sexual identities, while maintaining his right to be a "race man" or his commitment to a certain style of black masculinity. For every moment where Basil demonstrates integrity or proper "manhood," Harris juxtaposes the voice of a disheartened lover or distrusting character, who reminds us of his betrayal. Or often Basil's self-conscious reflections highlight his lack of remorse for his duping of others—almost prompting a spectatorial punishment for his unapologetic arrogance. The problem becomes not that he passed, but that he duped a woman using heterosexual privileges that were, to his future wife and society in general, not his property to possess. In this instance, heterosexuality, like whiteness, is a property whose ownership affirms a certain hierarchical relation (in this case, between "queer" and normal) (Harris 1998, 118). Thus, in order to own "straightness," one cannot embrace queerness. To do so would inherently disrupt any notion of stability attached to our assumed categories of identification. Thus, Basil becomes not only the man who Yancey finds "in the arms of another man," but also the man whom she "must let go." Though, while Yancey sings of letting go, she seeks to literally destroy the manhood Basil has built over the years as a public emblem of masculinity. This is not only her revenge, but also her attempt to un-queer herself. For if Yancey embraces and/or accepts Basil and his queer sexuality, she must admit that she loved queerly.[20] In this way, Yancey tries to "pass" through her admonishment of Basil's passing performances. It is necessary that she make this strategic move, showing the gravest disdain through framing Basil as the grossest and most disgusting "faggot" she can, in order to purify her own self-image. Ironically, when Yancey attempts to create a song about Basil—making him the spectacle of a song lyric—she jump-starts her own musical career. On the one hand, his sexuality is the deceptive and problematic presence that causes her pain; on the other, it is his DL status that becomes the conduit for her own success and economic wealth.

In many ways, Harris predicts the conundrum that has become a part of the DL madness that has taken black and popular press by storm since the

New York Times article in August 2003. For many, criticism of the DL has become a therapeutic device that not only provides emotional benefits but financial gains as well. Though Harris constructs Yancey as a character who would not be opposed to this criticism—as her greed for money and wealth has been ever present from her first appearance in his novels—he justifies her acts with claims of hurt and revenge. However, Harris does not grant such redemption for Basil's acts of deceit and/or secrecy. Instead, Harris paints Basil as a character who is simply burdened with "masculine anxiety," who outrageously attempts to compensate for his absent manhood through irresponsible and unapologetic acts. Almost unrealistically, Basil hardly shifts in character and his sexual agenda remains, even after numerous anonymous e-mails and phone calls questioning his DL status, as if he is unmoved by the potential of being discredited.

Harris's figuring of Basil's unnerving boldness dismisses what is central to the passing subject's performance: "controlling the disclosure of discrediting information about oneself to conceal the stigma entirely" (Blinde and Taub 1992, 286). Basil, as the literary embodiment of the "DL brotha," confounds the performance of sexuality as simple betrayal, thereby legitimating acts of homophobia within Harris's text and by his readers as statements, thoughts, and doings of innocent fear and frustration. Harris further perpetuates the cycle of homophobia, as Basil's acts of "deviance" produce masculine anxieties within himself and are repackaged as a deep internal homophobia, where queer sexuality is situated as a lesser, meaningless, and valueless activity for strict self-gratification. This need for Basil to lessen the value of queer desire, or to reposition his homoerotic relations to a level of insignificance, speaks to the masculine performance that is privileged by many DL men. Here, we see evidence of the complex dilemma with which black men are faced as they attempt to subscribe to accepted gendered roles that often produce more societal rewards.

A similar dilemma is articulated by Johnson's ex-colored man when he says: "It's no disgrace to be black, but it's often very inconvenient" (155). He speaks with a disregard for the contextual contingencies that mark blackness as "no disgrace," but admits to its compromising potential in his everyday life. What makes being a "Negro" inconvenient for the ex-colored man is the constant markedness of those who are identifiably black. Nonetheless, such iteration also calls attention to the convenience and absence of shame felt when the narrator is allowed to be "ex-colored," or perceived as white. On these "unmarked" occasions, he is able to walk the world with individual governance over his travels and can better manage his identity reception. His admission of the "inconveniences of being a Negro" draws attention to a kind of DuBoisian "double-consciousness," whereby a Negro is always already trapped by "being at once negro and American" (DuBois 1965, 215). The "inconveniences of being a Negro" implies not only his acknowledgment of being part black, but also an unspoken, unwritten feeling of obligation to the race. Concomitantly, in Harris's novels Basil exemplifies the dynamic tension of being caught between two sexual worlds: DL men are "cursed" with "twoness"—the desire to know (in the biblical and literal sense) men and women. However, Basil's situation is not a question of a sexual allegiance, but rather how to act out sexual desires in a discreet, unmarking way that would allow him to remain credible and respectable. Basil and the ex-colored man reveal that in "twoness" (or even multiple-ness) there is pleasure and pain, pride and shame, hope and despair. Indeed, both subjects express the pleasure in moving between worlds, while also understanding that they are "stepping always on the edge of danger." The level of the "danger" is often contingent upon what role either subject chooses to play in the racial-sexual theater and who acts as spectators for their gender, racial, and sexual performances.

While racial and sexual economies are different, the force-fitting societal solution to "choose" is the burden of both racial- and sexual-passing subjects. The major difference between the two passing subjects is that the racial passer must selectively edit his racial past, while the sexual passer conceals his sexual present. Harris attempts to privy the reader to some of the internal struggles of Basil's sexual present, where he seems oddly placed between what the world wants him to be and what he feels he should be. Unlike Johnson's careful construction, Harris's honesty about the social rules and laws are often left unspoken. Consequently, we only understand Basil's position as one of deception and deviance, never understanding the difficult reality of the sexual line that for many men is never to be crossed. It is the critical absence of the sociopolitical circumstance that encourages a reading of the sexual, or even racial, passer as possessing self-hatred and a harmful interior that is selfish and self-destructive. Additionally, due to the absence of a more generative and complex discussion of sexual passing, the importance of the external gazer on the constitution of the passer's identity is discounted and DL men are reduced to arbiters of their own sexual desire and disclosure, performers of extreme and grotesque individualism. A pivotal moment in *Any Way the Wind Blows* is when Basil explicitly disavows his sexuality. This moment can be read easily as an act of selfishness or as an example of his "internal homophobia." In a conversation with Sallye—one of his many "sexual flings"—she inquires about their relationship, in turn scrutinizing his sexual orientation:

"Are you gay or bisexual?"

I tried to keep my cool. "Damn baby, if you thought that was the case, then why did you come home with me?"

"My girlfriends and I always ask these questions. You don't look or act gay or bi, but answer the question," Sallye said as she stopped unzipping her skirt from the back.

"No, I'm not either one of those things," I said confidently. As far as I was concerned, that was the truth. I wasn't gay or bisexual. She didn't ask if I was on the down low and I didn't tell her. Besides, she wasn't looking at my lips but at the bulge in my pants. I could have said "hell yeah" and Sallye would have heard "hell no." (46)

Sallye's gender stereotypes notwithstanding, the sociopolitical situation that prompts this interrogation is left unexplained. Most importantly, no part of the narrative explicates Basil's reaction or his internal dialogue thereafter. The picture of the passer is incomplete and paints Basil as having sole control over his actions and their interpretation. This inaccurate reading removes responsibility from those who contribute to the necessity of certain performances of discreet identity through verbal judgments and punitive gazes—and random and unwarranted interrogation—while placing the central focus on what Basil did not say. This has been the case largely for public imaginings of the passer in general, but for DL men specifically. In this passage, however, we witness an explicit confession from Basil. I argue that this is an example of Harris's literary heavy-handedness, as he attempts to explain most candidly what the DL is for his reading audience. As Basil conceals his attraction toward men, based on the misnaming of his positionality by Sallye, the reading public is provided with an implicit definition of the DL: men who don't claim a "gay" or "bi" identity in order to avoid being denied male-female sexual opportunity. Indeed, this may be one aspect of DL men's objection to embracing these terms. However, it detaches Basil's dis-identificatory move from a history of minoritarian individuals disconnecting themselves from terms that do not fit their understandings of themselves. Furthermore, it also relinquishes the public of its accountability in terms of constructing a sociosexual climate where such terms signify both emasculation as well as sexual abnormality.

In the context of reading Harris's novels, such inaccurate understandings of the sexual passer's circumstance is highly dangerous, as individuals attempt to better understand themselves, as well as the complex sexualities of others. In the next example, as Harris illustrates the consummation of Basil's "relationship" with Bartholomew, he successfully characterizes the tension created on the trapeze of sexual desire. Yet, I argue, in the context of Harris's construction of Basil, a reader is more likely to pathologize than to engage productive discussions of Basil's marginality. In *Any Way the Wind Blows*, Basil first meets Bart when Bart answered a modeling call advertised by XJI Sports Management firm. Their sexual attraction turns this modeling call into a booty call. The heat leads them to Basil's home, where they engage in an episode of sexual intercourse. When they finish, Bart inquires:

> ". . . when can we 'hit it' again?"
> "Leave me your number and I'll get back with you," I [Basil] said. . . .
> "Can I have your phone number?"
> "I'll give you a call. You see, my shit is on the down low. I'm dating a female pretty seriously," I lied.
> "I don't date bisexual men," Bart said.
> "Then we're on the same page," I said.
> "But sometimes I make exceptions when they look like you," he said.
> "Hey, let's just take it slow and see if we gel. But you'll get your chances," I said as I walked toward the bedroom. I went to my closet and pulled out a dress shirt and began to put it on. I figured if old dude saw me getting ready for work he would finish dressing himself and hit the road. (67)

Not only is Basil dishonest in this passage, but he also uses the "down low" to scapegoat any definitive answer for Bart's inquiry for further meetings. When Bart tells Basil, "I don't date bisexual men," Basil responds, "Then we're on the same page." While Basil's complacency with this recategorization of the DL as synonymous with bisexual seems displaced, the larger message here is clear. Basil is not interested in dating at all, and here he and Bart have met on common ground. The episode above demonstrates Basil's post-sex anxiety, in which he attempts to escape his sexual reality. This attempted escape exposes the heavy burden placed on Basil's body whenever he engages in same-gender sex. Most interestingly, Harris poses Basil's post-sex ponderings as "in the closet." This moment is fascinating. It is in this space where Basil waits for the exit of his queer reminder—a waiting room par excellence. Like the ex-colored man's children, young Bart becomes the constant reminder of what Basil wishes to escape, evade, or ignore.

While the temporal placement of male-male sex "on the down low" is an area of inquiry that I will explore in another project, it is important to make note of it for my purposes here. On the one hand, Harris suggests the compatibility of the closet for Basil's sexuality. However, he reconstructs the epistemological closet since Basil is constantly returning to it within each of the novels. I argue that this constant return to or residential status in the closet reconfigures Eve Sedgwick's and popular understandings of the closet—pointing toward its possible permanence and comfort, rather than its temporality and torture. Michael Hardin, in his brief discussion of racial sexual-passing subjects in Harris's early texts, presumes that all those in the closet want to be "free" (2004, 116–17). This assumption, I argue, is guided by contemporary readings of sexual subjects as always being in search of freedom. While "freedom" may be a common desire of humanity, the characteristics of such desired freedoms seem to differ. In *Any Way the Wind Blows*, I suggest that the character Basil is free in the closet, "on the down low," and enjoys navigating the sexual line. Though it is not all pleasure, Basil never suggests that his circumstances would be improved if he were to establish an open "bisexuality." In fact, in the passage above, he rejects such an assertion; rather, he chooses to disidentify with this label and opt for a discreet sexual identity. This may be one of the most critically queer moments in Harris's construction of Basil's character as an agent who subverts normative structuring of the discreet performance of identity. Instead of opting for the simple, less culturally specific closet, Harris attempts to complicate the sexual position of Basil through a clear act of disidentification. Harris, through the character Basil, reconstructs the closet—known as a space of so-called captivity—as a location of potential freedom and possibility. Nonetheless, much of this passage's critical possibility is lost because Harris places greatest emphasis on the play rather than the complexity of the DL as a "remixing of the closet."

The aforementioned passage accentuates Basil's skill and appeal. Though Basil clearly treats Bart like a "trick" for the night, Bart still insists on continuing relations with him. As Bart expounds on Basil's good looks, it becomes apparent that Basil's aesthetics play a major role in his attraction. Basil's asides to the reader make us most aware of his ability to keep an emotional distance from his male partners, still acting upon his desires and ensuring future sexual encounters. Harris's reliance on the "playa" rhetoric and performance, most popular in heterosexual contexts, warrants a discussion of Basil and Bart's relational dynamics. First, the "relationship" between Bart and Basil seems to posit the former as non-masculine and the latter as masculine. This seems necessary, as Harris clearly is attempting to create contrasts between these two characters.

Such a gendered dynamic is instructive in terms of the reproduction of heterosexual norms within a homoerotic, or homosexual, context. Basil is clearly performing as the "man" in control, while Bart is positioned in a submissive, non-dominant role. This role construction is amplified when looking closely at Basil as "the man" who holds the future of Bart's career in his hands. In the patriarchal culture in which we live, such relational dynamics are clearly complicit with certain conventional understandings of hetero- and homonormative relationships. This characterization in a queer context only reifies the "top/bottom" binary that has been passed down from hetero-patriarchy. David Buchbinder asserts:

> Patriarchal masculinity derives much of its power through the exercise of a particular logic. By imposing . . . a system of oppositions—for instance, male/female, masculine/feminine, heterosexual/homosexual—which not only give meanings through difference, but equally give those meanings certain social, moral, ethical values. . . . (1998, 74)

In the sexual realm of the Basil-Bart saga, the installation of this top/bottom binary allows Basil to reconstruct a female-male fantasy while performing his "alternative" sexual relations. This illusion offers him an opportunity to be masculine, while also engaging in queer sex—in short, normalizing the queer not to feel, or appear, *too* queer. Before Bart departs for home, he alludes to seeing Basil another time. Basil interrupts his assertion and chimes in with "I don't think so." Basil continues to tell him, ". . . a good-looking brotha like yourself can have your pick of dudes and bitches." By opening this discussion, "bitches" assist him in transitioning out of Bart's homonormative ideals into a more heteronormative and misogynist mind-set. This need to recontextualize this situation demonstrates his desire for Bart to partake in heteronormative performances—a desire to normalize their relations as more homosocial than homoerotic. When Bart does not concede to his wishes, Basil pushes Bart to leave. As Bart is departing, he inquires, "So I got the job?" and Basil responds, "If you think so. It's a good thing to think positive." Bart, thinking he has landed a winner—like everyone else before him—has been duped. Basil winks.[21]

As Basil winks—performing the ultimate "playa" persona or the duper extraordinaire—we are distracted from the work involved in his performance of a masculinity shaped to shadow Basil's queer sexual desire. Yet no matter how much we are distracted by Harris's representation of Basil or Basil-like figures, their presence forces us to recognize not only the existence of DL men, but also the pressures on black men in general. As Mae Henderson explains, "By rewriting modernist notions of a constative, immutable, unified notion of self-hood with a conception of identity that is fundamentally performative, the narrative of passing interrogates the idea of a transcendent or essentialized identity" (2002, xxxix). Thus, the very presence of a contemporary passing sexual subject calls attention to the instability of sexual identities. As a result, we are seduced into thinking about the actual movement between two fictionally stable identities—seeing their fractures, ruptures, and fissures. Unfortunately, however, Harris's representations tend to be more linear than expansive, more "cool and sexy" than complex—reducing societal pressures to insignificant forces rather than the force-fitting, fiery presences that they are. Consequently, his writings are more likely to prompt a less sophisticated reading of the circumstances of DL men and those in their lives. Harris, more often than not, conveys the idea that DL men are men who prey on the gullible and survive on their insatiable lust, which serves to destroy all with whom they come in contact. Basil is the embodiment of the ex-colored man's fiancée's gross imaginary at the close of *Autobiography*. Basil, in *Any Way the Wind Blows*, is always framed as the "ex-straight man"—he is the sexualized reflection of the racial conundrum that the ex-colored man was. As the ex-colored man sought after a move to a different racial and class hierarchy, Basil longed for the masculine stability and the privilege of heteronormativity.

In Harris's construction of this hypersexual DL figure, Basil is the victim of our punitive gaze. Basil, as the quintessential black male representative in what is undoubtedly a queer novel, sets us up as readers. As Basil is critical and conscious of his own sexuality and sexual games, the reader is left to conclude that Basil is no more than a pretender or impersonator. The disapproval of Basil's behavior is unquestionable among readers of Harris's novels.[22] Consequently, our cultural ethos forces us to understand Basil as a criminal impostor, and we are only satisfied when he is punished within the novel. When *Any Way the Wind Blows* begins with Basil concluding "pulse-popping" sex with his new girlfriend Rosa—who fools him into believing she is pregnant with his child—we are left to enjoy the trickster being tricked. For the many who read Harris's books religiously, it is not surprising that Rosa confesses to Basil that she is pregnant by someone else. This is the classic moment where Harris's trickster is framed, making him a pun of the reader's joke. Basil has been tricked, and his heteronormative masculine status is challenged by Rosa's announcement that she is carrying a child that is not his. Here, Basil is the witness to a different type of passing—Rosa has shifted from "baby's momma" to "not your baby's momma." Yet in Basil's imaginary, she was—for the initial moment when she announced her pregnancy—the mother of his child. The parallel that Harris constructs between other forms of passing and that of Basil's is significant. In this opening, he clearly articulates what I have argued earlier is the pain of dominant understandings of passing: general perceptions of identity as singular always disappoint and disarm the spectator. Where typically passing ends in surprise and disappointment, Rosa's passing sends Basil on the path to deviance: in Harris's novels, it is common that moments of crisis lead Basil to engage in unapologetic and uncontrolled sex and rash acts.

In *Any Way the Wind Blows*, Basil commits to the "freeway of lust," where he is going to be "sexing everybody, and the good ones twice." Rosa's rupture of Basil's masculinity produces in him a desire to reaffirm his manliness through lascivious sex. This, of course, leads to the earlier discussed episode with Bart. Following that sexual escapade, Basil sets out on other sexual endeavors. Basil's sexual conquests, indeed, help move the narrative forward. However, such acts also shape the DL discourse and ultimately elicit a punitive gaze by those who are reading witnesses to his sexual adventures. Throughout the novel, he is continuously persecuted for his own "fleshly sin" by his own articulated guilt and various criticisms and accusations from others. Our (the readers') eyes have constant surveillance on Basil's body in (sexual) motion. Our eyes are guided to not only persecute Basil, but also to be constantly titillated by his ability to "stunt" not one but multiple individuals in one narrative episode. Within this novel, Basil's movement between two sexual worlds is constructed as stunts—deceptive acts driven by individualistic impulses that work for his own self-gratification. Once again, because Basil is the *essential* DL character within the text, he performs the master narrative of black male discreet sexuality. In this case, this form of passing is understood as only able to produce problems, rather than offering numerous possibilities that include privacy and upward mobility within a racist, homophobic society.

In the end, according to Harris's plot graph, the only way that Basil can redeem himself from his deviant (read: queer) behavior is to embrace heteronormativity—the voice that haunts him throughout the novel. With every female encounter, there is a deep desire to articulate his "comfort" with women. For example, in the chapter titled "Breakfast at Tiffany's," he holds Tiffany and reflects on how much more comfortable he feels sleeping with her than when he was with Bart. These smaller episodes foreshadow the ultimate redemptive moment, which arrives when Rosa returns to disclose that she is, in fact, carrying Basil's child. Basil assures her that "we gon make this work for the baby." Initially, this comment may suggest that Basil may give up his "double life" for the sake of his child. However, as an avid reader, one knows that there are no Harris novels without the DL subject as the central figure. Therefore, Basil's comment can be understood as a concern for the welfare of the child, his affirmation that he and Rosa will raise the child together. It is in the final chapter that Basil shares the true intent behind his original response to Rosa's admission that he is her "baby's daddy":

> When Rosa, with tears streaming down her face, passed Talley to me and I looked into the baby's face, I cried, but this time the tears that streamed down my face were tears of pride and joy. This crying thing ain't that bad after all. I know I might be alone again in my life, but I will never be lonely. The girl I've been waiting for has finally arrived. (342)

The melancholic tone underneath this passage strikes me as odd. On the one hand, it sounds like a sensitive, supportive dad who takes pride in seeing a part of himself in the world. On the other hand, however, the tone signifies a certain selfish fulfillment found in the birth of Basil's newborn child. He speaks as if he finally got the "thing" he always wanted. I am sure there is a hint of both. Nonetheless, in the frame of the novel, such a dramatic episode serves to redeem Basil in his own eyes. I am less certain, however, of the extent to which he is redeemed in the eyes of the reader. Indeed, by this point in the novel, Basil has lost most readers' favor, rendering this particular "Kodak moment" nothing short of disturbing.

This passage reveals that Basil, in his reproductive bliss, is like the ex-colored man, who presents his children as a major impetus for his final "pass." In *Any Way the Wind Blows*, Basil's daughter gives him the ammunition to abandon worldly confines, at least for the moment, and to perform ex-straight, being comfortable with whatever. As Basil states, in the close of the novel, "Any way the wind blows is fine with me." This final statement has double meanings. Of course, it is a gesture toward the idea that with his newfound love in his newborn daughter, nothing really matters. However, the statement also suggests that because he has performed the penultimate act of heteronormativity—that is, fathering a child—he can be more comfortable with his sexual oscillation. In contrast to the ex-colored man's decision to pass for white, Basil's choice is to remain queer. In this sense, Basil completely inverts dominant paradigms that deem queer as abnormal and non-queer as normal. Basil, the ex-straight man, may reconfigure this structure, with his move out of queerness being read as an escape from that which he deems uncomfortable and unfairly mandated. On the flip side, his move into normalness is an arrival in a comfort zone where he can be a subject who controls, condemns, and owns desire. In this construction of the world, Basil can desire both men and women without shame.

Indeed, this reading is generous and may possibly sound utopic. However, the ending suggests a utopic possibility, where the subject can potentially navigate, rather than pass, between identities. Basil finds some normalcy in being queer, while in other instances finding queer those things that society has deemed as "normal." This moment predicts a time where "passing" is a historical construction of the movement in and out of identity. Here, I am suggesting that Basil's desire to live as a man who happens to be bisexual, rather than as a man who "passes as straight," reconstructs our present narrative of identity. Unfortunately, ill-informed readings of sexual passing influenced by racial-passing constructs deem DL positionality as wholly problematic, rather than potentially instructive and even progressive in terms of dominant notions of sexuality. Our cultural subscriptions to the politics of visibility create unrealistic and unnatural expectations of sexual stability, instead of allowing us to see the natural multiplicity among us. Consequently, we categorize sexual and racial multiplicitousnness as "passing," as opposed to performances of identities that are extensions of what we may think we already know.

"Passing for Straight": Aberrations in Black Contemporary Narratives

When reading contemporary accounts of DL men and their "lifestyles," I am often struck by the many references to these men as "passing for straight." This consistent call back to "passing" as a historical-contemporary construct confirmed my intellectual suspicion that DL discourse is largely a combination of historical understandings of racial passing and Harris's pedagogy through his sexual-passing novels. The construction of passing within historical and contemporary public rhetoric clearly contributes to broader conceptualizations about sexual-passing subjects. The July and August 2004 issues of *Essence* magazine contained a two-part "report" entitled "Passing for Straight" and "Deadly Deception." These are two examples that illustrate the impact of such constructions on a very narrow and limited understanding of the sexual-passing subject, now understood in black society as the "DL brotha." Yet the classification of "brotha" is misleading and disguises the marginalizing tendency of the black press in their discussions of black male discreet performances of (bi)sexuality.

In *Inventing Moralities: Sexual Values in an Age of Uncertainty*, Jeffrey Weeks argues that society's ambivalence toward uncertainty creates great anxiety over sexual values (1995, 28–34). In many ways, this explains the overwhelming demonization of DL men within the black public sphere, as well as in the mainstream press—the DL confounds the certainty that has become traditionally attached to heterosexuality.[23] This historic tradition of understanding heterosexuality as a stable identity has produced great angst over the presence and pronouncement of any sexual performance that would suggest sexual instability. In this context, Tracy Vaughn's reminder that "whenever there is a seeming crisis in some assumed stable category, passing figures appear in discourse—and public anxiety prevails," becomes most insightful.[24] The truth of Weeks's and Vaughn's claims are recognizable in many contemporary texts addressing the down low and sexual passing. For my purposes here, I shall examine a contemporary exposé on black men who "pass for straight" in *Essence* magazine's 2004 two-part series.

The first article in *Essence* covering the seemingly ubiquitous subject of the "down low" is entitled "Passing for Straight" (Harris and Roberts 2004) This "report" introduces a discussion group appropriately hosted by E. Lynn Harris, who is framed as one of two popular "experts" on the DL,[25] and a resident reporter for *Essence* magazine. The article begins with an attempt by the authors to historicize the DL. Yet their efforts are undermined by the "beware: they are still here" tone with which the article is imbued. Such a discursive combination discounts not only the role of history in the lives of these black men for the sake of moral panic, but also shapes the discussion around deception rather than navigation. With this intention, the second article is entitled "Deadly Deception" (Smith 2004) and addresses the dangers of the "fatal secret" that DL men carry when they "sleep with other men." Like most discussions of the DL subject, there is a reduction of male-male sex to disease-prone behavior. Together, these articles are responding to the crisis of a shortage of available black men for heterosexual relationships and the predominance of unstable sexuality among black men, not to mention the coupling of this crisis with disease. The mythologized direct relationship between HIV and the down low serves to explain a long-ignored cycle of disproportionate rates of infection within African American communities.[26] Yet it is important here to highlight how disease is called upon to incite community awareness, while also distilling community homophobia. While such reports do make readers more conscious of HIV and move these specific health concerns beyond the historical "gay men's disease" paradigm, they also encourage homophobia and comments that become central to popular angst about these men who "pass as straight."

These "reports" are important in my discussion of passing for several reasons. As the first article utilizes the term "passing for straight," it calls attention to the connection between race and sexual passing. It demonstrates the ways that historical tropes of "passing" have made their way into contemporary discourses. As explained earlier in this chapter, passing is often employed as a movement toward a singular identity and simply marking passing identity performances as artifice. The problematic logic of viewing passing as almost always deceitful creates a situation where this is the default analysis of the DL circumstance. In addition, the use of E. Lynn Harris as the "expert" facilitator of this dialogue with DL men—and indirectly with the female readership—is an invocation of all the cultural baggage that his books have brought into the DL discourse. In Harris's narratives and contemporary conversations on the sexual-passing subject, claims that these men are putting on a "false identity," which serves to "dupe" rather than to deter stigma, becomes the dominant construction. Hence, this discussion of passing continues to excise the most important aspects of identity politics: the sociopolitical circumstances that warrant certain identifications. Because Harris's texts began as novels to entertain rather than inform, his "DL men" are decontextualized and recalled for the gaze of the *Essence* readers who may be familiar with his work. Thus, his role in the dialogue becomes pivotal to the readers' understanding of the conversation being performed on the printed page. Indirectly and directly, Harris's presence and literary texts endorse a linear reading of DL men and consistently characterize the DL as always "deadly" and "deceptive." Consequently, what may be potentially gained through reading the article closely is lost or reduced, as most readers have an established preconception of DL men and their practices.

When examining the second article of the report, "Deadly Deception," we can see a direct attempt by author Taigi Smith to calm black female anxieties, panic, and angst through the invocation of "passing" for the purposes of critique rather than critical conversation. While the first part of *Essence*'s report was a descriptive essay of the "illness" within the black community, this second look is a prescriptive section for those who have been affected by the "DL syndrome." The author attempts to psychoanalyze DL participants and their behavior and provide "new rules of engagement" for black women in what she calls "these confusing times in African-American history" (Smith 2004, 148).[27] Consistent with *Essence*'s "mission for the women" politics, this article provides a salve for black women's anxiety but misrecognizes what is essentially the force that is at the core of black male secrecy. Together, these "reports" are not reports at all. Instead, they are continuations of misled investments in understanding passing as "fakery," suggesting that we may still be embracing modernist notions of identity. Thus, the postmodernist view of the sexual subject may be better equipped to handle performances of sexuality that are more fluid, evolving, and not racially specific.[28] The presence of the DL and other alternative ways of being in the world demand that we must account for the multiplicitous nature of all communities. Rather than continue to embrace "passing" as a way to describe the movement between identities, we may want to consider the present as a "post-passing" moment—where such a description for managing identity may be too historically loaded to be useful. If we understand this moment as an "age of uncertainty" or a "postmodern" moment, identity is always fluid, and thus "passing" as a functional operation is deemed obsolete. In this equation, we are all postmodern subjects moving between identities that are never stable or fully coherent.

Indeed, DL men are not conventionally straight. However, the circulation and invocation of this maxim of "passing for straight" marks a significant component to the DL discursive construction. *Essence*'s article "Passing for Straight" and other texts on the DL topic easily call these men "closeted homosexuals," "gay," and "bisexual." Why do we attribute so much elasticity to queer categories but limit the expansiveness of "straight"? If DL men are doing "straight" during the majority of their lives—and most people identify them as such—then isn't their predominant performance heterosexual? The fact is that most DL men do not identify, mingle, or even often associate with "gay" individuals. Therefore, it is odd that these men are often placed in relationship to this sexual category. However, when DL men do identify with queer social settings, why are there no claims that they are "passing as gay"? The logic suggests that "straightness" is equated with fixedness and is deemed a pure form, while gayness is framed as a tainting presence that is eternally stigmatizing. Nonetheless, at best it seems most appropriate to consider DL men as practicing "bisexuals." "Gay" and "homosexual" seem to be inaccurate and unfair descriptors, as these associations of DL men with gayness connect these men with more marginal identities and further away from so-called categories of normality. Such willingness to box DL men in with the "decadent homosexual" comes with great rewards to those who are attempting to maintain their sexual purity and normality, while enforcing the sexual hierarchy that has homophobia at its base. In addition, associating DL men with gay men delimits the possibility for heterosexuality to be considered queer, or deviant. It seems that Harris's character Yancey Braxton, Basil's ex-fiancée, may have been a symbolic representation of the larger society and its treatment of all that lies outside normative sexuality. Her individual use and popular installations of "gay" to describe Basil, and subsequently DL men, simplify more complicated notions of sexuality—such as bisexuality—where the definitions are often blurred between desires and actions. Yancey, like other readers of DL performances of sexuality, is uncomfortable with more complicated—dare I say, more honest constructions of identity—finding it easier to situate these men in what may seem like more legible sexual categories.

Many who criticize the DL attempt to make use of the more visible, popular, and coherent identity of "gay," in order to more easily lump these men in a category that has been marked intelligible and readable. Interestingly, the public ambivalence over the DL subject clearly reveals that coherency and continuity are largely absent from the discourse. In fact, the "crisis" and "anxiety" over the DL are the result of what many can't interpret, read, or understand about men's travels across sexual borders. Yet the employment of the phrase "passing for straight" suggests that these men are impostors who borrow identity for their own benefit and discard the border that marks who does and does not belong in the "straight" community. Therefore, ascribing the term "gay" to describe DL men's sexuality frames these men as outside of black cultural belonging, while placing them inside a sexual identity that has been historically depicted as "other." Through the naming of those who want to remain unnamed, Smith attempts to give visibility to the decidedly invisible. This move, coupled with the claim that DL men are impostors, reaffirms what Corinne Blackmer (1995) notes about the major difference between racial and sexual passing—that is, in general, it is difficult for blacks to pass as white, but gays/lesbians are often able to pass for straight because they are always already assumably heterosexual until proven otherwise.

This reality in post-segregated civil rights America significantly explains the anxiety over sexual passing. Herein lies the problem of the naming of subjects as "heterosexual" or the verbal claim of this identity, which sets spectators' expectations. The challenge of naming, as Gayatri Spivak has made clear, is that "names we are given are not anchored in identities, but rather secure them" (1993, 53). So whereas racial passing, or renaming ourselves, was thought to confuse, confound, and corrupt white society's optic accuracy—the sexual passer (DL man) mystifies certain coherent, comfortable sexual securities. What is most striking in Blackmer's passage is how she recognizes that people both choose to pass or are named as heterosexual. In *Essence*'s discussion group led by Harris, it is this naming that prompts a participant named Jason to exclaim, ". . . understand that my sexuality is not all I am . . . don't label me this bisexual bogeyman" (210). His pleading for people to see beyond his sexuality calls attention to the saliency of this issue in society and the ability for sexual postionality to become the totality of one's being. Through his admission of being labeled a "bisexual bogeyman," Jason highlights how DL men are thought to be ghosts—deviants lurking in the shadows of heterosexual black America. "Passing for Straight" attempts to expose the "bogeyman" through an "open" dialogue. I argue that in the context of the agenda-driven setting, at the self-proclaimed gay author's dining-room table, these men are indeed "passing for straight up." Due to ample editing, tailor-made questions, and the minimal opportunity for sustained commentary by any one participant, the information obtained is extremely generic. This article not only serves as another shallow introduction to the down low, but also offers a reductive summation of sexual passing in the context of contemporary society. Indeed, "Passing for Straight" reintroduces black women and other readers to the DL as a subject of inquiry but does not effectively inquire into DL subjectivity.

In *Essence*'s second report, "Deadly Conception," DL men move from being "passers" to "liars." Smith explains that she is seeking "to explore why men on the down low view dishonesty as survival" (2004, 148). The deception here is that the "dishonesty" is the source of survival. Historically and in the contemporary moment, as I have argued earlier, acts of passing can be seen as "struggles over racial (or sexual) representation in a context of the radical unreliability of embodied appearances" (Wald 2000, 6). Yet in this article, there seems to be a conflation of passers with liars. This collapse signifies what Patricia Hill Collins (2004) has called a "past in the present" performance—where this contemporary text appropriates historical treatment of passing identities by reducing them to falsehood. While there is truth that passers are often dishonest, as they selectively edit information about their multiple identities, "liar" connotes an act of violence with no reasoning. The ex-colored man's fiancée's alarm and anxiety in *Autobiography* were heightened because she was blind to the impact that racial constraints placed on individuals with multi-racial backgrounds who appeared aesthetically white. Likewise, this article and several other critics of the down low suffer from the same blindness. Those who simply charge DL men as liars or deceivers seem to possess a selective amnesia about the sociopolitical climate of queer sexual agents in a homophobic and heterosexist society. The term "liar" is too reductive, as the truth of DL men's sexual doubleness is neither socially acceptable nor without consequence. Such assessments of the DL deny the social reality of both the larger black and white communities, as they promote and privilege a respectable heteronormativity that does not include a queer subjectivity.

Smith speaks in the voice of the collective "we," demonstrating that she knows her concerns are those of many black women.[29] Her emphasis on the impact of the DL on black women leads to a very limited and incomplete discussion about sexual passing and the DL in general. In fact, I argue that this discursive focus tells us more about black women and their cultural concerns than about DL men. As Smith laments about the new issues facing African American history, her hyperbolic call reveals a growing anxiety among black women caused by their absence from history. As *Essence* considers passing as a part of African American history, sexual passing is situated as dangerous in the age of HIV and sexually transmitted diseases. However, as a brother said in "Passing as Straight," "the issue is cheating." These articles, and many similar writings for mostly female readerships, reveal that homophobia and the conjoining of HIV with male-male sex are as pervasive among women as with men.

When Smith attempts to appropriate a neo-liberalist stance on sexuality as she remarks that gay men and gay sex are often imbued with "shame and stigma," she follows up with a poor psychoanalytic assessment of "why now more black men are having sex with other men." Her answer? The "oversexualization" of American culture: sexual images of video girls, women shaking their booties, and sex set to music. While I can see how these things could possibly "desensitize" men to sex with women, in this complicated web we call sexual desire, such an assessment for the general population of black men seems quite absurd, particularly in a context where such sexual imagery serves as the impetus for male-female attraction, or at least conversations that erotically address what the eye consumes. Put simply, her claims seem shortsighted when one looks ethnographically at what images are privileged by black men and also what conversations (in barbershops, gas stations, public streets) men engage in. This article seems to suggest that passing is an easy choice. Indeed, the leading of a "double life" may sound appealing; it is, however, a physical and logistical nightmare. This reality continues to be unacknowledged in all constructions of DL men as dangerous sexual passers. Smith, in her commitment to black female health and safety, denies black DL men the care and consideration necessary to fully understand their sexual subjectivity, or even the "true" ethos involved in their passing performances.

Together, "Passing for Straight" and "Deadly Conception" offer little more than dangerous information for the reading public. Passing, for these authors, is always an act of betrayal. Each article assumes a specific intentionality by the passer—to deceive those who are witnesses to their everyday lives. Neither article addresses the role of the spectator's vision in establishing if, or if not, a subject passes. For example, is it the DL man's fault that we continue to understand race, gender, class, and sexuality according to visible traits that we believe are guarantees of identity? The articles also suggest that sexual passing is the cause of high rates of HIV infection among black women. Is it not the act of "unprotected sexual activity between the DL man and his female partner" that creates such tragic circumstances?[30] Because these and many other articles are more fascinated by simplistic understandings of passing, more sophisticated and productive conversations about identity, passing, and spectators are often elided within contemporary interpretations. Unconsciously, there seems to be a reproduction through discourse of the cultural situation that produces the necessity for men to live "down low." As the public continues to embrace linear notions of sexuality, consume linear fictional narratives, and misunderstand passing as a performance of fakery, the DL will remain a secret.

As passing is a performance always in motion, it is only through the engagements with actual bodies and texts that we can best understand how subjects navigate racial and sexual lines. Indeed, my reading of these sexual-passing performances is informed by the history of racial passing in the U.S. context. This allows for a more nuanced reading of how people perform as sexual-passing subjects, as well as locates the origin of how they are interpreted by society. I understand the DL as not only a contemporary manifestation of the passer in sexual terms, but also as a subject who refutes notions of sexual purity and stability—while attempting to balance his multiple identities. Nonetheless, the pedagogy of historical approaches and contemporary representations of passing play a significant role in how we understand sexual passing and, particularly, the DL.

Conclusion: From Sexual Discretion to Sexual Suspicion

We demand that sex speak the truth . . . and we demand that it tell us our truth, or rather, the deeply buried truth of that truth about ourselves which we think we possess in our immediate consciousness.

—Michel Foucault, *The History of Sexuality,* Volume 1: *An Introduction*

While magazines and newspapers ignited the public interest in black sexual discretion, television shows such as *ER, Girlfriends, Soul Food,* and a few others have pursued the topic of the down low in their episodic narratives. Yet none have received quite the acclaim that was given to *Law & Order: SVU's* "Lowdown" segment, which originally aired in April 2004.[1] Indeed, the excitement around Oprah Winfrey's exposé of the DL contributed to this *Law & Order* episode's popularity. "Lowdown" tells the story of white district attorney Jeffrey York, who is killed by his black colleague Andy Abbott, after York threatens to disclose their sexual relationship if Abbott refuses to leave his wife and family to pursue a committed relationship. This highly compelling narrative rearticulates the DL story I have excavated in the previous chapter, but highlights most importantly what Darnell Hunt names as a "raced way of seeing." This construction iterates how certain bodies, because of their race and racial history, are positioned in discourse in different ways (Hunt 2003, 11). At the outset of the episode, we are witnesses to black and Latino female and transgendered prostitutes—sexual dissidents—walking the "strip" and being harassed by the police. While cruising this location, the police find the body of York and conclude that one of "them" (meaning the prostitutes) probably killed him. Though it was not one of the prostitutes, we later learn that it is another deviant subject, a "DL brotha." This framing figures criminality as not only being a natural act of minoritized people and sexual dissidents, but also a relevant threat toward those who reside in dominant categories.

These racialized ways of seeing sexual deviance continue throughout the episode. The first suspect in the murder of Jeffrey York is Kevin Brown, "aka Keisha Brown," a transvestite prostitute who has a criminal record. After she proves her innocence, the investigators are led by York's gym partner to the second suspect—York's last client, whose name is reduced to simply Alvarez. Here, we see a pattern of suspects—all of whom are individuals of color—only to arrive at the actual killer, who is yet again a man of color, Andy Abbott. Abbott is a criminal on two accounts: he is the murderer of the district attorney, and he is a married man who was not only having an affair with York, but also with several men on his ritual "poker night." As the detectives become aware that Abbott is possibly the last person York saw the night he was killed, they interrogate Abbott at his home. In this conversation, they ask, "Did you know Jeff York was gay?" and Abbott responds, "He didn't seem gay." The female investigator then replies, "Sometimes you can't tell." Her look is suggestive, as if she is reading Abbott or inferring that as Abbott pretends to be unaware of York's sexuality, she knows something more. Thus, the investigation continues as the detectives follow up on Abbott's alibi: he was at poker night with the guys.

As the drama continues, it is the "poker night" that becomes suspect. The detectives proceed to interview several black men who attend the Wednesday-night poker game. They confirm Abbott's alibi. When they return to the police precinct, they review the facts and are baffled by why these men would protect Abbott—until Detective Fin Tutuola, played by rapper-turned-actor Ice-T, explains:

TUTUOLA: Maybe they all have something to hide . . .

DETECTIVE: Like what?

TUTUOLA: I think they're on the down low.

CAPTAIN: Down what?

TUTUOLA: The down low. Black men having sex with other men.

DETECTIVE: Every one of these guys is married. Some have kids.

TUTUOLA: That's sex on the down low. They say it doesn't mean they're gay.

DETECTIVE: What does it mean?

TUTUOLA: It's just sex. They hang out, have a few drinks, pretend that what goes on downstairs isn't who they are. You grow up being black, you're supposed to be a man, become a father. Church, your family, your friends, they *all* see being gay as a white man's perversion. (*emphasis added*)

Tutuola is situated as an insider who seems to know everything about the "down low" because he is black. Somehow his racial belonging privileges him to know all about a culture to which he doesn't belong. Consequently, this is an awkward moment in the episode—not because of his supposed knowledge of DL culture, but how he is situated as the "official" on this topic, while his white colleagues stand like empty vessels waiting for the word. In an interview on the *Tavis Smiley Show*, Ice-T commented on his role of teacher in this scene, stating that the producers had to explain to him what the DL was—he originally believed it was "sneaking around."[2] This serves as a testament to what is most troubling about how this scene configures race—a biological trait that privileges one to have some omniscient gift of understanding all aspects of black life. Interestingly, after Tutuola's black history lesson, there is no association of the white district attorney with the "down low." He is understood as gay, while the black men who play poker are some peculiar group—an oddity of sorts—who not only have male-male sex, but who also corroborate in a murder case. Seemingly, this DL culture is a black thing that white people cannot understand or practice. Because of the assumption that it is impossible for whites to understand blackness or DLness, Ice-T quickly volunteers to interrogate a key player in the poker group a second time—to bring the down low out front.

It is Detective Tutuola who secures a confession from a famous ex–football player, DuShawn McGovern, who is a part of the poker group. Yet more significant than the confession he draws out is the conversation, or confrontation, he engages in with McGovern, where the detective informs him that not only is he on the down low, but that this makes him gay. When McGovern says, "I have relationships with women, and sex with men," it sounds like the writers lifted a line from J. L. King. Nonetheless, Tutuola responds, "I got news for you, that means you gay." The detective removes the power of naming from McGovern, calling forth the same categorical imperative that Oprah called forth from J. L. King. This consistent act, of forcing men who consider themselves down low to embrace gayness, is a move to not only control nomenclatural choices but also levels of anxiety caused by sexual ambiguity. Yet Tutuola's provocations force a confession, almost as if to suggest McGovern's concession to the detective's argument, or at least his being silenced by it. In this moment, McGovern reveals that he, Abbott, and other men engage in same-sex acts, though he says, "Nobody mentions sex." He continues to explain that Abbott killed York because he started "talking love" and "he wanted Andy to leave his wife." It is the first part of the writing that deserves attention: Do DL men not want love? Do black men not want love from others? This goes unexplained. However, in this world of "just sex," as Tutuola teaches us, we are left to believe that not love but lust is the only thing that exists in DL relationships.

Abbott killed York, then, because York loved him. Until we hear Abbott articulate his motive, we never know that the impetus for the murder was York's threats to disclose his sexuality—the fear that York would make public what Abbott understood as private. In the scene after McGovern unleashes the silence on the poker group as a sex club, Abbott is arrested, and, ironically, the only audible line of the Miranda rights is "You have the right to remain silent." This, indeed, is allegorical. As York (who represents both whiteness and gayness) attempts to force Abbott (who represents blackness and sexual nonconformity) to conform to his mode of doing sexuality, there is great resistance—and a greater desire for silence. While York wants to announce their sexual relations as a relationship, Abbott wants to silence those moments, marking them as situational and temporal. It is only through the disavowal, or the killing of York, that Abbott can feel most normal. We know from Michael Warner, however, that the "trouble with normal" is that it produces an opposing category of "shame" (1999, 6). Abbott erroneously believes that by killing York the shame of loving another man will disappear. Unfortunately, when one murders, or kills a part of oneself, there is always some trace. This drama is not just an allegory; it is a dilemma.

In this episode of *Law & Order: SVU*, HIV is the trace that announces Abbott's sexual relationship with York; thereby, confirming his motive and guilt. York had infected Abbott, who then transmitted the virus to his wife. Yet because we do not get to know York in this dramatic structure of events, his role in this triangle of infection is marked insignificant. The focus here is on DL men. Thus, the precautionary tale continues, affirming the mythology that these men pose major "risks" for black women. More specifically, the irresponsible acts of black men lead to dangerous outcomes. Or, more accurately, the sexual activities of some DL men produce "risks" for women. It is worth noting here the ways in which the narrative is similar to the *Oprah Winfrey Show* and King's *On the Down Low*, as it focuses on middle-class "DL brothas." In the context of something as heinous as murder, however, "Lowdown" facilitates degradation by mainstream media of upwardly mobile black men. As these men engage in social activities traditionally associated with white men, we are reminded that these men are intruding on white territory. This becomes the explanation for why they cannot behave—their blackness, or biological inferiority, is always present or lurking in the shadows. In addition, the "Lowdown" seems to suggest that as black men become more manicured, more in power, and more middle class, they become more white, gay, and low-down. The latter, which is the title for the episode, is most problematic. As the show illustrates its knowledge of this network of men as "down low," the choice to title the show "Lowdown" seems, at best, judgmental. As a result, the final scene of the episode should be viewed with much resistance.

The episode closes with Abbott's wife's visit to her husband in prison, begging him to admit his wrongdoing to avoid the case going to public trial. In the process, she grants him forgiveness:

> I forgive you . . . for what you did. But I cannot forgive you, if you let our children, and your friends, and their families be destroyed. A trial will drag all of us through the mud. I am asking you, Andy, to be man, and admit what you have done.

However, rather than forgive him, we the audience are left to ask, "How could this 'low-down' man put his family at risk?" The use of the term "low-down," I argue, manipulates our assessment of the circumstances. We are led to believe that it is his intention to "put her at risk," by way of having unsafe sex. The "low-down" act, in this context, is not only Abbott's sex outside of his marriage but, most significantly, his sex with other men. Even if one is unaware of the episode's title, the discourse that we have consumed within media tells us that these types of men are often unremorseful, selfish, and unconcerned with black women's health. Thus, when Abbott tells his wife, "He wanted me to leave my family, I couldn't. I couldn't . . . admit I'm 'gay,'" it raises several potentially transgressive questions. Is a subject gay only when he makes public his male-male relationships? Is there a way to be gay and down low? Or is Abbott's use of "gay" here an indicator of the limited nature of the language used to describe sexuality? Either way, we are left with something that often is unspoken within discourses surrounding the DL: at the core of discretion is a concern for "respectability." This is obvious as Abbott's wife asks him to save the family's face. Likewise, it is apparent when Abbott informs her that he could not leave his family, nor could he embrace a "gay" identity. These two dilemmas have at their nexus a concern for public opinion and personal privacy. While the episode may be entitled "Lowdown," we learn that both Abbott and his wife utilize the down low—politics of sexual discretion—in order to negotiate their public and private selves.

One of the most striking moments in the *Law & Order: SVU* episode is when Abbott's wife urges him "to be a man and admit what you've done." The black woman is utilized to not only elicit a confession, but to discipline the black man for "acting out." With her verbal and physical pain, he is called to apologize for his doubly criminal acts of murdering his colleague and potentially murdering his wife. She "calls him out" not only for his sexual impropriety, but also his masculine malpractice. Here, the DL man is most clearly understood as not simply low-down, but dangerous and dysfunctional. This episode anticipates how years later "suspect" would not be a noun to describe suspicion, but an adjective to connote men who may have sex with men, or non-traditional performances of heterogender.

The "Suspect" at Starbucks: Everyday Encounters, Fears for the Future

I often sit at Starbucks—with my books, my laptop, and my pomegranate green tea—crafting and editing my academic scholarship. At the close of this book, I sit, once again, at Starbucks. The coffee shop environment, in a Habermasian way, seems to be a generator of conversation, intellectual stimulation, and exchange. Often individuals inquire as to what I am doing "with *all* those books." I respond, "Working on a book." Then they inevitably ask, "A book about what?" After I distill my project in the two-minute spiel I have mastered, they always have an experience they wish to share. Two of these shared experiences illustrate what I have deemed as the queer future of the DL.

The first conversation was with a young black woman who had initially engaged me in conversation about my research when she recognized J. L. King's now-infamous book *On the Down Low: A Journey into the Lives of "Straight" Black Men Who Sleep with Other Men* on my table. She was primarily shocked to witness a "brotha" reading this book. I quickly explained that I was critiquing and reviewing the text, far more than I was enjoying it. This began a lengthy conversation. After a long discussion, within which she also verified my sexuality, she commenced to survey the men in the Starbucks. As she sat, she pointed to about five or six men who she considered "suspect." By this, she meant that these "brothas were acting one way when they were really another." These were the type of brothers she said she would have to either keep a close eye on or "cut them off!" I have noticed that the DL discourse has women in a state of constant paranoia around "their" men's sexuality, while inadvertently pre-scripting what qualifies for being a "real man"—what he looks like, talks like, dresses like, and acts like.

My conversation with a black man in his mid-forties verified what I feared were the effects or future of the DL within black discourse: a string of suspects and a heightened self-consciousness or greater paranoia among black men in general. As I sat at my small round table, sipping my tea, he inquired as to the type of work I was doing. Quickly seeing this as an opportunity to hear a presumably "straight" black man's reaction to the DL, I eagerly obliged his request. After I explained the gist of my project, I added to my spiel that I was concerned about the impact that dominant discourses surrounding the DL would have on the black male population. He immediately responded, "Now, that's what I'm talking about—'cause a brother can't even try to nurture or be nice to a black woman without being 'suspect.'" He then continued to share how he tries to "wine and dine" women, as well as maintain his hygiene (such as getting manicures and pedicures), to ensure the comfort of women he dates.[3] These acts, he lamented, were seen as "less than masculine endeavors" by many of the women he would date. In addition, he also indicated that his interests in "opera, shopping, and less 'get your hands dirty' activities" deemed him even more questionable. After all this, he exclaimed, "Can a brotha ever win?!"

Indeed, he can win. But only if he adheres to certain stereotypes that many black men have attempted to deconstruct in their everyday lives— which, of course, now will position him as a potential "DL brotha." Black manhood here is a trap. The DL is invoked exclusively to signify those men who deceive female counterparts while having relations, or relationships, with other men. As "suspects" in these ideologically incriminating times, the possibility for positive outcomes is rare for black men. On the one hand, black men who elicit certain characteristics that would deem them sexually suspect are framed as dangerous agents unfit for fair treatment. On the other hand, as so many black men are judged with arbitrary rubrics, they often further delineate themselves from their actual gay/bisexual/DL/queer "brothas." As a result, black men who perform queer "straightness" or those who engage in discreet practices of homo- or bisexuality are not afforded the privilege of defining themselves or keeping their sexual acts contained to the privacy of space. Instead, they are subject to public scrutiny and criminal framing in all spaces—invalidating their reasons for opting for discretion rather than visibility. Thus, this discursive situation for black men enacts more of a necessity for cool posing and sexual passing, rather than encouraging social-sexual freedom of choice. Like Foucault's epigraph above makes clear, when it comes to sex in our society, it is deemed as truth-telling in the moment of making the sexual visible rather than allowing each individual to construct their own versions of truth. In the case of the DL, black men are always already "suspect" and subject to potential scrutiny rooted in a host of discursive mythologies perpetuated in and outside of media. Outside the realms of sex, however, black men are major figures of "suspicion," often framed as criminal and violent within the news, television shows, and pop-cultural film and video. Consequently, the narrative of the DL as "deviant" and dangerous" is more sellable, appealing not only to the racist mytholo-gies of our society, but to the optic biases that are products of the mass circulation of the deviant black male body.[4]

The fact that DL men are now commonly referred to as being "suspect" is not surprising when considering the etymology and cultural baggage of the word itself. The word "suspect" derives from the Latin word *suspicere*, which means "to look at." In essence, at the core of marking the suspect is the gaze—which is always already instructed by cultural bias and expecta-tions. Consequently, within the history of racism and black doubt, black men are often looked at in ways that are almost always suspicious. Likewise, the cultural usage of the "suspect" within contemporary usages inflects a scopophilic tendency to inscribe criminality upon the black male body. As we learn of suspects in the context of contemporary media, the proliferation of images of "black men" within the frame of criminality deems this a natu-ral image. DL men, as sexual suspects of deviance, extend the ascription of criminality from juridical acts to sociosexual disobedience. Indeed, this ex-plains why the greater concern surrounding the DL centers on "black men who have sex with female partners, while participating in male-male sexual acts." The central criminal act, for the general public, is not only that DL men act outside of what has been deemed naturally masculine, but also that DL men act as heterosexual impostors. In this light, the labeling of men as "suspect" is not a move of suspicion, but a sign that the spectator has acquired enough "truth" within the given performance by the male figure under scrutiny. Consequently, the black male is subject to being a suspect of "deviance" not because of something that he has done or actual evidence of misconduct, but largely because of his relation to deviance by the nature of "acting out." In this sense, I use "acting out" to signify the notion of acting out of character, which assumes that there is an essential way for black men to behave. When black men do not subscribe to certain modes of perfor-mance, they are deemed "other," a code word for "suspect," or a signal of their masculinity being in question or being understood as potentially "queer."

As individuals attempt to decipher the "truth" of the DL within the pub-lic sphere, black men are discursively reduced to mere abstractions, a col-lection of distorted fragments. However, this book has demonstrated how men (re)embody themselves through performance, language, and queer world-making, countering the active discourse by allowing them agency and humanity. As DL men perform within spaces—queer clubs, phone chat lines, Internet sites, and within literary discourse—their "doings" disrupt simplistic narratives of sexuality. In this sense, the DL becomes a kind of counterpublic. Contesting Warner's claim that "counterpublics" are queers who denounce the language of heteronormativity (1999, 86–87), DL men dismiss the notion that queerness must be predicated upon a politics of visibility and repudiation of discretion. Seeing the shift among black queers as of late toward outness as premium, the DL population might be better understood as a counter-counterpublic to the black queer public sphere. While, on the one hand, the black queer population is a counterpublic by the very nature of its existence, DL men penetrate spaces with a discourse of discretion that marks their racialized sexual experience as distinctively different from white and privileged black queer communities. Thus, it counters the counterpublic where black queerness is articulated as something to be "seen"—the sense of sexuality that is aligned with the dominant mode of expressing sexual identity within America.

This countering force is akin to José Muñoz's explanation of "disidentification [as] meant to be descriptive of the survival strategies the minority subject practices in order to negotiate a phobic majoritarian public sphere that continuously elides or punishes the existence of subjects who do not conform to the phantasm of normative citizenship" (1998, 4). While DL men enact a dis-identificatory politics, they are continuously framed as queer "strangers"—situated outside of the dominant black queer paradigm, perpetrating an untruth rather than evidence of the opposite. If anything is apparent, it is the fact that the DL is a positionality that has a central role in the lives of not only queers of color, but also within black communities more generally.

Indeed, *Sexual Discretion* begins a critical conversation about the architexture of masculinity and its dubious relationship to black male sexuality. As the first project to really examine the DL as more than a "phenomenon," it attempts to shed more light on a population with historical and contemporary significance. This book has attempted to move the DL from a discourse of "suspect" to subject—recognizing the potential for these men to inform a more sophisticated understanding of race, gender, and sexuality. Through an interdisciplinary approach, taking performance as a central paradigm for inquiry, this project better facilitates a discussion of the fluidity and complexity of sexuality. Through the critical aims of this book, DL men move from the distorting gaze of suspicion; rather, here they are situated within an intellectual discourse that understands the "doing" of gender and sexuality as an always already shifting apparatus. DL men, in the precarious position of being subject to public scrutiny and pitted against the confines of the ideals of black masculinity, are too often framed in an illusory coherent, cohesive sexual narrative. Indeed, the punitive public gaze and self-regulating tenets of black masculinity encourage the creation and maintenance of DLism.[5] Nonetheless, the manifestations of this positionality have multiple dimensions. This project has only begun to unveil the nuances of DL positionality and all of its complexities—disallowing for reductive, moral-driven assessments of discreet performances of non-normative sexuality.

Research that studies sexual performances and rejects what may be referred to as normative approaches to sexuality is necessary. For me, the greatest importance of this project is to identify the ways in which intersecting identities shift sexual politics. Recently, I have discovered various manifestations of this shift through the incorporation of the DL within various cultural groups. For example, in San Francisco I located a group of Asian men who have appropriated the DL under the nomenclature *Downe*, to not only express their affinity for discretion but also hip-hop culture. Several conversations have pushed me to incorporate a discussion of DL women, of all races—many of whom I have met during research for this project. Indeed, a new project exploring black women's sexual discretion would be appropriate—moving beyond filmic representations, though powerful, such as *The Aggressives* (2005) and *Pariah* (2011). Outside of those who explicitly embrace DL in modified versions, there are several communities of men and women who "remix the closet" and create other ways of being in the world without ever coining a term or using the terms being ascribed to them. All of these communities deserve critical attention within academic research, as they illustrate the ways in which marginalized communities "make do," or create their own worlds with their own discretion.

Indeed, David Eng, Judith Halberstam, and José Muñoz's inquiry "What are the social costs of this new visibility?" (2005, 2) is still an apt one. While the growth of queer visibility for those who desire it is praiseworthy, it is as important to recognize the error in its establishment as the privileged or desired state. Such revelry over queer visibility often excludes those who operate outside the seemingly popular paradigm. This tendency to exclude these experiences gives license to marking men suspect. In this case, as visibility is seen as the norm, invisibility and discretion are viewed as signs of abnormality or underdevelopment. Consequently, as queers of color embrace other ways of doing sexuality, they are marked as outsiders, while the dominant mode of doing is deemed as normative and most rewarding. Nonetheless, the discreet way of doing sexuality allows black men to retain the ideals of masculinity while engaging in queer desire. Whether DL men discreetly participate in relations with only men or with both sexes, the location of themselves within the DL continuum acknowledges their desire to practice desire in "low-key" ways that avoid public scrutiny. Indeed, the DL as a community may be under discursive fire. Nonetheless, public discussion on DL men focuses on abstract figures rather than individuals. Consequently, the damage that is done through discourse is that of the demonization of black men and, more generally, black people. The men with whom I spoke have illustrated the minimal influence of discourse on their DL journey. As one man told me, "It gives the DL a bad rep, but it don't really affect me . . . 'cause it's not me."

Still, the discourse of "suspicion" continues to fuel national momentum. While there is some logic to women's desire to expose DL men, too little time is spent deconstructing the systems that perpetuate dangerous sexual practices and discreet sexual behavior. The former is most worrisome for me. As the larger public focuses on those who commit the "crimes of identity," as D. Marvin Jones has put it (2005, 103),[6] I am concerned about the crimes against humanity that prevent individuals from making the best choices for themselves and others. For example, what makes an individual believe "I'm clean—look at me, how can I be HIV-positive?!" Such assurance, based in masculine sincerity, perpetuates a belief that one's gender protects one from the perils of disease. These myths create some dangerous behaviors, which are known to bring about unfortunate results—which have implications for scholars, health-care providers, and those involved with maintaining the welfare of society.

Medical practitioners and scholars like David Malebranche and Gregory Millett are beginning to ask these questions on the medical front. However, in order to affect change, how do we get these issues to be a larger part of academic and popular discourses on sexuality? As we move to concern ourselves with the workings of the DL, let's unveil the "discreet" sexual choices that are costing people their quality of life. It seems too easy to resort to the old scripts of black male disease and demonization, rather than addressing the more complicated conundrums of sexuality. Those types of questions are central to solving the issues of sexual unhealthiness within all communities. Rather than invoking discussions of "suspect" sexuality in racialized closets, we may be better served to discuss how the "target-group approach" to epidemiology may not be most conducive to research within marginal populations. We may be better served to begin to unpack the boxes in our ideological closets—a queering, of sorts—discovering more nuanced ways to discuss the interplay between race, gender, sexuality, and class.

As this book ends, a new chapter in American history is being made. Black men and women "coming out" seem to be the page-turning discourse:

hip-hop and R&B star Frank Ocean, active NBA player Jason Collins, and WNBA rookie star Brittney Griner all have taken the public stage.[7] Such acts of bravery have been lauded as doings of a public good; anticipation of other artists and sports stars' "public confessions" seems at its highest. In these cultural spaces, where masculinity runs amok among women and men, such acts are without a doubt courageous and commendable. However, the public celebration and subsequent discourse that makes such confessions seem easy must be met with pause. How might we think of these "exceptional" black figures within a particular genealogy? How do their celebrations facilitate further (mis)understanding of black queer life broadly? What does their "out" postionality assume? Particularly, as each of these public figures still commit to a modicum of discretion—as we know nothing of their desires, their sexual relationships, or very little of their process of coming to know and understand themselves. But most significant here is that the ideological pressure present in the lives of those who work in the factory or community bank is different than those who have multimillion-dollar contracts in the music and sports industries. Inadvertently, this idea of those who do public service through coming out versus those who selfishly remain "closeted" criminalizes the latter in hopes of creating a community that mirrors white queer ideals. This is the way that the media and popular queer politics work together, deeming black articulations of sexual discretion as not only selfish, but self-sabotaging to community life. In turning attention away from the "outness" that is not affordable to many black men and women, this book attempts to capture what may be dismissed as simple deviance, rather than complex doings that "create a space where normative myths of how the society is naturally structured are challenged in practice" (Cohen 2004, 38).

This book has attempted to distill sexual discretion as a complex presence that has historical and cultural significance in the survival of people of color, in the face of surveillance. This book, through its exploration of DL men in the press, novels, and everyday life, reveals how sexual discretion and black masculinity collaborate in the process of its own queer world-making. Like odd bedfellows, sexual discretion and black masculinity create a new cultural paradigm for understanding how some black men (un)consciously critique, speak back, and challenge what we think we know in the age of modern sexuality. Here, in this book, the voices and spaces through which men perform a different style of "deviance" are examined closely—revealing the many ways that our demonic discourses brand subjectivity and also create pedagogies that continue to oppress. Being attentive to DL narratives—both spoken and written—enlivens a rich story of the nuances of black masculinity and sexuality in black communities. And instead of affirming a universal understanding of sexuality and black masculinity, *Sexual Discretion* through its interdisciplinary means unveils the dynamic lessons we gain to learn when we move from seeing the "low-down" to goin' down low.

NOTES

PREFACE

1. In order to best include the multiple ranges of sexualities and genders represented heretofore, I will utilize the term *queer*. While jarring to the ears of those exposed to the more pejorative articulations of this term, I incorporate it here to best encapsulate the diversity of non-dominant performances of gender and sexuality that are impossible to be accounted for with the common descriptors (i.e., gay, lesbian, bisexual, etc.). *Queer* as a term here functions not as noun, but as a remark on the "doing" of sexuality to interrupt all that is commonly understood as "normal," "right," "proper." Queer things destabilize the perceived function of an established situation, institution, or understood reality. In essence, the term *DL* functions queerly, as it tries to create space for another way of articulating discreet sexuality without reverting to the claustrophobic closet.

CHAPTER ONE

1. In Alex Hinton's film *Pick Up the Mic*, he interviews poet and activist Tim'm West about the inability of black people to "come out of the closet," or elect to engage in visible queer identity politics.
2. Due to the length of this introduction and the aims of this example, I will not narrate every episode in the video series. However, a more detailed narration of each chapter can be found at http://en.wikipedia.org/wiki/Trapped_In_The_Closet#Synopsis.
3. With the rise of media attention, particularly coverage on the *Oprah Winfrey Show*, the euphemistic "sista" that references black women is transmogrified to hail all women forth, as an audience for these black male "deviant" performances.
4. See Venable 2001; Edwards 2001. As these articles focus on the inability to decipher the sexuality of DL men, it illustrates a frustration and anxiety over these "passing" performances.
5. The DL now shadows the black popular discourses about HIV/AIDS. Over the last ten years that I have been writing this book, it has shifted from the household bogeyman to a recognized villain that always haunts public health conversations.
6. See Madhubuti 1990; Wallace 1990; Duneier 1992; Connor 1995; Blount and Cunningham 1996; Ross 2004; Hine and Jenkins 1999; Booker 2000; Clark 2001; Wallace 2002.

7. Here, I riff on Nicole Fleetwood's brilliant troubling of "trouble" in *Troubling Visions: Performance, Visuality, and Blackness*, where she takes seriously how black bodies and subjects are *made* in the visual apparatuses and processes. For her, "blackness becomes knowable through performance, cultural practices, and psychic manifestations" (2011, 6). This is what, I argue, happens as the DL is being reproduced and manufactured in the public sphere—disallowing for independent or nuanced readings of black men's employment of sexual discretion.

8. Centers for Disease Control and Prevention, *HIV/AIDS Surveillance Report*, 2001, vol. 13, no. 2.

9. I am reminded of Hiram Perez's critique of "gay shame" discourses that "sustain the impossibility of a private black sexuality" (2005, 186)—by offering practices of discretion, or understandings of a black "re-mix of the closet," as evidence of sexual embarrassment or devaluing. Also instructive is Jack Halberstam's important recognition of how "gay shame stabilizes the pride/shame binary and makes white gay politics the sum total of queer critique, gay shame also has a tendency to universalize the self who emerges out of a 'shame formation': at the microlevel, the subject who emerges as the subject of gay shame is often a white and male self whose shame in part emerges from the experience of being denied access to privilege" (2005, 223). As I think through the presence of shame and the strategies created by men of color in this study, I have to work outside of this overdeterministic "formation" and make room for what I discussed earlier as a "down-low way of being in the world" that has become a naturalized response, disconnected from any affective register of shame.

10. When looking at the hyper-surveillance of black people in the media, within institutions, and in everyday life, it is not surprising that conventional understandings of "liberation" are inapplicable. Instead, black people—as bodies always on the auction block of sorts—often seek privacy.

11. Jason King's 2003 *Village Voice* article "Remixing the Closet: The Down-Low Way of Knowledge" was very influential in providing a frame for what was transpiring in the media and within this video series. I use this notion of remixing throughout the book, as I believe this signature phrase captures so much of how the DL is translated within and across cultural communities.

12. I was involved and interviewed in the "His Secret Life" episode of a WLS-TV, Chicago ABC news segment with Cheryl Burton, which led to the now oft-cited Oprah Winfrey exposé of the subject (February 17, 2004).

13. It is important to highlight that all DL men did not give primacy to traditional gender performances; thus, I made myself unattractive to some. In fact, at a 2005 public forum where public health officials were discussing the "real" issue that DL men posed to the black community, I attracted a man who was clearly uninterested in someone who mirrored his same gendered presentation of self.

14. See Kroeger 2003. Brooke Kroeger use of this phrase as the subtitle of her book, *Passing: When People Can't Be Who They Are*, frames her text around the idea of "truth" of one's being. In my work, I am less interested in ontological arguments, but rather how it is that these men employ passing to not suggest a true self, but a desired self; one that is largely preoccupied with masculinity and its cultural and performative demands.

15. George Marcus's multi-sited ethnographic approach is the most cohesive and rigorous for more fully understanding the dynamics of DL cultural activity. He defines the multi-sited approach as a "mobile ethnography that takes unexpected trajectories

in a cultural formation across and within multiple sites of activity that destabilizes the distinction . . . between life-world and system" (1998, 80). In Marcus's conceptualization, the ethnographer moves in and out of multiple sites of interest and recognizes the individual's relationship to certain spaces, while also being attentive to the role played by specific ideological commitments. For example, DL men can be found in multiple sites from traditionally gay clubs to Internet chat rooms, phone chat lines and public restrooms. While this multi-sited method to ethnography clearly offers insight as to the various levels of risks and/or activities that DL men engage in, it also suggests something very fundamental about the larger social structure. Indeed, an inability to express certain desires as a "straight" man requires explorations and experiences outside of the heteronormative gaze.

16. See Jackson 2006. In *Scripting the Black Masculine Body: Identity, Discourse, and Racial Politics in Popular Media,* Jackson details the process of how "xenophobic tendencies . . . are redistributed and recycled in mass-mediated cultural practices" (9). This framework makes room for not only a conversation about textual inscriptions, but how the body responds and performs to regulatory agents such as media constructions.

17. See Mankekar 1999, Robertson 1998, and Kulick 1998 for excellent examples of how ethnography illuminates the value of subjugated knowledge.

18. As I worked with the late Dwight Conquergood as a graduate student, he would reiterate this hierarchical structure of the ethnographer as an "uninvited guest" who needed to be aware of his/her place. This was important, particularly as sexual secrets and discrete ways of being in the world are sensitive matter, to be handled with care and constraint. Many of the men with whom I spoke often asked repeatedly, "Can you make sure this is not connected to me?" In other words, can you frame my words, in order that my identity is not unveiled; fearing to be found out or exploited by my ethnographic distillation.

CHAPTER TWO

1. Here, I employ Eric Watts and Mark Orbe's term "spectacular consumption" to signify what they refer to as "the process through which the relations among cultural forms, the cultural industry, and the lived experiences of persons are shaped by public consumption" (2002, 225).

2. Centers for Disease Control and Prevention, *HIV/AIDS Surveillance Report,* 2001, vol. 13, no. 2.

3. "Things . . . script actions" (Bernstein 2009, 69). I am using Robin Bernstein's idea to signal how the DL as a "thing," becomes a way to understand black men, their actions and inaction.

4. Though I am indebted to Amy Robinson for her coinage of the term "sexual passing" in her essay "It Takes One to Know One," I employ the term in this book differently. I am much more interested in how these particularly moves in and out of categories— and the whole idea of this particular construction of this mobility-based logic—can better explain how hierarchies in identity categories become functionalized. Thus, the men with whom I spoke had moments where they passed into/out of queerness, while simultaneously maintaining their pass into straightness, or normative culture. For me, Robinson's explication for passing may not be fully helpful here. This is taken up in detail in chapter 5.

5. The idea of the black family as threatened by external forces has been an ongoing dialogue, which is maintained as new discursive formations arise to create fear among

blacks, as well as facilitate further homophobia within black communities. In the previous chapter, racial mixing was the threat that was seen as a potential pollutant, or contaminant, of white and black family purity. Similarly, present discursive renderings of DL men suggest that they endanger the stability of the black family, particularly through the transmission of disease to black women.

6.   Here, I am suggesting that black women are rewarded by this reconfiguration in two ways. First, it relinquishes them from being the unfit figure in heterosexual relationships—as deemed in welfare reform and the historical treatment of their role in the black family—by placing focus on the disruptions of DL men. Second, it extends narratives of the "deadbeat dad, boyfriend, father" to include actions that challenge not only black men's loyalty to their family, but also to heterosexuality. For those black women invested in such narratives, it further constituted their sentiments of frustration and anger.

7.   By "mission work," I mean the labor that people do "for the people's advancement" and the work that exoticizes the "other" for pleasure or profit.

8.   Here, I reference the oft-cited Moynihan report and certain (mis)appropriations of E. Franklin Frazier's *The Negro Family in the United States*.

9.   This is borrowed from Ed Guerrero, as he discusses how the monster is called upon in times when uncomfortable "energies, memories, and issues" surface (1993, 43).

10.   In an unpublished essay and a public lecture at the Black Gay Research Summit on August 3, 2005, David Malebranche described DL men as being a discursive product of the same type of mythology afforded to Bush's justification for the war in Iraq, the search and apprehension of the "weapons of mass destruction." Likewise, the black community searches for DL men, walking phallic symbols, who are understood, but not proven, to be contaminants and dangers to the black community.

11.   I use "thug" to identify what Michael Jeffries has called a "performative trope [that] is born from mainstream society's revulsion and characterized by nihilism and mercenary capitalist impulses" (2011, 78). Such an understanding likens the construction of the thug within hip-hop media, particularly how *Vibe* attempts to deal with the juxtaposition of "homo" and "thug." Likewise, "homo" is always already understood as a being that which is most disparate from the thug, rather than potentially a part of its public circulation. Nonetheless, homo-thug represents a doubling of deviance that signifies the intensity of such a coupling.

12.   This is a quote from someone I was speaking with about the state of hip-hop. These remarks are akin to the oft-cited quote from Ice Cube, that "Real Niggas ain't faggots."

13.   Most recently, discussions of middle-class men who are not "thugs" have arisen in response to the mass hysteria among middle-class black females in America contracting HIV/AIDS. The class implications here are quite interesting when we think about the historical black agenda that often has taken flight as a result of middle-class concern and anxieties. For this reason, the recent proliferation of popular press articles on the subject of the "down-low brotha," rather than the "thug" or the "bisexual," is quite suspect—a cyclone induced by the presence of the DL topic in middle-upper-class suburbia via the *New York Times*, as well as middle-upper-class black media sources. Nonetheless, the predominant picture of the "dreadful bisexual" remains to be that of the thug-like black male sexual deviant. Though I argue that the momentum of DL discourse was a result of middle-class black men's discreet practices, it is the working-class "deviant" who infects middle-class purity and represents the greatest threat to the "black community."

14. This point is taken up in more detail in the ethnographic component of this book.

15. While the DL discourse has significant effects on black female representation, this issue is taken up in a later section of this chapter.

16. Indeed, this notion of the uninformed and uninterested black public is troubling. Rather than positioning black people as being uninterested and in need of a simple fix, it may be better to propose that the culture of sexually transmitted infection prevention has produced an attitude within the public of disinterest and the need for simplicity. Boykin's reading suggests that this is something culturally specific to black people. This is simply not the case.

17. It is worth noting how the notion of "Living (and Dying) on the Down Low" divorces these men from HIV/AIDS and appears to blame the "down low" for their potential death. In addition, it assumes that the DL body is always already infected or at risk.

18. Few articles provide a substantive inclusion of black female narratives and experiences during their discussion of the DL. However, see Vargas 2003; Glanton 2004. Both of these articles give women central voices in discussing the issue of HIV/AIDS.

19. During a conversation, discussed later in this chapter, J. L. King credited this article for the interest of Broadway Books in his story.

20. I would argue that actual physical images of DL men allow people to do more than piece together fragments of an idea, but to believe that they have all the evidence they need to not only recognize but reprimand particular "types" of black men.

21. Indeed, my choice of the term "Messiah" is loaded. However, my use of the term is not to invoke all the historical cultural baggage, but to more accurately describe *how* J. L. King is situated within DL discourse, as *the* voice of authenticity; therefore, seen as providing the most "official knowledge" from within the inside.

22. This rendering of analysis of the heightened DL scene in Chicago could be read as more of a way to bring relevance to his discourse in this particular venue. The pinpointing of Chicago as a central hub of DL culture incited not only interest, but panic within the eyes, faces, and body language of the audience.

23. In this dialogue, J. L. King claimed that DL men have threatened him and that he had received several criticisms from the black gay community for his "demonization" of them. In the August 1, 2004, *Houston Chronicle*, he made similar claims—asserting that because of such hostility, he has bodyguards. Interestingly, in all of my encounters with King, there had been no bodyguards. In fact, there was typically a group of gay men with him.

24. This is extracted from previous field notes at the Spoken Word Cafe's relationship chat.

25. The transcript of this special segment can be found at http://abclocal.go.com/wls /news/specialsegments/021704_ss_hissecertlife.html. I was given the honor of being one of the academic consultants for this project.

26. This has been validated by several attendees, who in confidence contend that King's investment in the DL is largely a financial one—yet an investment that comes with great costs.

27. This is in conversation with a point made in the introduction of this book, where Marlon Ross challenges the critique of black male constructions of sexuality that lie outside of dominant norms.

28. See Kant, *The Groundwork of the Metaphysics of Morals*, where he explains this imperative as an unconditional obligation to perform a certain action—in this case, identifying one's "self"—which is required and justified by the law. Here, the social law of categorization is imposed on King and DL men by Oprah.

29. It is important to note that the *Oprah Winfrey Show* is broadcast nationally and globally, while the after-show is a part of a more limited cable television station, Oxygen. Thus, more people have access to the problematic rhetoric within the *Oprah Winfrey Show* than they would to the after-show.

30. Phill Wilson's comments remind me of the last line of Dwight McBride's provocative essay "Straight Black Studies," where he states: "Whenever we are speaking of race, we are always already speaking about gender, sexuality, and class" (2005, 87). For a specific discussion of "intersectionality," see Crenshaw (1989).

31. In the post-show talk of the *Oprah Winfrey Show,* King posits that he wrote this book for the accessibility of both of these audiences.

32. In a personal interview with J. L. King in 2002, he told me that E. Lynn Harris is not a close friend of his, but a writer whom he often reads.

33. This is the taken from the Centers for Disease Control's webpage, where they outline their stated objectives and goals. See http://www.cdc.gov/about/default.htm.

34. This website no longer exists, presumably as the niche market of DL materials has eroded.

35. After substantial success with two *New York Times'* best-selling books, J. L. King shifted his focus from a website centering on the "down low" to the appropriate http://www .jlking.net. In other words, he became the focus of his campaign. After all, he was now the "messenger." (This website is no longer functional. One might mark the demise of the website as correlating with the centrality of King as DL spokesperson.)

36. This mission statement can be found at http://www.cdc.gov/about/mission.htm.

37. This image was originally found at http://www.livingdownlow.com/html /prevention.html, but can now be ordered from the Centers for Disease Control directly.

38. See White 2001 and Higginbotham 1993.

39. I recognize the possibility of reading her statement as contradictory. Yet her voice told me that she understood the complexity of her statements. She was rendering her own honest truth about what was happening.

40. Unfortunately, I have been unsuccessful in locating this poster. It was a local ad campaign. Nonetheless, I believe its significance is worth citing here.

CHAPTER THREE

1. Often men would give me a brief moment of their time, stating their disinterest in a longer interview but a willingness to simply chat with me for a minute or two. These moments often gave me what I call soft data; not a lot to extrapolate a fortune of meaning, but yet illuminating of the threaded presences within the Dl experience of club space and even everyday life handlings of desire.

2. The late Charles Clifton, as he explored historical presences of homoeroticism, illuminated the importance of recognizing the role and service that discreet sexual identity has played in the lives of black men. See Clifton 2000, 342.

3. The name of this club has been modified, to secure confidentiality for the men with whom I speak, as well as the club and its other patrons.

4. Like the name of the club, I have used pseudonyms to protect subjects' anonymity.

5. As a student of Dwight Conquergood, this was one of his common sayings.

6. For more information on the transition from house to hip-hop and its effects on the club space and its business, see Kai Fikentscher's *"You Better Work!": Underground Dance Music in New York City* (2000).

7. See Berlant and Warner 1998, 558.

8. Here, I contest William Hawkeswood's discussion in *One of the Children: Gay Black Men in Harlem*, where he mislabels the population of men with whom he speaks as "gay black men," when they clearly prioritized blackness before gayness (1996, 11–12). "Black gay men" seems to better articulate the way in which many understand themselves and often (even in Hawkeswood's study) show strongest allegiance. Such recognition further explains the black gay affinity for hip-hop, as it assists in an authenticated blackness.

9. Though Robert speaks generally about the Gate as a club, I would suspect that his sentiments are his interpretation of his experiences in the hip-hop section of the space.

10. Note how the uninhibited, self-expressive, and energetic gets read as being feminine or over the top.

11. See Mark Simpson's *Male Impersonators: Males Performing Masculinity* (1993) for a broader discussion on the art of gender impersonation.

12. In Michel de Certeau's *Practice of Everyday Life* (1984), he refers to this viewpoint as a (dis)advantage point above the city, away from the masses. While this perspective provides a place to feel the energy and activity in the space, it also positions me outside the participatory realm, in a place of power and privilege that I often find too titillating or, at times, troubling.

13. Usually, those who elicit initial eye contact or conversation are not interested in my research questions. Most often, they are interested in me as an object of attraction. For this reason, there are many more dead-ends than there are live wires. However, I can sometimes turn their attraction into a fruitful conversation with minimized flirtation.

14. This term is an indirect admission that one has sexual relations with men. Typically, "to get down" suggests a temporal queer experience; whereas the person who "gets down" only does this periodically, or when it is convenient for them.

15. Often when faced with issues of sexuality, nonverbal expression can provide greater clarity; while language often creates greater tensions and even over-articulates what the subject desires. In this case, erotic physical performance clarifies homoerotic desire.

16. Here, Houston Baker's discussion of disco music has great resonance when he states, "There are gender-coded reasons for the refusal of disco. Disco's club DJs were often gay, and the culture of Eurodisco was populously gay" (1995, 198). This may also explain the consistent disdain for "house" music as it often queers spaces and carries a queer aesthetic.

17. Interestingly, Shawn has admitted to me several times that he often performs both roles, as active and passive participant in sex. This contradiction is consistent within all initial conversations with men on the DL, but often operates the same way in traditional black gay discourses.

18. For more on gentrification and its effects on black people, see Mary Pattillo's *Black Picket Fences* (1999), as well as her recent book, *Black on the Block* (2007).

19. For more information on this dance form and the musical significance of the "Ha!," see Marlon Bailey's *Butch Queen Up in Pumps* (2013).

20. It is important to note that this relationship with "femmes" or transgendered individuals is not peculiar to DL men. For example, many gay men prefer relationships with "femme" men or transgendered women. However, since I have been doing this research, the investment in these relationships are often predicated on something very different from those of many gay men. It seems that many DL men engage in

a gender attraction, whereby they are captivated by certain ideals that are grounded in hetero-patriarchal ideals. It is also important to note that my use of the term "relationship" is by no means to suggest that Tavares has ever sustained relationships with those with whom he shares interests. "Relationship" is used to describe the connection or association between Tavares and those he desires.

21. While one could argue that male-transgender relationships are a part of homonormativity—the lack of acceptance of this relationship within black queer "communities" counters this supposition. More specifically, for Tavares the only way he can even fathom a relationship with a "man" is if he appears to be a "woman" or "womanly."

22. Philip Brian Harper (1999) highlights the ways in which certain leaders within the black community have continued to create heterosexual anxiety over queer presences.

23. bell hooks (2003) illustrates the detrimental effects of this structure on black male understandings of self and also locates white supremacist patriarchal culture as the hidden culprit in perpetuating and legitimating both sexism and homophobia. It is important to recognize how these forms of domination reward black men for acting out in sexist and homophobic ways, reiterating its use value and almost necessity within black male life.

24. One of the cited reasons for attendance by many DL men, in spite of the possibilities of being "found out," is that the Gate typically attracts the same "type" of people. In other words, the likelihood of incidentally encountering a spouse, family member, or friend is unlikely. In addition, many have said that their anxiety is lessened because those who would frequent the Gate are probably more likely to "be cool" with what men do at the Gate.

25. There are multiple rumors circulating as to what caused the party's demise. Some attribute the Gate's party closure to mismanagement of funds by party promoters and organizers. Others have concluded that the Gate's owner began to demand more money to utilize the space and the party was not generating enough revenue to be profitable. Many have speculated that the party become too much of an eighteen-and-up club, which meant less revenue to be generated—as the demographic shift produced a more unpredictable presence and profit. And many have told me that they believed the owner saw more profit in "straight parties" than "gay parties." Whatever the truth here, what is for certain is that this brand of black queer world-making in this underground industrial space has not been matched in the Chicagoland area.

CHAPTER FOUR

1. This was taken from a conversation with a twenty-two-year-old young man who was an avid user of the Internet, as well as phone chat lines for male-male erotic encounters and conversation.

2. While these texts employed the term "queer" to describe the language and culture of men, they often reduced the queer experience to that of gay and lesbians. More specifically, the subjects and their acts were called queer because they involved admittedly gay subjects. This project challenges this move, as it attempts to make queer inclusive of not only minoritized subjects but also those experiences that are described outside the context and container of traditional sexual categories. In this sense, this chapter moves to make queer a bit queerer, rather than employ simplistic and linear understandings of the term.

3. This space would later be called the Bi-Blade.

4. "Gag" is a black gay vernacular term that expresses a sense of comedy and jest in dialogue for entertainment purposes.

5. While my conversations with Charles were in 2002, the DL had begun to be used as a descriptor of positionality quite frequently. Interestingly, the name of the party line was shortened and abbreviated, as is common in black vernacular. However, most striking are the similarities between "DL" and "PL."

6. While openly gay men traveled the space, my attention here is on how DL men bracket themselves as sexual subjects within the CB space.

7. This is extracted from an interview conducted on April 29, 2003.

8. Dwight Conquergood, in his classroom and one-on-one tutorials, encouraged deep listening as a way of interacting within space, especially when the activity in sites was more covert and inexplicit.

9. Many of the men with whom I spoke referred to the CB as more private than any other part of the "line." In addition, they highlighted that they had control over how they moved within these spaces. In other spaces, there were not only other callers, but also technical issues such as disconnection or "bumping" that eliminated callers' opportunities to communicate.

10. This will be discussed further later in the chapter. However, I mention it here to draw a parallel between the operation of certain styles of masculinity for DL men and black gay men.

11. Throughout this book, I have made a distinction between the various manifestations of the DL. Here, I separate the DL from those who prefer discretion because they indicate two different identifications but similar desires. Though DL men use a specific label to gain masculine authenticity, those who are discreet in sexual practices are also deemed masculine. For most men I have encountered in either category, there is a preference for a certain style of masculine performance that aligns itself within a heteronormative trajectory.

12. Due to his unstable housing situation, Tavares would often compensate his payment for sexual favors for temporary food and shelter.

13. This is much like "trade" of the 1990s, as Edwin Greene describes in "Thoughts on Trade/Ending an Obsession" (1999), where it is about money/food in exchange for sex. While DL men may not identify themselves as "trade," many gay men who are familiar with the history of the term ascribe them this title. Indeed, some DL men do "trade" for sex—an indicator of the value given to heterogendered performances.

14. Though I have not spoken with anyone who received money to actually perform the non-dominant role in intercourse, many I have spoken with have noted this as a part of the tradition. The presence of this role reversal, so to speak, among gay and DL men's relations would only seem fitting as there is an erotic power in penetrating those who have been deemed to possess the most masculine positions within a community. In fact, there is often a sort of boastful presence among gay men, who typically perform the non-dominant role, when they top the "top."

15. This caller identified his DLness by his affiliation with women (his heterosexuality). While this is common within the CB space, this is not the only or predominant construction of the DL. In fact, most definitions are centered around a commitment to discretion and privacy.

16. In Chicago there seems to be limited spaces for demonstration of everyday queer desire (e.g., street, bus, clubs, parks, etc.). In New York City, the openness of sexuality seems to be more visible and available in public spaces. For example, in cities such as New York City and Atlanta, there have been many instances where I have

been propositioned in subtle and explicit ways in public places. In a sense, sexual tourism, in terms of geography, seems to be more common in some cities more than others—Chicago is not one of them. I do realize, however, that even in more metropolitan and inviting city cultures, many men do choose to tour virtual spaces as they provide greater security and selectivity.

17. This commonality of showing only parts of the self divorces these men from the personal or personable, but also relegates them to opposition for being interested in nothing more than the sexual-physical aspects of queer life. Consequently, the space itself is ridden with interactants who make such announcements as "if you only have a dick/ass shot, you will be blocked." In addition, many participants indicate that they want to have access to "private pics"—which usually unveils a nude photograph or image.

18. Though this study focuses and examines the narrative of DL men who are black, there were several men with whom I spoke who did not fit this category. For example, there was a white interactant named DLWhiteBoi_26, who explained his use of the term as signification of "keeping his business to himself." In addition, it was also to signal viewers of his profile that he was interested in "certain types of masculine guys." In addition, there was also DL_LatinBro, who also articulated similar reasons for his use of the term. However, he said that he felt that the DL really spoke to how he and others like him (meaning Latino men) "kept a low-key lifestyle." Many of his ideas illustrated that he felt that the DL gave a name to something he was always doing. Unfortunately, my interactions were contained to one or two conversations. I am not sure why men from other cultural-racial backgrounds were less willing to sustain contact. However, I sometimes felt that my approach may have been too culturally specific in terms of the textual voice I would use and the questions that I would ask. Indeed, the cultural knowledge of the ethnographer impacts the outcome of his dialogue with "others," even within cyberspace.

19. Indeed, the men who utilize their pictures are also often interested in "relationships" rather than just "1-on-1 sex." This is significant as male-male relationships are a conventionally gay manifestation. Thus, many gay men in the space have begun to admit disinterest in those without face pictures.

20. The last statement—"if he is a send off"—is a reference to whether the caller will actually meet when and where he says he will.

21. This may be the greatest irony of DL men's operations within this space. As they disavow themselves as "fags," their comfort is largely predicated upon the large presence of gay men within the Steve4Steve site. Yet this is an unacknowledged observation by those men who perpetually use "fags" to define themselves outside of a queer community.

22. In addition, there are several codes and choices in constructing profiles that would prove most outsiders to be invaders to the site, rather than actual members of the "community."

23. The absence of a discussion of these men is odd—as I have witnessed several men and women who have accepted various "arrangements" to account for the presence of spouses who prefer the company of the opposite sex and the sexual company of the same sex. Often couples no longer sleep in the same bed or even sometimes in the same household. Yet they maintain their legal marriages for the benefit of the children and the fiscal resources gained through the perpetuation of their "institution."

24. While this was only one example of a response, it is akin to the multiple responses that my counterparts have shared with me.

CHAPTER FIVE

1. I use the term "spirits" to speak to what many people consider the core of them-selves. However, I am not trying to make a move toward an essence of blackness, but rather a communal feeling that is often the result of injustice.

2. Michel de Certeau refers to this in *The Practice of Everyday Life* (1984) as "makeshift creativity." In his conceptualization of this strategy, those who are without make do with what they have. This has been a historic presence within African American communities.

3. I am alluding to Werner Sollors's discussion of the primary role that "social and geo-graphic mobility" plays in the lives of passing subjects. He argues that while certain social, geographic, and political arrangements sustain the color line, passing allows for performances of resistance, in which those who may be traditionally exiled are welcomed (1997, 247–48).

4. For critical perspectives on the role of intersectionality in queer lives, see their respec-tive essays in the anthology *Black Queer Studies* (Johnson and Henderson 2005).

5. By 2000 Harris had sold one million copies of his six novels, all of which explored the lives of black queer men. Specifically, novels that took as their central character what is now understood as "DL brothas." See the Q&A section of *Ebony* magazine's October 2000 issue.

6. The writing of these novels during these specific era were significant, according to scholars Gayle Wald (2000) and Hazel Carby (1998), as these writings acted as de-vices of agency during the racially and gendered turbulence of the times. The resur-gence of such novels and narratives at the close of the twentieth century should not go unnoticed. Recent examples include James McBride's *Color of Water: A Black Man's Tribute to His White Mother* (1996), Danzy Senna's *Caucasia* (1999), Gregory Howard Williams's *Life on the Color Line: The True Story of a White Boy Who Discovered He Was Black* (1996), Colson Whitehead's *The Intuitionist* (2000), and Patricia Jones's *Passing* (1999). As Tracey Vaughn has done in her work, I argue that the return of passing novels is an indicator of crisis and a heightened visibility of the instability of identi-ties thought to be stayed or stable.

7. Such a response is not foreign to the genre of passing novels. Charles Chestnutt's *House Behind the Cedars* also confronts the material internal struggles of the spectator of the "pass." Through his telling of the white aristocrat George Tryon's falling for Rena, a female passer, he demonstrates the extremes of the American racist imagi-nary—not only its effects on those of mixed race, but also on those who are white. Such recognition of the emphasis on the "signs of race" signals the great dependency of the interpreter on the visual, as well as acknowledges the sheer value of interpre-tation in the passer's achievement in attaining an authentic, or legitimate, place in society more generally.

8. Both Siobhan Somerville (2000) and Philip Brian Harper (1996) argue that the inter-racial romance is both fleeting and peripherally placed in *Autobiography*. While this is a possible reading, I read it as central, while still finding their points about ho-moeroticism and gender performances instructive.

9. Here, Michael Warner's (1999) critical discussion of normal and queer is instructive. Although he focuses primarily on sexuality, I appropriate his use of "normal" in regards to that which is hegemonic with regards to race, gender, class, or sexuality.

10. E. Lynn Harris's official website describes Basil as a "terminal bisexual"—a label very much akin to the historical "tragic mulatta." In this case, the modifier "termi-nal" is used to indicate the everlasting, yet painful quality most obvious in Harris's

construction of Basil's desires for men and women. The difference in historic portrayals of the mulatta is that her life usually ends in death and anguish, whereas Basil's life may be complicated but is always allotted outcomes that benefit his own secrecy and sanity.

11. It is important to note that in this novel Basil is described as "being on the down low," but it is not a positionality claimed by him specifically. However, Basil's gender performance and discreet sexuality—his subscription to a legible "heterogender"—prompts others, including the author, to give him such a label.

12. See Venable, Ballard, and Edwards for examples of the popular media representations of the down low in 2001.

13. On the one hand, I mean the possibilities for DL men within certain black contexts. While on the other hand, I mean his acknowledgment of what interest his reading public would have in the DL subject.

14. It must be noted that the final two novels in Harris's trilogy, with Basil as the central character, debuted second on the *New York Times'* best-sellers list. This speaks to both the thirst for and the popularity of this passing character in the public imagination.

15. This was a common response on his website and among women whom I have spoken with about his novels. In addition, when visiting Amazon.com, I found several reviews that found much pleasure in the scandalous nature of the writing. One reviewer even stated that she felt that these novels would be good educational material for teens.

16. In *The Boundaries of Blackness: AIDS and the Breakdown of Black Politics* (1999), Cathy Cohen discusses the trope of the "dreadful (male) bisexual" within the context of HIV/AIDS as almost always the configuration of the main vector of contagion. Such a historical trope plays out in the DL narrative as well. In many senses, the DL in discourse is a re-articulation of the "dreadful bisexual" figure.

17. This is not to suggest public alarm and warning cannot be useful. However, his literary voice lends itself to an incomplete and empty interpretation and representation of the circumstances of DL men and black people, in general. Due to Harris offering exaggerated and sensationalized characters and contexts, readers are left with literary work that rarely appeals to intellect, but instead to homophobia. His passing characters, particularly in *Any Way the Wind Blows*, are reductive and simplistic. Nonetheless, his constructions of the DL have been the most influential and effective in terms of the years that he has dedicated his writing to this topic, both directly and indirectly.

18. I frame this character in this way because it accents the unidimensionality that Harris often ascribes to his female characters. Typically, the female characters serve to give greater volume to the central male figure, who also sees her value as minimal or insignificant.

19. In addition, often the in-group representatives are the readers who are "in the know"—as we are the only witnesses to the many honest asides that each character provides for readers. In these moments, characters confess their most honest secrets, feelings, and concerns.

20. Thank you Jennifer Devere Brody for her insight here.

21. While this discussion does not take issue with Harris's portrayal, I must note that Harris's focus on the "dupe" interferes with his ability to convey the greater complexities of DL life. My discussion attempts to critically engage "passing" discourse to illuminate the complexity of DL sexuality.

22. In one review on Amazon.com, a woman commented that "Basil is not a good rep-

resentative for gay, bi, or any people." This sentiment was shared by several other reviewers—as they expressed their "disgust" with his actions.

23. I specify heterosexuality as being the assumed stable category because in Western constructions of sexuality, homosexuality is often thought to be a temporal state or simply a detour from its heterosexual other.

24. This quote is taken from personal communication but can also be found in Tracy Vaughn's dissertation (2005), which takes as its central focus racial passing and the role of externals in constructing and maintaining identity.

25. The other, of course, is J. L. King—the author of *On the Down Low: A Journey into the Lives of "Straight" Black Men Who Sleep with Men* (2004)—who has been deemed the man who "blew the lid off the DL." His significance in the discourse will be discussed extensively in the following chapter.

26. By calling the impact "mythologized," I am not marking concerns about HIV insignificant, but incomplete and inaccurate. Indeed, the discussion of the DL and its potential relationship to the rise of HIV is important. However, such conversations must come equipped with recognition of the multiple contributing factors to the present circumstance of health. The significance of HIV in DL discourse will be discussed more fully in a later chapter.

27. It is important to note how "history" is called upon to exaggerate the importance of the DL in *Essence's* report. Such hyperbolic connections to history impose a specific centrality to the DL that unfortunately marks sexual passing as a racially specific move. Furthermore, "these confusing times" suggests that there has been a critical change in the clarity of African American history. Such ponderings deny that African American history has always been a confounding and conspicuous construction of narratives.

28. The modernist tendency often assigns characteristics and behaviors to bodies based on the finding of certain practices among specific groups. I critique this tendency by making a brief remark about the tendency to see not only the DL as unilateral "fakery," but also black. Indeed, sexual passing, like racial passing, is beyond the "fake and real," as well as the white and the black.

29. In terms of facilitating a more healthy discussion about women, HIV, and the DL, Taigi Smith does well. In her article, she uniquely gives women helpful facts that will assist them in remaining healthy and safe. This health component in the context of the DL conversation is one of the most productive. However, her aim to discuss the DL specifically is shortsighted and highly agenda-driven.

30. This is not to simplify the role of gender roles in the sexual relationships between individuals. However, I am attempting to move away from the act of passing as culprit to the act of "unprotected sex" as criminal.

CONCLUSION

1. This episode had the highest rating on network television during its airing; see www.tv.com/law-&-order-special-victims-unit/lowdown/episode/310631/summary.html. In addition, this episode was awarded the SHINE Award—an "honor for those in the entertainment industry who do an exemplary job incorporating accurate and honest portrayals of sexuality into their programming." See http://www.themediaproject.com/shine/.

2. In an interview on the *Tavis Smiley Show*, Ice-T commented on his role of teacher in this scene, stating that the producers had to explain to him what the DL was—he originally believed it was "sneaking around."

3. It is important to note that the acts he engaged in with women required a certain type of economic stability and positionality. In essence, his framing of the "dilemma for brothas" was one that was essentially about a middle-class identity being a masculine performance that can be scrutinized.

4. The power of the construction of the "suspect" is at the forefront of my mind, as I reflect on George Zimmerman's acquittal after killing Trayvon Martin—who was clearly deemed suspect and treated accordingly. For me, DL men's mark as *suspect* cannot be disaggregated from the larger ways in which this becomes a marker that legitimizes discursive and physical violence.

5. However, it is important to note that I am not certain that the DL would become extinct if these structures were not active. Admittedly, part of the idea that the DL is a by-product of certain systems is based in an assumption that DL has some pathological impetus. In fact, I would argue that with or without the mandates of visibility and invisibility, individuals would still practice discreet sexual acts. As many men have indicated, there is as much pleasure in the ability to not be seen as there is to be always visible. Nonetheless, with these two major operating regulating factors, the DL seems an apt positionality for individuals who wish to avert surveillance and demonization.

6. While D. Marvin Jones's use of the term "crimes of identity" is specifically concerned with race as a criminalizing factor, my use here attempts to draw a parallel with sexuality. I argue that sexuality is often a demonized identity, which is framed as a crime against the conventions of dominant paradigms.

7. Though it is significant that Brittney Griner's media coverage has been minimal and may remark upon cultural fascination with men's sexuality—which is at the core of this book's critique. In many ways, our preoccupation with men—this book included—misses not only opportunities to incorporate women, but to speak to the role of female masculinity in productions of sexuality.

REFERENCES

Alcoff, Linda. 1995. "Cultural Feminism versus Post-Structuralism: The Identity Crisis in Feminist Theory." In *Feminism and Philosophy: Essential Readings in Theory, Reinterpretation, and Application*, edited by Nancy Tuana and Rosemarie Tong, 434–56. Boulder, CO: Westview Press.

Alexander, Elizabeth. 2004. *The Black Interior*. St. Paul: Graywolf.

Alexander, Michelle. 2012. *The New Jim Crow: Mass Incarceration in the Age of Colorblindness*. New York: New Press.

Altheide, David L. 2002. *Creating Fear: News and the Construction of Crisis*. New York: Aldine de Gruyter.

Anderson, Benedict. 1991. *Imagined Communities: Reflections on the Origin and Spread of Nationalism*. Rev. ed. London: Verso.

Bailey, Marlon. 2013. *Butch Queens Up in Pumps: Gender, Performance, and Ballroom Culture in Detroit*. Ann Arbor: University of Michigan Press.

Baker, Houston A., Jr. 1995. *Black Studies, Rap, and the Academy*. Chicago: University of Chicago Press.

Baker, Paul. 2005. *Public Discourses of Gay Men*. New York: Routledge.

Baldwin, James. 1985. "The Black Boy Looks at the White Boy." In *The Price of the Ticket: Collected Nonfiction, 1948–1985*. New York: St. Martin's.

Ballard, Scotty R. 2001. "Why AIDS Is Rising among Black Women." *Jet*, July 23.

Barrett, Rusty. 1997. "The 'Homo-Genius' Speech Community." In *Queerly Phrased: Language, Gender, and Sexuality*, edited by Anna Livia and Kira Hall. New York: Oxford University Press.

Barthes, Roland. 1993. *Image, Music, Text*. London: Fontana Press.

Battle, Juan, and Sandra L. Barnes, eds. 2009. *Black Sexualities: Probing Powers, Passions, Practices, and Policies*. Brunswick, NJ: Rutgers University Press.

Beam, Joseph. 1986. "Brother to Brother: Words from the Heart." In *In the Life*, edited by Joseph Beam. Boston: Alyson.

Bell, Derrick. 2001. "The Sexual Diversion: The Black Man/Black Woman Debate in Context." In *Traps: African American Men on Gender and Sexuality*, edited by Rudolph P. Byrd and Beverly Guy-Sheftall. Bloomington: Indiana University Press.

Berlant, Lauren, and Michael Warner. 1998. "Sex in Public." *Critical Inquiry* 24, no. 2 (Winter): 547–66.

Bernstein, Robin. 2009. "Dances with Things: Material Culture and the Performance of Race." *Social Text* 27, no. 4: 67–94.

Bersani, Leo. 1987. "Is the Rectum a Grave?" *October* 43 (Winter): 197–222.

Betsky, Aaron. 1997. *Queer Space: Architecture and Same-Sex Desire.* New York: William Morrow.

Blackmer, Corinne. 1995. "The Veils of the Law: Race and Sexuality in Nella Larsen's *Passing.*" *College Literature* 22, no. 3 (October): 50–67.

Blasius, Mark, ed. 1999. "An Ethos of Lesbian and Gay Experience." In *Sexual Identities, Queer Politics.* Princeton, NJ: Princeton University Press.

Blinde, Elaine, and Diane Taub. 1992. "Women Athletes as Falsely Accused Deviants: Managing the Lesbian Stigma." *Sociological Quarterly* 33, no. 4: 521–33.

Blount, Marcellus, and George P Cunningham. 1996. *Representing Black Men.* New York: Routledge.

Boling, Patricia. 1996. *Privacy and the Politics of Intimate Life.* Ithaca, NY: Cornell University Press.

Booker, Christopher B. 2000. *I Will Wear No Chain!: A Social History of African American Males.* Westport, CT: Praeger.

Bourdieu, Pierre. 1991. *Language and Symbolic Power.* Cambridge, MA: Cambridge Polity Press.

Boyd, Todd. 2004. *The New H.N.I.C. (Head Niggas in Charge): The Death of Civil Rights and the Reign of Hip Hop.* New York: New York University Press.

Boykin, Keith. 2005. *Beyond the Down Low: Sex, Lies, and Denial in Black America.* New York: Carroll & Graf.

Brooks, John. 1976. *Telephone: The First Hundred Years.* New York: Harper and Row.

Browning, Barbara. 1998. *Infectious Rhythms: Metaphors of Contagion and the Spread of African Culture.* New York: Routledge.

Buchbinder, David. 1998. *Performance Anxieties: Re-Producing Masculinities.* Sydney: Allen and Unwin.

Buckland, Fiona. 2002. *Impossible Dance: Club Culture and Queer World-Making.* Middletown, CT: Wesleyan University Press.

Butler, Judith. 1999. *Gender Trouble: Feminism and the Subversion of Identity.* New York: Routledge.

———. 1996. *Bodies that Matter: On the Discursive Limits of "Sex."* New York: Routledge.

Campbell, John Edward. 2004. *Getting It on Online: Cyberspace, Gay Male Sexuality, and Embodied Identity.* Binghamton, NY: Harrington Park.

Carby, Hazel. 1998. *Race Men.* Cambridge, MA: Harvard University Press.

Centers for Disease Control and Prevention. 2006. "Vision, Mission, Core Values, and Pledge." http://www.cdc.gov/about/mission.htm. Accessed August 6, 2006.

———. 2001. *HIV/AIDS Surveillance Report* 13, no. 2.

Chestnutt, Charles W. 1900. *The House behind the Cedars.* Boston: Houghton Mifflin.

Clark, Keith. 2001. *Contemporary Black Men's Fiction and Drama.* Urbana: University of Illinois Press.

Cleaver, Eldridge. 1999. *Soul on Ice.* New York: Delta.

Clifford, James. 2002. *The Predicament of Culture: Twentieth-Century Ethnography, Literature, and Art.* Cambridge, MA: Harvard University Press.

Clifton, Charles. 2000. "Rereading Voices from the Past: Images of Homo-Eroticism in the Slave Narrative." In *The Greatest Taboo: Homosexuality in Black Communities,* edited by Delroy Constantine-Simms. New York: Alyson, 2000.

Cohen, Cathy J. 2004. "Deviance as Resistance: A New Research Agenda for the Study of Black Politics." *DuBois Review: Social Science Research on Race* 1: 27–45.

———. 1999. *The Boundaries of Blackness: AIDS and the Breakdown of Black Politics*. Chicago: University of Chicago Press, 1999.

Collins, Patricia Hill. 2004. *Black Sexual Politics: African Americans, Gender, and the New Racism*. New York: Routledge.

———. 2000. *Black Feminist Thought: Knowledge, Consciousness, and the Politics of Empowerment*. New York: Routledge.

Connell, R. W. 1995. *Masculinities*. Berkeley: University of California Press, 1995.

Connor, Marlene Kim. 1995. *What Is Cool?: Understanding Black Manhood in America*. Chicago: Agate.

Conquergood, Dwight. 1991. "Rethinking Ethnography: Towards a Critical Cultural Politics." *Communication Monographs* 58: 179–94.

———. 1985. "Performance as a Moral Act: Ethical Dimensions of the Ethnography of Performance." *Literature in Performance* 5, no. 2: 1–13.

Danet, Brenda. 1998. "Text as Mask: Gender and Identity on the Internet." In *Cybersociety 2.0: Revisiting Computer-Mediated Community and Technology*, edited by Steven G. Jones. Thousand Oaks, CA: Sage.

de Certeau, Michel. 1984. *The Practice of Everyday Life*, translated by Steven Rendall. Berkeley: University of California Press.

DeFrantz, Thomas F. 2004. "The Black Beat Made Visible: Hip Hop Dance and Body Power." In *Of the Presence of the Body: Essays on Dance and Performance Theory*, edited by Andre Lepecki. Middletown, CT: Wesleyan University Press.

Denizet-Lewis, Benoit. 2003. "Double Lives on the Down Low." *New York Times Magazine*, August 3: 28–33, 48, 52–53.

Dodd, Aileen D. 2005. "Black Journalists Criticize Media Coverage of 'Down Low' Phenomenon, Articles Wrongly Link Behavior to Blacks, Increase in AIDS." *Atlanta Journal-Constitution*, August 6: 2C.

Douglas, Mary. 2002. *Purity and Danger: An Analysis of the Concepts of Pollution and Taboo*. New York: Routledge.

———. 1992. *Risk and Blame: Essays in Cultural Theory*. New York: Routledge.

Drewal, Margaret T. 1991. "The State of Research on Performance in Africa." *African Studies Review* 34, no. 3: 1–64.

DuBois, W. E. B. 1965. "Souls of Black Folk." In *Three Negro Classics*, edited by John Franklin. New York: Avon.

Duneier, Mitchell. 1992. *Slim's Table: Race, Respectability, and Masculinity*. Chicago: University of Chicago Press, 1992.

Edwards, Tamela. 2001. "Men Who Sleep with Men: AIDS Risk to African American Women." *Essence*, October 1.

Edwards, Tim. 1999. *Men in the Mirror: Men's Fashion, Masculinity and Consumer Society*. London: Cassell.

Eng, David L., Judith Halberstam, and José Esteban Muñoz. 2005. "Introduction." *Social Text* 23, nos. 3–4 (Fall–Winter): 1–17.

Fabi, M. Giulia. 2001. *Passing and the Rise of the African American Novel*. Urbana: University of Illinois Press.

Fairclough, Norman. 1995. *Media Discourse*. New York: Bloomsbury Academic.

Fanon, Frantz. 1952. *Black Skin, White Masks*. New York: Grove Weidenfeld.

Favor, J. Martin. 1999. *Authentic Blackness: The Folk in the New Negro Renaissance*. Durham, NC: Duke University Press.

Ferguson, Roderick A. 2004. *Aberrations in Black: Toward a Queer of Color Critique*. Minneapolis: University of Minnesota Press.

50 Cent. 2003. "In Da Club." *The Massacre*. Interscope.

Fikentscher, Kai. 2000. *"You Better Work!": Underground Dance Music in New York City*. Hanover, NJ: Wesleyan University Press.

Fiske, John. 1996. *Media Matters: Race and Gender in U.S. Politics*. Minneapolis: University of Minnesota Press.

Fleetwood, Nicole. 2011. *Troubling Visions: Performance, Visuality, and Blackness*. Chicago: University of Chicago Press.

Foucault, Michael. 1988. *Power/Knowledge: Selected Interviews and Other Writings, 1972–1977*. Trans. Colin Gordon. New York: Pantheon.

———. "Of Other Spaces." Trans. Jay Miskowiec. *Diacritics* 16, no. 1 (Spring): 22–27.

———. 1978a. *Discipline and Punish: Birth of the Prison*, translated by Alan Sheridan. New York: Pantheon.

———. 1978b. *The History of Sexuality, Volume 1: An Introduction*, translated by Robert Hurley. New York: Pantheon.

Glanton, Dahleen. 2004. "HIV Quietly Sweeps through Rural South." *Baltimore Sun*, March 28.

Goffman, Erving. 1963. *Stigma: Notes on the Management of Spoiled Identity*. New York: Touchstone.

Gordon, Avery. 2008. *Ghostly Matters: Haunting and the Sociological Imagination*. Minneapolis: University of Minnesota Press.

Green, Edwin. "Thoughts on Trade/Ending an Obsession." In *Fighting Words: Personal Essays by Black Gay Men*, edited by Charles M. Smith. New York: Avon.

Grosz, Elizabeth. 1994. *Volatile Bodies: Toward a Corporeal Feminism*. Bloomington: Indiana University Press.

Guerrero, Ed. 1993. *Framing Blackness: The African American Image in Film*. Philadelphia: Temple University Press.

Guy-Sheftall, Beverly, and Johnetta B. Cole. 2003. *Gender Talk*. New York: Ballantine.

Halberstam, Judith (Jack). 2005. "Shame and White Gay Masculinity." *Social Text* 23, nos. 3–4 (Fall/Winter): 219–33.

Hammonds, Evelyn. 1995. "Missing Persons: African American Women, AIDS, and the History of Disease." In *Words of Fire*, edited by Beverly Guy-Sheftall. New York: New Press.

Hardin, Michael. 2004. "Ralph Ellison's *Invisible Man*: Invisibility, Race, and Homoeroticism from Frederick Douglass to E. Lynn Harris." *Southern Literary Journal* 37, no. 1 (Fall): 96–120.

Harper, Philip Brian. 1999. *Private Affairs: Critical Ventures in the Culture of Social Relations*. New York: New York University Press.

———. 1996. *Are We Not Men?: Masculine Anxiety and the Problem of African-American Identity*. New York: Oxford University Press.

Harris, Cheryl. 1998. "Whiteness as Property." In *Black on White*, edited by David Roediger. New York: Schocken.

Harris, E. Lynn. 2001. *Any Way the Wind Blows*. New York: Anchor Books.

———. 1994. *Invisible Life*. New York: Anchor Books.

Harris, E. Lynn, and Tara Roberts. 2004. "Passing for Straight: Brothers Who Secretly Have Sex with Men Explain the Attraction Plus, Women Talk about the Price of Loving a Man on the Down Low." *Essence* (July): 156–210.

Hawkeswood, William. 1996. *One of the Children: Gay Black Men in Harlem*. Berkeley: University of California Press.

Hazard-Donald, Katrina. 1996. "Dance in Hip-Hop Culture." In *Droppin' Science: Critical. Essays on Rap Music and Hip-Hop Culture*, edited by William Eric Perkins. Philadelphia: Temple Press.

Healy, Murray. 1996. *Gay Skins: Class, Masculinity, and Queer Appropriation*. New York: Continuum International Publishing.

Henderson, Mae. 2001. Foreword to *Passing*, by Nella Larsen. New York: Modern Library.

Herring, Scott. 2007. *Queering the Underworld: Slumming, Literature, and the Undoing of Lesbian and Gay History*. Chicago: University of Chicago Press.

Higginbotham, Evelyn Brooks. 1993. *Righteous Discontent: The Women's Movement in the Black Baptist Church, 1880–1920*. Cambridge, MA: Harvard University Press.

Hine, Darlene Clark. 1998. "Rape and the Inner Lives of Black Women in the Middle West: Preliminary Thoughts on the Culture of Dissemblance." *Signs* 14 (August): 913–20.

Hine, Darlene Clark, and Ernestine Jenkins, eds. 1999. *Questions of Manhood: A Reader in U.S. Black Men's History and Masculinity*. Bloomington: Indiana University Press.

Hollinshed, Denise. 2002. "Some Gay Black Men Are Keeping a Deadly Secret." *St. Louis Post-Dispatch*, April 21.

hooks, bell. 2003. *We Real Cool: Black Men and Masculinity*. New York: Routledge.

———. 1992. *Black Looks: Race and Representation*. Boston: South End.

———. 1981. *Ain't I Am Woman? Black Women and Feminism*. Boston: South End.

Hunt, Darnell M. 2003. *Screening the Los Angeles "Riots": Race, Seeing, and Resistance*. New York: Cambridge University Press.

Jackson, John L., Jr. 2005. *Real Black: Adventures in Racial Sincerity*. Chicago: University of Chicago Press.

Jackson, Ronald L., II. 2006. *Scripting the Black Masculine Body: Identity, Discourse, and Racial Politics in Popular Media*. Albany: State University of New York Press.

Jeffries, Michael P. 2011. *Thug Life: Race, Gender, and the Meaning of Hip-Hop*. Chicago: University of Chicago Press.

Johnson, E. Patrick, and Mae Henderson, eds. 2005. *Black Queer Studies; A Critical Anthology*. Durham, NC: Duke University Press.

Johnson, James Weldon. 1989. *The Autobiography of an Ex-Colored Man*. New York: Vintage.

Jones, D. Marvin. 2005. *Race, Sex, and Suspicion: The Myth of the Black Male*. Westport, CT: Praeger.

Jones, Patricia. 1999. *Passing*. New York: HarperCollins.

Julien, Isaac, dir. 1988. *Looking for Langston*. DVD. British Film Institute.

Kant, Immanuel. 1998. *The Groundwork of the Metaphysics of Morals*. Edited by Mary Gregor. New York: Cambridge University Press.

Kelley, Robin D. G. 1997. *Yo Mama's Disfunktional!: Fighting the Culture Wars in Urban America*. Boston: Beacon.

Kellner, Douglas. 1995. *Media Culture: Cultural Studies, Identity and Politics between the Modern and the Postmodern*. New York: Routledge.

King, Jason. 2003. "Remixing the Closet: The Down-Low Way of Knowledge." *Village Voice*, June 25–July 1.

King, J. L. 2004. *On the Down Low: A Journey into the Lives of "Straight" Black Men Who Sleep with Men*. New York: Broadway Books.

Kiritsy, Laura. 2002. "The Naysayer of the Nation's Black Male AIDS Epidemic." *Bay Windows*, March 7.

Kroeger, Brooke. 2003. *Passing: When People Can't Be Who They Are*. New York: Perseus.

Kulick, Don. 1998. *Travesti: Sex, Gender, and Culture among Brazilian Transgendered Prostitutes*. Chicago: University of Chicago Press.

Lancaster, Roger N. 1992. *Life Is Hard: Machismo, Danger, and the Intimacy of Power in Nicaragua*. Berkeley: University of California Press.

Law & Order: Special Victims Unit. 2004. "Lowdown." NBC.

Leap, William L., ed. 1999. *Public Sex/ Gay Space*. New York: Columbia University Press.

———. 1996. *Word's Out: Gay Men's English*. Minneapolis: University of Minnesota Press.

Lefebvre, Henri. 1991. *The Production of Space*, translated by Donald Nicholson-Smith. Oxford: Blackwell.

Madhubuti, Haki R. 1990. *Black Men: Obsolete, Single, Dangerous?: Afrikan American Families in Transition: Essays in Discovery, Solution, and Hope*. Chicago: Third World Press.

Majors, Richard, and Janet Mancini Billson. 1992. *Cool Pose: The Dilemmas of Black Manhood in America*. New York: Touchstone.

Mankekar, Purnima. 1999. *Screening Culture, Viewing Politics: An Ethnography of Television, Womanhood, and Nation in Postcolonial India*. Durham, NC: Duke University Press.

Marcus, George E. 1998. *Ethnography through Thick and Thin*. Princeton, NJ: Princeton University Press.

McBride, Dwight A. 2005. *Why I Hate Abercrombie & Fitch: Essays on Race and Sexuality*. New York: New York University Press.

McBride, James. 1997. *Color of Water*. New York: Riverhead Trade.

McDowell, Deborah. 2007. "Black Female Sexuality in Passing." In *Passing*, by Nella Larsen. Edited by Carla Kaplan. New York: Norton.

Mercer, Kobena. 1994. *Welcome to the Jungle: New Positions in Black Cultural Studies*. New York: Routledge.

Millet, Gregorio, David Malebranche, Byron Mason, and Pilgrim Spikes. 2005. "Focusing 'Down Low': Bisexual Black Men, HIV Risk and Heterosexual Transmission." *Journal of the National Medical Association* 97, no. 7 Supplementary: 52S–59S.

Mitchell, W. J. T. 1994. *Picture Theory: Essays on Verbal and Visual Representation*. Chicago: University of Chicago Press.

Mumford, Kevin. *Interzones: Black/White Sex Districts in Chicago and New York in the Early Twentieth Century*. New York: Columbia University Press.

Muñoz, José Esteban. 1998. *Disidentifications: Queers of Color and the Performance of Politics*. Minneapolis: University of Minnesota Press.

Nakamura, Lisa. 1995. "Race in/for Cyberspace: Identity Tourism and Racial Passing on the Internet." *Works and Days* 13: 181–93.

Neal, Mark Anthony. 2005. *New Black Man*. New York: Routledge.

Nero, Charles. 2005. "Why Are the Gay Ghettos White?" In *Black Queer Studies*, edited by E. Patrick Johnson and Mae G. Henderson. Durham, NC: Duke University Press.

———. 1991. "Toward a Black Gay Aesthetic." In *Brother to Brother: New Writings by Black Gay Men*, edited by Essex Hemphill. Boston: Alyson.

Osborne, Duncan. 2004. "The Down Low Goes Down." *Gay City News*, April 19–25.

Pattillo, Mary. 2007. *Black on the Block: The Politics of Race and Class in the City*. Chicago: University of Chicago Press.

———. 1999. *Black Picket Fences: Privilege and Peril among the Black Middle Class*. Chicago: University of Chicago Press.

Perez, Hiram. 2005. "You Can Have My Brown Body and Eat It, Too!" *Social Text* 23, nos. 3–4 (Fall–Winter): 171–91.

Phelan, Peggy. 1993. *Unmarked: The Politics of Performance.* New York: Routledge.

Poulson-Bryant, Scott. 2005. *Hung: A Meditation on the Measure of Black Men in America.* New York: Harlem Moon.

Quiroga, José. 2000. *Tropics of Desire: Interventions from Queer Latino America.* New York: New York University Press.

Reddy, Chandan. 1998. "Home, Houses, Non-Identity: Paris Is Burning." In *Burning Down the House: Recycling Domesticity,* edited by Rosemary Marangoly George. Boulder, CO: Westview Press.

Reid, Elizabeth M. 1996. "Communication and Community of Internet Relay Chat: Construction Communities." In *High Noon on the Electronic Frontier: Conceptual Issues in Cyberspace,* edited by Peter Ludlow. Cambridge, MA: MIT Press.

Ringer, R. Jeffrey. 1994. *Queer Words, Queer Images: Communication and the Construction of Homosexuality.* New York: New York University Press.

Robertson, Jennifer. 1998. *Takarazuka: Sexual Politics and Popular Culture in Modern Japan.* Berkeley: University of California Press.

Robinson, Amy. 1994. "It Takes One to Know One: Passing and Communities of Common Interest." *Critical Inquiry* 20, no. 4 (Summer): 715–36.

Rosaldo, Renato. 1993. *Culture & Truth: The Remaking of Social Analysis.* Rev. ed. Boston: Beacon.

Rose, Tricia. 1994a. *Black Noise: Rap Music and Black Culture in Contemporary America.* Middletown, CT: Wesleyan University Press.

———. 1994b. *Microphone Fiends: Youth Music and Youth Culture.* New York: Routledge.

Ross, Marlon B. 2005. "Beyond the Closet as Raceless Paradigm." In *Black Queer Studies: A Critical Anthology,* edited by E. Patrick Johnson and Mae Henderson. Durham, NC: Duke University Press.

———. 2004. *Manning the Race: Reforming Black Men in the Jim Crow Era.* New York: New York University Press.

Russo, Vito. 1987. *Celluloid Closet: Homosexuality in the Movies.* New York: Harper.

Sanchez, Maria Carla, and Linda Schlossberg, eds. 2001. *Passing: Identity and Interpretation in Sexuality, Race, and Religion.* New York: New York University Press. Scott, David. *Refashioning Futures: Criticism after Postcoloniality.* Princeton, NJ: Princeton University Press, 1999.

Sedgwick, Eve Kosofsky. 1990. *Epistemology of the Closet.* Berkeley: University of California Press.

———. 1985. *Between Men: English Literature and Male Homosocial Desire.* New York: Columbia University Press.

Senna, Danzy. 1999. *Caucasia.* New York: Riverhead Books.

Shabazz, Rashad. 2009. "So Low You Can't Get Under It: Carceral Spatiality and Black Masculinities in the United States and South Africa." *Souls* 11, no. 3 (July): 276–94.

Shaw, David. 1997. "Gay Men and Computer Communication: A Discourse of Sex and Identity in Cyberspace." In *Virtual Culture: Identity and Communication in Cybersociety,* edited by Steven G. Jones. Thousand Oaks, CA: Sage.

Simpson, Mark. 1993. *Male Impersonators: Males Performing Masculinity.* London: Cassell.

Smiley, Tavis. 2004. "Ice-T." *Tavis Smiley.* PBS. May 13. http://www.pbs.org/kcet/tavissmiley/archive/200405/20040513_icet.html.

Smith, Barbara. 1982. "Toward a Black Women's Feminist Criticism." In *All the Women Are White, All the Blacks Are Men, but Some of Us Are Brave: Black Women's Studies,* edited by Gloria T. Hull, Patricia Bell Scott, and Barbara Smith. New York: Feminist Press.

Smith, Pamela. 2000. "Failing to Mentor Sapphire: The Actionability of Blocking Black

Women from Initiating Mentoring Relationships." *UCLA Women's Law Journal* 10, no. 2: 373–449.Smith, Sidonie and Julia Weston, eds. 1998. *Women, Autobiography, Theory: A Reader*. Madison: University of Wisconsin Press.

Smith, Taigi. 2004. "Deadly Deception: Men on the Down Low View Dishonesty as Survival." *Essence* (August): 148–51.

Smitherman, Geneva. 1994. *Black Talk: Words and Phrases from the Hood to the Amen Corner*. New York: Houghton Mifflin.

Sollors, Werner. 1997. *Neither Black nor White yet Both: Thematic Explorations of Interracial Literature*. New York: Oxford University Press.

Somerville, Siobhan. 2000. *Queering the Color Line: Race and the Invention of Homosexuality in American Culture*. Durham, NC: Duke University Press.

Sontag, Susan. 1989. *AIDS and Its Metaphors*. New York: Farrar, Straus and Giroux.

Spivak, Gayatri. 1993. *Outside in the Teaching Machine*. New York: Routledge.

Thompson, Robert Farris. 1966. "An Aesthetic of the Cool: West African Dance." *African Forum* 2, no. 2: 85–102.

Tucker, Cynthia. 2004. "Blacks Flee Gays, Can't Flee AIDS." *Atlanta Journal-Constitution*, March 14: 8D.

Turner, Victor. 1988. *The Anthropology of Performance*. New York: PAJ.

———. 1982. *From Ritual to Theatre: The Human Seriousness of Play*. New York: PAJ.

Vargas, Jose. 2003. "HIV-Positive, without a Clue." *Washington Post*, August 4.

Vaughn, Tracy. 2005. "(W)rites of Passing: The Performance of Identity in Fiction and Personal Narratives." PhD diss. University of Massachusetts, Amherst.

Venable, Malcolm. 2001. "A Question of Identity." *Vibe* (July): 98–108.

Wald, Gayle. 2000. *Crossing the Line: Racial Passing in Twentieth Century U.S. Literature and Culture*. Durham, NC: Duke University Press.

Wallace, Maurice. 2002. *Constructing the Black Masculine: Identity and Ideality in African American Men's Literature and Culture, 1775–1995*. Durham, NC: Duke University Press.

Wallace, Michele. 1990. *Black Macho and the Myth of the Superwoman*. New York: Verso.

Warner, Michael. 1999. *The Trouble with Normal: Sex, Politics, and the Ethics of Queer Life*. Cambridge, MA: Harvard University Press.

———. 1993. *Fear of a Queer Planet: Queer Politics and Social Theory*. Minneapolis: University of Minnesota Press, 1993.

Watney, Simon. 1989. *Policing Desire: Pornography, AIDS, and the Media*. 2nd ed. Minneapolis: University of Minnesota Press.

Watts, Eric King, and Mark P. Orbe. 2002. "The Spectacular Consumption of 'True' African American Culture: 'Whassup' with the Budweiser Guys?" *Critical Studies in Media Communication* 19, no. 1 (March): 1–20.

Weeks, Jeffrey. 1995. *Invented Moralities: Sexual Values in an Age of Uncertainty*. New York: Columbia University Press.

West, Tim'm T., perf. 2005. *Pick Up the Mic*, directed by Alex Hinton. DVD. Planet Janet Films.

White, E. Frances. 2001. *Dark Continent of Our Bodies: Black Feminism and the Politics of Respectability*. Philadelphia: Temple University Press.

Whitehead, Colson. 1998. *The Intuitionist*. New York: Doubleday.

Wiegman, Robyn. *American Anatomies: Theorizing Race and Gender*. Durham, NC: Duke University Press.

Wightwick, George. 1847. *Hints to young architects: Comprising advice to those who, while yet at school, are destined to the profession*. New York: Wiley and Putnam.

Williams, Gregory Howard . 1996. *Life on the Color Line: The True Story of a White Boy Who Discovered He Was Black.* New York: Plume.

Winfrey, Oprah. 2004a. "A Secret Sex World: Living on the 'Down Low.'" *Oprah Winfrey Show.* ABC. April 16.

Winfrey, Oprah. 2004b. "A Secret Sex World: Living on the 'Down Low.'" *Oprah after the Show.* Oxygen. April 16. http://www.oprah.com/tows/after/200404/tows_after _20040416.jhtml.

Ziller, Robert C. 1990. *Photographing the Self: Methods for Observing Personal Orientations.* London: Sage.

INDEX

West, Tim'm, 1, 14
Weston, Julia, 60
White, E. Frances, 70
Wiegman, Robyn, 134
Wightwick, George, 96
Wilson, Phil, 59, 62–63

Winfrey, Oprah, 22, 25, 52–65, 162, 165
women, 21, 24–26, 28–29, 35, 43–46,
62–63, 66, 114, 125–27, 141, 143, 151,
156, 159–60

Ziller, David, 120